YOUNG
MEN
GO
NORTH

Joe Upton

Epicenter Press Inc.
Alaska Book Adventures™

Kenmore, WA

Epicenter Press

6524 NE 181st St., Suite 2, Kenmore, WA 98028

Epicenter Press is a regional press publishing nonfiction
books about the arts, history, environment, and diverse cultures
and lifestyles of Alaska and the Pacific Northwest.
For more information, visit www.EpicenterPress.com

Library of Congress Control Number: 2022936024

ISBN: 978-1-684920-49-5 (Trade Paperback)
ISBN: 978-1-684920-50-1 (Ebook)

Cover and interior design by Scott Book & Melisssa Vail Coffman

To Mickey Hanson, long gone now, mate on the Sydney, in 1965.
Who sat up with me in that big pilothouse on my night watches
and shared with me a lifetime of stories about the Northwest Coast.

CONTENTS

"Whenever a bunch of fellows would get together, someone would start to talking about going up North.

Things were pretty much settled to the south of us. We didn't seem to be ready for steady jobs. It was only natural we'd start talking about the North. We'd bought out the Russians. We'd built canneries up there. The fellows who hadn't been up was hankering to go. The rest of us was hankering to go back."

—*The Trail Led North: Mont Hawthorne's Story*

My own journey started far to the south . . .

Our tuna seiner, Iquique, Chile, 1965. Previously the boat had operated out of West Africa, and there was a six foot by six foot blackened concrete pad on the deck, near the big seine winch. I asked what it was for, was told that in Africa, the black crew weren't allowed inside, that they slept on the net pile and cooked on a fire on the concrete pad. On the bleak hill in the background you can see the switchbacks of the rail line that brought nitrates from the big mines back in the desert to Iquique to be loaded into square rigged sailing ships waiting to take it to Europe. When World War I came along the Germans invented atificial nitrate and the mines closed.

PART I – A YOUNG MAN LEARNS A TRADE

A NOVEMBER NIGHT, 1964, EASTERN PACIFIC, south of the Equator: I am restless, step out of my cabin, walk out on deck. Our big tuna seiner rolls slowly in the low swell, the rest of the crew asleep, bright deck lights on, less a wandering ship come our way in the night. I walk to the rail, step back, startled. For the water around our little ship is alive, full of strange fishes attracted by our lights from the mile deep water beneath us. Weird looking squid, bright tuna, schools of finger-sized anchovy, others that I have never seen. After a while I go back into my cabin, sleep. But uneasily; something about that mass of life churning around us silently in the night made me uncomfortable.

At first light our spotter pilot dives on us, pulls up sharply just over our mast: time to get to work, boys! And so our day begins: skiff man ready, crow's nest manned, big tuna binoculars on the bridge scanning back and forth. After an hour we set: big seine skiff's engine roaring, the net paying out behind us in a big circle. And finally we peer down as the bottom of the net is slowly pulled toward the surface and suddenly the water boils with tuna, squid, even a few seals.

It's a big enough set, but mixed: maybe 2 tons of big squid mixed in with 8 of tuna. And at the very end, when we roll the rest of the catch aboard, a big—probably at least fifteen hundred pounds—sea lion flops aboard as well, and we give him plenty of room until he finds the lowest place in the rail, and wriggles over it and back into the ocean. Then there's nothing for us but to wade knee-deep through the mess of tuna and squid, try to throw the squid over the side before they can muckle onto us with their suckers, and work the tuna into the open hatches.

Four months earlier, I had stepped off a four-engine DC-6 in Iquique, a small dusty fishing town on the desert north coast of Chile. I was an American teen, hoping for redemption from a poor high school academic record, with a recommendation from an "interesting job," as a college admissions officer had put it. Found lodging in a once elegant but then shabby mansion, left over, my new roommate said, from Iquique's glory days. When square riggers from Europe filled the harbor, come to load bags of the whitish power—salitre, nitrate—dug from the mines in the vast Atacama Dessert above town, to fertilize fields in Germany, France, Holland and the rest of Western Europe. And to make gunpowder, that fueled the Great War, that stopped the nitrate trade in its tracks, when German scientists invented a way to make artificial nitrate.

The big square riggers, that also brought food to that remote coast, simply stopped coming, and Iquique, as my roommate put it in his mix of English and Spanish, "was abajo. For many years, muy poor. People they clap when a car go down the street."

The first night I was there, this same roommate, an entrepreneurial guy named Miguel Huidobro, asked me to help him. At midnight. We drove his pickup through the dark and empty streets, but with no lights, our way lit by the moon.

"Porque no luces?" (Why no lights?) Said I, hopefully practicing my high school Spanish.

"Vas a ver." (You'll see,) came the answer.

We went to the airstrip, on the outskirts of town. A mile or so west, out over the ocean, I could see the lights of a plane, making wide circles. Miguel drove to the end of the runway and flashed his headlights three times, and the lights swung in toward the land.

It turned out to be a beat up twin engined DC-3, landing and swinging around at the very end of the runway to head out again, ready to take off. The engine on the side of the plane with the door coughed to a stop and we backed up to it as it opened. Miguel handed the men inside a thick manila envelope and they started to drag out sides of beef that we pulled into the back of our truck until the springs were totally flattened out. We spent the next hour knocking on doors, delivering the heavy sides of meat.

"I am contrabandista," said my friend, explaining that it was way cheaper to buy beef from Bolivia, a short flight away, than it was to have it delivered from the south of Chile, where the cattle producers were.

Iquique was abajo, Miguel explained, until just a few years earlier when upwelling in the rich north flowing Humboldt current moved closer to the coast, bringing the great schools of anchovies near enough for small Iquique based seiners to reach them. The first three, steel 55 footers, came down as deck cargo on a big freighter from Louisiana, were launched cautiously with a combination of the ship's booms and a big crane on shore.

Those first three boats found an amazingly abundant resource—often getting two or three full loads in a day. Within a few years, fish meal plants were built and two local shipyards were building steel seiners as fast as they could, and by the time I arrived, the fleet was around 300 new boats, 70 and 80 footers, dwarfing the first three, the *Nina*, and *Pinta*, and the *Santa Maria*.

The fish meal plants needed workers and the seiners needed crews: jobs that paid cash money. At that time the farm economy of Southern Chile was semi-feudal in nature. You rented farm-owned housing, maybe got a tiny plot of land for a garden, bought what you needed from the company store. You were paid to work there, but what with the rent and expensive food from the store, most folks never managed to actually save much money.

Without sophisticated electronics, it was fishing the old fashioned way—using our eyes with the big tuna binoculars.

So they came to Iquique, 2,000 plus miles north over bad roads in rattle trap buses, their belongings in cardboard suitcases, their chickens strapped to the roof. To live in shack towns of packing cases or discarded corrugated steel roofing. Luckily there was no rain and the climate was mild. And bit by bit, these farm peasants slowly made the way into what even might be described as the middle class. With a wife working in the fish meal plants and the husband on a boat, with perhaps the neighbor watching the kids, there might be income enough for more than just the basics, maybe they might even get one of the government built cinder block real houses.

And in the fleet, like in much of Latin American culture, the macho tradition ruled. Here's how it worked on the boats. Skippers, jealous of their prerogatives, ruled the engine controls, the throttle and the reverse gear levers to be totally off limits: no one beside the skipper could even touch them, nor even ask how they worked. And so the stage was set for a night that became planted in Iquique history and legend.

The fish were distant that night: 100 miles offshore, much farther than usual. In order to arrive at daylight, the fleet then totaling perhaps 90 boats, steamed out of the harbor around 7 p.m. After clearing the breakwater all

TUNA TALES

On the tuna boat, when we got in from one of our long trips off-shore, each member of the crew would get two fish. These were hand-some 12-15 pound bonita, hard frozen. The married men would take them home to their families; one at a time. Each would be a feast for the neighborhood or extended family. For us single men, in that poor town, a single fish could be traded for a night on the town, complete with drinks, dinner, and a lady to share it all with. So we'd put on our good clothes and walk down the dock with a smile on our face and a frozen tuna on our shoulders, ready for a wicked good time.

the skippers except for the leader, gave strict orders to their crew: "Follow the boat ahead, don't touch the controls under any circumstances and wake me at daylight."

About an hour after that, one of the first boats in the line developed some sort of engine issue and turned around for town. In a dutiful procession all the boats behind that one, slowly turned 180° and headed back to the harbor, essentially a cul-de-sac with a small entrance. I was on shore that night and woke to the sound of engines racing and steel hulls clanging into one another as the returning fleet ran out of room and the terrified helmsmen, afraid to do anything but follow strict orders, frantically maneuvered to avoid other boats as they too ran out of maneuvering room. It came to be known as "The Night The Fleet Turned Around."

The gathering place for foreigners in Iquique was the bar at the Hotel Pratt, on the main plaza. Occasionally when I was in town between tuna trips, I would sit in there, nurse my cheap local beer. Often the group was a bit like who's who in world fishing. Harvey Smith, the fish meal magnate from Louisiana, might stop in. American Peter Schmidt, whose Seattle company, Marine Construction and Design both was building seiners in Iquique and manufactured critical deck equipment was a regular. There were South Africans, Germans; even the big pharmaceutical company Pfizer, had a small fleet in Iquique—not sure why—and sometimes they had guys there too.

There were also some skippers from Washington State and Alaska, working on contract to instruct Chilean skippers in the intricacies of purse seining. I was an anomaly to them: a 19-year-old American kid, working on the anchovy and tuna boats for local wages.

The first immigants to Iquique built modest homes out of whatever they could find, like these abandoned sheets of corrugated steel. Baking hot during the day, and cold at night, they were little more than just shelter.

And their talk of Alaska fascinated me. The men spoke of fishing crab in the pack ice, of whirlpools that could suck down big boats, of fish runs that make even the great anchovy boom seem puny. Places with names like False Pass, Yuculta Rapids, Seymour Narrows, Fords Terror. Names spoken, it seemed to me, with reverence. So after a while, by listening to the tales, Alaska came to seem like a mythic place, bigger than life.

"You fish in sailboat days?" A conversation started one evening. I moved a little closer, not wanting to appear nosy, but wanting to catch it all. Roger, one of the oldest of the men begins a tale.

"I went up to Bristol Bay on the *Star of India* in '18. We came up from San Francisco, Alaska Packers had a whole fleet of them square riggers, sent 'em north every year for salmon. The last of the snow was still on the shore when we sailed into the Ugashik River and dropped the hook."

He explained how they launched the pile driver and drove a forest of pilings, then everyone turned in to help the carpenters: working with hammer and saw every day: the big dock appearing over the pilings, then the buildings for the fish house and can line. Bunkhouse and cook houses on the shore, one for the Chinese, another for the rest.

The days getting longer, the bushes greening up, the great tides surging in and out of the river. And always in the distance, the looming jagged cone of 4,400' Aniakchak volcano, steam ominously venting from near the top, watching over all that they did.

The flurry to get the can line ready: the boiler and steam engine installed, the overhead shafts and bearings bolted to ceiling joists, the wide leather belts looped down to the canning machines. The water lines hooked up and tested on the big Iron Chink: the pride of the cannery—the machine that revolutionized salmon canning, taking away the jobs of dozens of Chinese workers in each cannery. A big wheel-shaped contraption full of knives and brushes and squirting water hoses, it lopped off head and tail, eviscerated and cleaned fish after fish for hour after hour without a smoke or coffee break. In those early days Chinese workers cut the cans out of big sheets of tin and soldered the pieces to make a can.

Ice cream vendor with new subsidized housing behind. Before water and sewer lines were extended out to these neighborhoods, a daily water truck and a trench for sewage served their needs.

The first of the salmon flipping and stirring in the river off the cannery, the boats rigged and launched.

And finally what they had all come for: The Run.

The tug towing the line of sailing gillnetters out each morning, the Norwegian fishermen brewing coffee on their tiny stoves, getting ready to work the 14' oars, hoist the sails, lay out their nets and pick fish, and pick, and pick. Slow at first . . . the guys coming in with 500 . . . 800 . . . 1,000 pounds.

Roger was a carpenter, but then once the cannery was built, he was a 'puller' too—crew to a Norwegian captain, just two them on the 32' double ender.

"You couldn't believe all them fish," he said, "One day, you'd get maybe two . . . three hundred fish . . . then just a couple days later, there'd be so many your net would be sinking . . . and it was all you could do . . . both of us pulling for all we had, just to get that little rag of a net aboard, sometimes seemed like there was almost a fish in every mesh . . .

"Six days a week we fished, your hands and arms so tired at the end of the day, you could barely make it up the dock ladder, eating all you could stuff down at the mess-hall, and stumbling into bed in the bunkhouse with the sun still up and then getting up at 4:30 and staggering out there to do it all again.

"The good thing up there is that we fished the tides, see . . .? There wasn't no water at the dock at low tide, them days at most of the canneries . . . So when the low tide came around in the morning, we could sleep in!"

"But the crazy part was how quick it was all over. 25th of June it wasn't no point to even put your net in the water; you'd hardly get a fish. Then come 4th of July and there'd be so many your net might be sinking on each set and you'd be hauling them fish right off the shallow bottom and be falling asleep in the mess hall; once my chin fell right into my soup and I woke to see all the other fellas laughing around me.

"It was aways a bit of a contest to see who would make high boat at the cannery—they gave out a little bonus for that. When they were coming thick, it was just who could get them out of the net the fastest and get that net back in the water. It didn't hardly matter where you put your net when there was a big run—they was just fish everywhere . . .

"You had to be careful too . . . You put too many fish on and you'd sink your boat easy. Each season there'd be one or two boats lost like that. Though we were always fishing so close to each other, you'd get picked up quick."

"And Deadman Sands was always waiting. I never liked to fish much over by them Sands. Wasn't buoyed off or nothing—the ice'd take any buoys out anyway. When them big tides were high, you'd never even know they was there. But come down towards low, there they'd be, hundreds of acres of them sands just waiting for fellas who wasn't careful.

Author's collection

The Alaska Packers Association operated the last fleet of square riggers in commercial operation, sending the boats north until just before the start of World War II. The big steel ships could be had cheaply, packed a lot, and could be operated by the same men that built the canneries, caught and canned the fish as well.

"They'd be nothing but a death trap in a hard blowing southerly and a coming tide. The breakers on the edge of the Sands would just tumble your boat over and then no one could get in there to help you—it'd be just breakers all the way across. Even if someone knew you were in a pickle— no one had radios in them days.

"Nor motors either until '51 ; that was stupid: not letting us have engines.

"Season of '48 the Sands took ten guys; five boats and crews all lost. Big 24 footer of a tide and a hard blow southerly came up quick. Those boats didn't have no warning or nothing—we was over that way, but my skipper was scared of those Sands, and that was a good thing. We was all talking about it at supper that night. None of the guys was from our cannery, they were all from the Diamond M, but some of our guys were close enough to see those boats rolled right over by the surf, tumbled over and over until they just disappeared. One of the boats managed to anchor by the edge, but they was already in the breakers and they just got swept away. Everyone who fished the Bay that season knew someone on those boats. I knew a Swede the name of Kjell, nicest guy you'd want to meet. Gone just like that.

"The fishing would be pretty much done by the 20th of July, and the monkey boat would push the *Star* back aside the wharf again and the whole gang would turn to loading her with case salmon out of the big warehouse. I remember that first season was a big one and the can line worked day and night with hardly ever a breakdown and we'd filled that warehouse right up to the rafters.

"We'd empty that warehouse right out, take maybe four, five days, and each evening when we was done, around evening mug up, we'd like to go out to the face of the dock just to see how deep the old *Star* was in the water with all that case salmon. Some seasons the tides would be right enough we'd load her right at the dock until she was full, but if the tides were smallish, we'd only get her about two thirds loaded, but then we'd have to anchor her off out in the stream where it was deeper, and we'd have to load the rest of them cases with a little barge.

"Then once the warehouse was half empty, another gang would start to hoist the sailboats out. There was a little wheeled cart and we'd wheel each boat back into the warehouse, set her on blocks, and take the sails out and hang them so they wouldn't get mildewy or rot or rat chewed over the long winter.

"When we started putting the boats into that big warehouse, everyone knew the season was starting to wrap up and we'd all get to talking about home again and our gals and all. Leaving Day was always a big thing. There was **eight** Alaska Packers canneries in The Bay in the '30s, and each one had its own *Star* boat, all these big gorgeous square riggers. And we'd all be leaving about the same time, and when we saw the first one with sails up, headed home, we'd all get working Johnny-quick; there was almost a race to see who would be the first one to get home and through the Golden Gate.

"That was a sight I'll never forget. On the day we left, you could look out ahead and behind and there was four other *Star* ships plus us, all taking that big ebb, all deep loaded with cans and crews, and behind us was Aniakchak, blowing a big puff of steam like she was seeing us off."

"Two nights later we were working our way down the peninsula, down towards False Pass, light airs, I was just yarning on deck with some of the fellas and one of them other volcanoes, Pavlof or Shishaldin, or maybe Round Top gives a big puff of red stuff, ash and cinders I guess. Lit up the whole sky and the sea and our sails all glowing red with it, and you could see two of the other *Star* ships ahead, all lit up red, too.

"Going through Unimak Pass is always tough, seems like it's always blowing northerly when we try to get through before the season, and southerly when we're trying to get through at the end . . . Them big square riggers deep loaded like we was, wasn't very handy in tight places like the Pass. But in those days Alaska Packers always had a big tug that came up with the *Star* fleet. And one by one, they'd pass us a big hawser and tow us right through the pass until we were in the clear on the other side and let us go . . .

"Then it was running free 'fer home . . . Four or five'd leave Unimak on the same tide, but within a day or two we'd be all spread out and out of sight of each other. Sometimes if you went up to the top of the mast, you'd get a glimpse of one or two of the others, but pretty much it was a guess as to who'd be first through The Gate.

"Course all them fellas'd be anxious to get home to their gals and start spending their season's money and all. But to tell the truth, I was kind of jealous of the winter man, the caretaker who got to stay behind and see the seasons change and just work on cannery stuff and hunt all winter.

"So I went into the Alaska Packers Association office right there by their docks in Alameda and put my name on the list to be a winter man. They kind of give me a funny look when I asked, because I was single, and I could see that there weren't a lot of names on the list, even though it was hard times back then, and it was guaranteed grub and a warm cabin all winter and a bit of cash at the end. They liked it better when it was a couple or even a family to care take them big canneries. Heard tell there was one guy in the Diamond X, that was the most remote cannery in them days, up the Kvichak, went sort of cuckoo. When the gang arrived back in the spring, he hadn't tended to the place at all, and was just sitting there in that little house. Just sitting there by the oil stove, with the place filled up with trash and shit. Just the loneliness and them long, dark days made him wacko. Lucky he didn't burn down that nice house and the whole cannery.

"But guess no more families came along and they give me the job after the '33 season, at the old Diamond M, up in the Naknek.

"The season was good . . . It pretty much always was back in them days before the Japanese came in and took so many fish after the war. They was in such hard shape after we firebombed and then atomic bombed them so bad that heard tell that the 'gummint' figured it was better for them to keep catching our fish than for the US of A to try to feed a couple of million folks while they got back on their feet.

"Tell truth, I didn't really know what it would be like after all the ships left and winter came on hard. But up in the Naknek them days there was the Diamond O just downriver a few hundred yards. The old Diamond O had a family tending it for the winter, and we got to be friends. They had little kids and it did my heart good when they came around. But the best part was that there was a little band of natives there, and they like to took me in too, just like one o' them.

"They was Yup'iks, they spoke their own lingo. But some of them had worked in the cannery too and spoke a little bit of English, enough for us to understand each other just enough. One of the gals took a shine to me and after a bit she moved in with me. Made that winter go a lot easier, I tell you.

"But I got to like them Yup'iks and their ways. They showed me hunting tricks I never knew before. Fer instance . . . they treated bullets like they was almost sacred . . . There was a fair amount of caribou around, but they'd wait, maybe for hours in that cold in the winter, to get a good shot so they wouldn't use more than one bullet.

"They had this banyo they called it—really pretty much a sauna—but on some of those long cold dark days, half the village'd be crowded in there. It sure made those long dark cold days go faster.

"The old Naknek . . . She sure froze hard that winter. I never been around ice like that. The first couple of nights when it came off really cold and the ice started to snap and crack in the middle of the night, it woke me up, kind of sceered me to tell the truth . . . The winter house was built for the guy that tended all the cannery machines and it was set back from the big can building, but on the same deck built on pilings because the shore was so soft and muskegy there . . . Course the ice froze hard around all them pilings. And course even froze up on top with all that thick ice, the tide was still rushing in and rushing out underneath the ice, so sometimes in the middle of the night there'd be a big pop or creak and it would shake the whole cannery!"

P.A.F. Salmon gill net boats in Bering Sea district.

Getting ready—somewhere in Bristol Bay, probably around 1920. It is the beginning (or possibly the end) of the season, as the boat masts are still uninstalled except for the one in the foreground. In the background are what look like pilings for another building.

"And look," he said standing up and pointing to one of the big framed photographs on the wall of the bar of square riggers in Iquique harbor, " she was *here*, called the *Euterpe* in those days, but here in 1888!"

Later I had a close look at the old photo: a bunch of similar old sailing ships crowded into the harbor, almost identical dark hulls except some had three masts, others four. How he could recognize the ship he'd been on 30 years earlier was beyond me.

Ugashik, Naknek, Kvichak, Nushagak, Egegik. All those rivers with Russian names. No trees, volcanoes puffing out steam, Eskimos. I thought: "Alaska: wow; what a place it must be!"

One of the Americans there was George Fulton, who had an unique job: running a 80' steel boat demonstrating stern trawling to Chilean fishermen, a more efficient system than hauling the nets over the side on what were called side trawlers, the way the Chileans had been doing it for generations. He told me that once, when they were fishing in Southern Chile, down in those channels near Cape Horn, he'd found two pretty good-sized islands that weren't even on the chart.

We became friends and he explained about sailboat days; how the State of Alaska had rules that you had to use sail or oars for power in the Bristol Bay fishing boats until 1954, when engines were allowed for the first time.

I'd explained to George how I'd gotten into college for the next fall, but that I needed to make more money than the 75 bucks a month I was making on the Chilean boats.

"You should go to Alaska," he said. I told him it sounded great, but kind of like an impossible dream. But what he said next electrified me: "There's a couple of boats headed up to Seattle from here next month. I can get you a job on one of them."

And just like that, my life was totally changed.

A salmon purse seiner in Chatham Straits. Limited by Alaska law to 58', and with a typical crew of 5, around 200 such vessels operated summers in SE Alaska waters during the 1970s

THE LURE OF ALASKA

FOR MYSELF THAT SPRING OF 1965 and for thousands of young men and women before and since, Alaska commercial fishing was a powerful magnet. The idea of getting on a boat and heading north for a summer of adventure and hopefully a good paycheck at the end was enormously attractive and exciting.

And so I joined the dozens of other young folks, walking up and down the docks of Seattle's Fishermen's Terminal, the maze of stores, warehouses, and machine shops set on the fresh water of Salmon Bay, just a quarter mile from the locks that lead down to the salt water of Puget Sound.

Here's how it worked: you walked the docks, trying to get the attention of a busy skipper or a sympathetic crewmen, to ask if they needed a hand for the season. For most of the time it was a thankless and discouraging task: skippers were under the gun to get their boats ready and get out of town and headed north. Most boats were already crewed up, with hands returning from previous seasons, who had been already working for weeks, painting up and building nets. Plus most of the guys walking the docks were newbies, greenhorns with no Alaska or commercial fishing, or even boating experience.

But all the same we knew guys got sick, hurt, failed to show, and that many of the crewmen and more than a few skippers had started just like we had: walking up and down the docks.

As I walked around Fishermens Terminal, I saw boats like the Lucien B, *above, that were operated by just one guy or a couple. Maybe, some day, I thought, I might be one of those guys.*

For myself, after the grit and dirt of the docks of North Chile, the rough, company owned steel boats, the smell of fish meal and dead whales, Fishermen's Terminal was like something out of a dream. Gorgeous wooden boats, carefully maintained and painted by their owners, lined the docks; pride of ownership was everywhere.

But it was bittersweet as well—ten days passed chasing leads that never seemed to work out, while seeing other guys, less able than me, I thought, get on good boats just by happening to be in the right place at the right time. Day after day I walked the docks with many other eager young men and gals, chasing every lead, but not getting a job.

Workers load cans onto racks that will be rolled into the retorts, essentially pressure cookers that heat the cans long enough to cook the salmon and kill any bacteria. This size of can is called a "one pound tall" and are typically used for institutional and military markets.

THE CANNERY LIFE

Salmon canneries were the core business along the coast of much of Alaska for generations, starting in the 1880s.

It was seasonal. In the spring the mechanics and the carpenters would begin to get the equipment, the docks, and the buildings ready for the frenzy to come once the run started. Boats and crews would arrive from the 'lower 48,' (there aren't enough boats and crews in Alaska to harvest the big salmon runs.)

Then came the workers, often a mix of natives and Chinese at first, college kids in recent years, and today, often workers from many different countries, all there just for the season.

But more than just an industry, it was a culture that ran down through generations of fishermen and cannery workers, a way of life that defined the coast and those who lived there.

In the beginning, before refrigeration that allowed big fish transport vessels called tenders or packers, to bring the fish to town, the processing facilities were built out in the wilderness next to the fish runs, each a whole little town in itself.

Then the tenders allowed the canneries to move into towns where they didn't have the cost of maintaining a whole little village lost in the wilderness.

The Sidney was a 80' tender or fish packer, with refrigerated sea water in her holds. Note the big tank for the back deck—gas for the boats that fished for us. Her layout was a bit unusual—galley on the top deck behind the pilothouse, and a big storeroom on the main deck for groceries, etc.

The boat that I had come up from Chile on, the *Nick C II*, and where I was living as I looked for a job, was tied up at the edge of a busy waterway where fishing boats would pass on their way to the locks to begin their trip up the Inside Passage to Alaska and the fishing season ahead. Each evening as I sat outside on deck eating my modest supper, the boats would pass, crews standing on deck, beers in hand, and I could hear snatches of their excited conversations about all the fun they were going to have 'Up North.' It was torture.

Finally a tip, from a marine store cashier: "The *Sidney* needs an engineer," he said one day without fanfare. I thanked that man, you bet, and hustled over.

The *Sidney* was a handsome 80 footer loading boxes of freight into her hold. I called up to the man operating the winch controls: "I heard you're looking for an engineer."

He looked me up and down and finally said, "Aren't you a little young?"

"I've been second engineer on a tuna boat."

"How about gas engines? Most of the native boats that fish for us have big Chrysler Royal gas engines. Are you familiar with them?"

"Oh, sure," I said, more confidently than I felt, "no problem."

"OK," he said after a moment, "You got some kind of reference?"

I gave him the name of Steve Trutich who owned the *Nick C II*.

I couldn't sleep that night I was so excited. In the morning I hustled over to the *Sidney*. A truck was alongside with another load of freight. The skipper was at the winch controls again, waved me aboard.

"OK, kid, you're hired. How about a thousand a month?"

"Great," I stammered, and in an instant a whole new life opened up.

Just then a big Caddy pulled up and some guy waved to my new skipper.

"Here, take over," my boss said, and waved up at the rigging over me, "and don't two-block anything." And jumped into the Caddy and took off.

"Yo, kid," It was the driver of the truck. "Hustle up, we're burning daylight here."

I suddenly realized he was expecting me to run the winches. I looked down at the array of the six winch levers and froze.

Just then a kindly looking older man emerged from the hold below and climbed up the ladder to where I stood, muttering loudly enough for me to hear: "Ain't that like Lloyd, hiring a green engineer to save a few bucks."

He presented a big claw of a hand: "Hello, young fellow, I'm Mickey Hansen."

Just by chance I had stumbled into an epic Alaska fishing job: the shady skipper, the grumpy cook, the green deckhand, and the old Alaska salt as mate.

Mick turned out to be a wonderful friend and a true mentor. Born in Norway, like many of the older men in the Alaska fisheries, he'd immigrated as a child and gone to Alaska on his dad's boat at 12. He'd spent 50 years working the coast in all kinds of weather, in all kinds of boats. We took a shine to each other right away, and he taught me many of the skills that I needed to be an Alaska fisherman.

We spent another two days loading freight at the West Wall of Fishermen's Terminal, and I got a glimpse into the enormous logistical undertaking that was the Alaska salmon business. Ahead and behind us at the quarter mile-long wharf, were big boats like ours, absorbing truckload after truckload of food and supplies for ourselves and the smaller boats that depended on us, as well as freight for the remote canneries that we worked for. We'd work until dark, almost 10 at that time of year, and in the morning find the deck littered with packages dropped off after we'd hit the sack.

Behind us at the wharf that first evening were three 58' Alaska salmon seiners, tied together, bedecked with flags, a boozy party in progress on their decks. Taped on the flying bridge of one was "HAPPY ARE WE WHO FISH ON THE SEA." I was too, very much so.

In the morning they were gone, through the locks and down into the salt water of Puget Sound beyond to start their journey on the winding way north: the Inside Passage and Southeast Alaska. About which I'd already heard so much in the bar of the Hotel Pratt, far away in Iquique, Chile, just a few months before.

I couldn't sleep that night either.

A JUNE PRE DAWN MORNING: "Hey Kid, wake up, You gotta see this."

I stumbled out of my bunk, pulled on my clothes, stepped outside, climbed the ladder up to the pilothouse.

Two days earlier we had finally sailed and plunged into the vast island choked wilderness that is the Inside Passage to Alaska.

We were in a dark canyon of a channel, first light barely in the sky. The current pushed our big boat from side to side. Our skipper seemed anxious, checking the tide book as we approach a particularly narrow spot in the channel. A whirlpool the size of a tennis court, perhaps four feet lower in the center, swirled around a point in the narrow passage ahead.

Skipper spun the wheel sharply to keep us clear.

"This is Seymour Narrows, kid," Mick, the kind 65-year-old mate said, "it's only safe to go through at slack water, at the top or the bottom of the tide. Otherwise those whirlpools are big enough to suck boats under."

Our boat lurched suddenly sideways as we dropped into a big current boil. "Wow," I thought, "If this is slack water, what's it like when the current really gets ripping?"

"It used to be worse," Old Mick said, "there was a rock right in the middle of the narrowest spot. They blasted it the hell out of there; took near three million pounds of TNT."

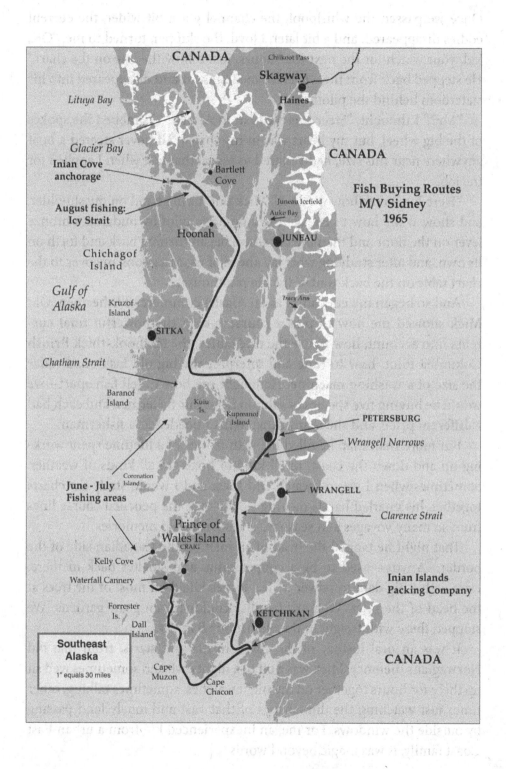

CANADA

Chilkoot Pass

Skagway

Haines

Lituya Bay

Glacier Bay

CANADA

Inian Cove anchorage

Bartlett Cove

Fish Buying Routes M/V Sidney 1965

Juneau Icefield

Auke Bay

August fishing: Icy Strait

Hoonah

JUNEAU

Chichagof Island

Gulf of Alaska

Kruzof Island

Tracy Arm

SITKA

Chatham Strait

Baranof Island

Kuiu Is.

Kupreanof Island

PETERSBURG

Wrangell Narrows

Coronation Island

June - July Fishing areas

WRANGELL

Clarence Strait

Prince of Wales Island

CRAIG

Kelly Cove

Waterfall Cannery

Inian Islands Packing Company

Forrester Is.

Dall Island

KETCHIKAN

Southeast Alaska

1" equals 30 miles

Cape Muzon

Cape Chacon

CANADA

Once we passed the whirlpool, the channel got a bit wider, the current eddies disappeared, and a bit later, Lloyd, the skipper, turned to me, "OK, kid, your watch for the next four hours. Just follow the line on the chart." He stepped back from the wheel for me to take it and disappeared into his stateroom behind the pilothouse.

"Me?," I thought, "Steer this big boat to Alaska?" I grabbed the spokes of the big wheel, but my heart was in my throat: I'd never steered a boat anywhere near this size, hadn't dared to reveal that fact when I applied for the job.

"Here Joe, here's how we do it," Mick put his big hand on my shoulder, and showed me how to engage the automatic pilot by nudging a bronze lever on the floor and then the big wheel began turning back and forth on its own, and after studying what lay ahead of us, Mick took me over to the chart table on the back wall of the big pilothouse.

And so began my education as an Alaska commercial fishermen. Old Mick showed me how to plot a course taking the powerful tidal currents into account, how to use the tide tables, the textbook-thick British Columbia Pilot, how to tune and interpret the big old fashioned radar the size of a washing machine. He taught me how to tell fish apart—we would be buying five species of salmon from our fishermen and each had a different price, and the many other skills I needed as a fisherman.

But more than that: he filled me with stories of a lifetime spent working up and down the coast, in all kind of boats, in all kinds of weather. Sometimes when I was on watch Old Mick and I would study the charts together, his gnarled hands moving slowly over the penciled course lines from so many voyages and seasons, as if stirring old memories.

That night he tapped the head of an inlet on the Canadian side of the border: "Anyox—used to be a copper mine and smelter back in there, even with a big dam to power it. The fumes killed off most of the trees at the head of the inlet. Worker's families couldn't even grow gardens. We stopped there with freight in the old *Minnie B* in '34."

It was an oral history of the coast, in fits and starts, from that old Norwegian's memory. Mick was a bit of a night owl, and sometimes we'd sit up there for hours together on my night watches, sometimes talking, other times just watching the dim shapes of that vast and lonely land passing by outside the windows. For me, an inexperienced kid from a urban East Coast family, it was magic beyond words.

With totem poles on the land and eagles in the sky, that summer was ALASKA in capital letters.

Three mornings after leaving Seattle, I stood on the bow taking it all in as we pulled into our home base for the 1965 salmon season: the Annette Island Packing Company cannery, in the Tsimpshian native village of Metlakatla, just 50 miles north of the Alaska-Canada border. Backed by snow topped mountains, the cannery, like many up and down the Northwest Coast, was a collection of low buildings built on pilings over the water with a long dock in front, to which a fleet of fishing vessels were tied three deep.

So began my introduction to what was the core industry of the Northwest Coast, especially Alaska for almost a hundred years. With the fishing season opening in just a few days, it was a beehive of activity: fishermen working on their nets and finishing up painting and preparing their boats for the season, cannery workers scrubbing the floors, mechanics testing and repairing the long line of machines that assembled the cans, cut and washed the fish, filled the cans, then sealed and cooked them.

A tidy native village spread out along the shore south of the cannery, with children playing on the gravel beach and dogs wandering freely. Noisy, busy, Seattle seemed a world away.

We got right to work, sliding in to tie up under the 'hoist'—the crane that would unload the freight that we had filled our hold with down in Seattle.

I soon realized that the arrival of a boat loaded with freight from Seattle was a big deal in an isolated native village like that one. Most of the stuff in our hold and in our big lower deck storeroom were pallets of supplies for the cannery itself. But many of the smaller packages that had been dropped off, sometimes late at night, were all for individual villagers: prescriptions, that box of Granny Smith apples that I had wondered about, and dozens of boxes, mostly from Sears, dropped off by friends or taxi.

For, as I discovered, the doorstop-sized Sears & Roebuck mail order catalog was a core staple of life in these isolated communities. Metlakatla did have a post office, but if you could get a friend or even a taxi if it was a big order, to drop off your order to a boat headed up from Seattle to the village, it got there faster and cheaper.

So barely had we gotten the lines on the dock when a procession of shy native women and gruff native guys began coming by, either down the ladder from the dock or by outboard skiff alongside to ask for a package and I'd rummage around in the big storeroom and deliver it. Most said a quiet thanks and moved on.

The oddest delivery that we received down in Seattle was on deck when we got up one morning: an old fashioned foot-powered Singer sewing machine, without any identification or information on who it was for. So I just lugged it up into the big storeroom and kind of forgot about it. Then late that first afternoon in Metlakatla, a battered wood skiff pulled alongside with a rough looking older guy and a grandmotherly woman with white hair in a bun and a shapeless blue pattered Mother Hubbard dress. They were by far the oldest natives I had yet seen.

She said something that I didn't understand, and it took me a moment to realize it wasn't English but Tsimshian, the local language. Then she said "sew-ing," making an up and down motion with her hand and I got it: that old sewing machine was hers.

The man passed me a line and jumped aboard. I pointed into the storeroom, where you could see the sewing machine among the cases of pop, cereal, candy, cookies, etc. And he came out with it in his arms, beaming.

"Ah," said the woman, crying out in a joy that you could understand in any language, and passed me up something covered with a cloth: a pie still warm from the oven. The man set the old Singer on our deck by the rail, clambered back aboard the skiff and I passed that old machine carefully down to where he already had a blanket on the bottom of the skiff to receive this precious possession. And without a word, they were gone, to some cabin, I supposed, so far out of town that the power lines didn't reach. Or maybe they just liked the old ways.

Commercial salmon fishing in Alaska was strictly regulated by what the locals called 'Fish and Game,' actually The Alaska Department of Fish and Game, or just ADF&G. By monitoring both the catch, and the number of fish escaping up the rivers and streams to spawn (and called escapement), they had been able to maintain good catches for many decades, while catches in places like Puget Sound and British Columbia declined. It helped that most of the Alaska salmon streams were essentially in wilderness areas.

To start the 1965 season, a three day opening, as these fishing periods are termed, was scheduled to start in two days, which meant that we had a long busy day to get unloaded, cleaned and fueled up, and load the hanging scales to weigh the fish we would be buying. Finally we left the cannery for the 7 hour steam around the south end of Prince of Wales island to an area known as the 'west coast' where our boats would be starting their salmon seine season the next day.

Seining is the process of using a long net set usually in a circle to catch salmon. Alaska seiners are limited by law to 58 feet and usually have a crew of five.

It was almost midnight before we finally anchored and I got everything shut down in the engine room except for the two cylinder diesel running the refrigeration system, chilling the sea water in our big hold for tomorrow's fish.

As I was wiping down the main engines and cleaning up my workbench, Skipper Lloyd came down the ladder with six small boxes and an odd request. The boxes held injectors, small, penlight-sized devices that squirted a fuel mist into diesel engines.

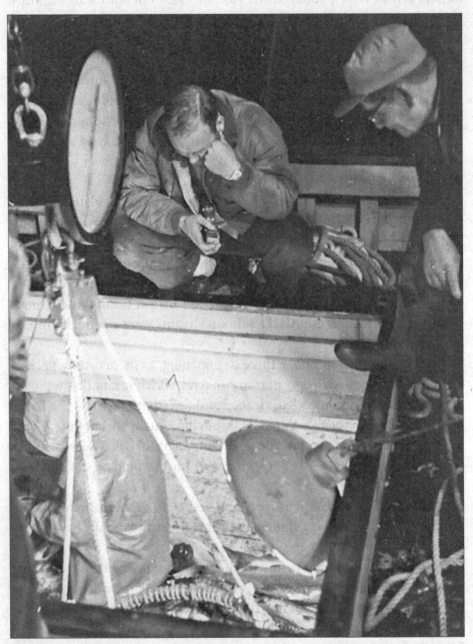

You had to be pretty sharp to tell reds from dogs when the guys you were buying from were trying to fool you.

"Here," he said, "put these in the starboard engine. And clean up the old ones really well and put them back in the boxes."

That was weird, I thought. The old injectors would have to be rebuilt anyway, why clean them up when the injector shop would do all that? The next evening, when our first boat of the season slid alongside to unload his fish, I found out.

"Hey, David," he called out to the skipper, "here are those new injectors you ordered." And passed over the boxed injectors that I had pulled out of our engine the night before. They were probably even still warm! Lloyd had many such tricks up his sleeve, which I came to call, "Secrets of the old time fish buyers."

The challenging part about fish buying was simply learning how to tell the five different species of salmon apart. There are kings (or chinooks), sockeyes (or reds), dogs (or chums), silvers (or cohoes) and humpies (or pinks). Of these, the most similar looking were dogs and reds in the early part of the season when both were just coming in from the ocean and had yet to undergo the dramatic physical changes that would occur when they got closer to spawning and the end of their lives.

Here's how it would go: Lloyd would squat on the deck of the boat that we were buying fish from, looking down into the fish hold where a circular net was hanging beneath our big scales, and several crewmen stood ready with their peughs, essentially one tined pitchforks, used to stab fish in the head and throw them into the scale basket. (In the interests of better fish quality, peughs are no longer used.)

"OK," Lloyd would call out to start the process, "any kings?" Occasionally the larger and most valuable king salmon would be caught in the net. Kings were uncommon. Next it was, "Give me your money fish." This was the call for reds or sockeyes, which might be 10-20% of the day's catch.

With that the guys in the hold would start peughing and flipping reds into the basket as fast as they could, and this was where the buyer had to be on his game. Because to the untrained eye, reds and dogs in June and early July were almost identical and as reds were worth four or five times as much as dogs, the crew would inevitably try to throw in a few dogs with the reds.

"HEY!" Lloyd would yell, and point to the offending fish. The action would stop, and someone would inevitably say something like, "Whad'ya mean.? They're all reds." But then the dog would be taken out and fish would fly until another dog was thrown in as a red and the process started all over again.

However, pretty soon the guys in the hold figured that they couldn't pull one over on Lloyd, and that trying to just slowed down the whole unloading process with other boats waiting, and got on with the reds, then the chums, perhaps 10% depending on when and where they were fishing, and then finally the smaller pinks, which typically accounted for most of the catch.

Approaching Point Retreat lighthouse from the east. Glacier Bay is on the other side of the distant mountains.

In his hand Lloyd had this wooden device about half a foot long which held five individual counters—which he used to keep track of the individual species in the basket, using average weights to figure out the totals later. This was called 'by the fish,' which was faster, but possibly a tiny bit less accurate than weighing each species separately, which would have taken more time.

When the basket had about a thousand pounds, Lloyd would call out the weight from the big circular scale, I would write it down, and then operate the winch controls to hoist it up, swing it over our open hatch, and then our deckhand would pull the line that opened the bottom of the net, allowing the fish to drop into the refrigerated seawater in our hold.

The *Sidney* was rigged with two booms with hydraulic winches on each boom which allowed us to be unloading two boats at the same time, with Mick counting the fish on the boat on the other side.

Icebergs in Stephens Passage: beautiful but possibly deadly at night if you hit one!

After each boat was finished—they might also need fuel or fresh water and we had both—we would pass them our high pressure salt water hose, and they would wash down their decks and holds while their skipper would come aboard us for a minute to sign and take his copy of the 'fish ticket,' as the receipt was called.

Our fleet was all seiners. There were three primary ways of catching salmon in Alaska, trolling—towing baited hooks and lines, gill-netting—setting a fence-like net in the water, and purse seining, With a crew of five including the skipper, seiners used a nylon net typically about 1,500' long by 90' deep with hard plastic foam floats on top and lead weights along the bottom. Additionally there were steel rings at intervals along the bottom of the net, through which a braided nylon line was threaded—the purse line.

When ready to fish, the net was stacked on the stern of the seiner with the end attached to the 'seine skiff' (actually a beefy 18x10 boat with a big gas or diesel engine). The skiff was towed directly behind the seiner attached by a quick release device. When the skipper wanted to start his 'set," he would yell something like "Let 'er go!," the skiff would be released, dragging the end of the net with it. Often a set would be made off a point of land where salmon were known to travel, with the whole net set in a big curving 'C' with the current pushing the fish into the middle of the net. After a period of time, the net would be closed up into a circle, and then both ends of the nylon line that ran through the rings at the bottom of the net would be winched in. The effect of this would be to close the bottom of the net, essentially making a rough circle maybe 380 feet in diameter with the fish trapped inside into a basket. Finally one end of the net would be taken aboard and hoisted up into the power block, a hydraulically op- erated pulley at the top of the boom over the center of the deck, and the net slowly stacked on deck, making the circle smaller and smaller, until the fish were concentrated tightly next to the boat where they could be brought aboard with a winch and a big dip net or brailer.

MY FIRST ICEBERG

Something woke me in the middle of the night, something big scraping our boat. I pulled on a sweatshirt and stepped out, shivering, into the night. I thought one of the big seiners in the anchorage had drug anchor, bumped into us.

But it was ice. Glacier Bay was just across Icy Straits to the north and sometimes bergs would drift across and into our anchorage.

This was a big one, its top even with our boat deck. The moon was full and the berg was illuminated by it, seeming to glow from within. I could see gravel inside the ice, probably scraped from some canyon wall a thousand years before I was born.

I reached out, tried to scrape off some of the gravel. But the ice was too hard and it slowly moved away in the tidal current.

It was magic.

WATCHING OUT FOR CASH BUYERS. ANOTHER element of fish buying that we needed to attend to was watching out for cash buyers. While our boats were usually owned by their skippers, canneries such as the one in Metlakatla would often essentially serve as banks for their fishermen— lending them money over the winter for boat repairs, insurance, net, gear, etc. In those days at the beginning of the season, an owner might owe easily $10 – $20,000 to the cannery.

In the normal course of things, the owner would deliver all his fish to the cannery, and get paid when he got back to town at the end of the season, less what he owed. In a slow fishing season, it might take much of the season for the boat to pay back the money that it had borrowed, but usually at no interest—a pretty good deal.

However, there were other fish buyers, not connected to our cannery, cruising around with big 'cash' signs—where a fishermen could deliver his fish and get cash on the spot. It was obviously attractive for a boat who owed a lot of money to a cannery to sell his fish for cash, often at a higher price, to someone else. Skippers would obviously prefer to do it on the sly, perhaps selling half of his catch for cash, and then coming to us to deliver the rest. So, we would be on the alert for cash buyers and make sure that we anchored up so that our boats couldn't deliver to another buyer without us seeing them do so.

After our last boat—we usually had seven or eight—we would square away the deck: wash the brailers that we had loaded the fish with, wash the whole deck down, coil the fuel and water hoses, etc. Then I would go below for an engine room tour that primarily consisted of making sure the refrigeration system running off its own small diesel was bringing down the water temperature in the hold, shut down the generator for the night, check the load on the batteries, and then the last thing was to pull up the thermometer that hung in the refrigerated water of the fish hold, and record the reading in my engine room log.

One of the best parts of fish buying was that during the typical three or four day fishing period, we would only be buying fish usually in the evening, when meant that often we had the treat of sleeping in! Plus we had a 16' aluminum skiff with a 25 hp. outboard motor, a pretty zippy combination. So if there were no engine room issues that needed my attention, or seiners that came in with a mechanical problem that fell to me to try to fix, I could jump in the skiff with a fishing rod to try and catch a king or nice silver salmon for supper, or simply explore that vast island-studded wilderness that surrounded us.

My favorite day of those summer weeks was always the last day of fish buying. It would usually be almost 8:30 or 9 at night when we'd finally bought our last fish, hosed all down, picked up the anchor and gotten underway for Metlakatla, six or seven hours away. I would spend some time in the engine room making sure all systems were good, wash up, put on a clean sweatshirt, stop at the galley for a coffee and a home made dough nut or cookie—our cook was wicked grumpy but he set a great table—and walk forward to the big pilothouse.

By then Lloyd trusted me enough to let me steer through the night, so he'd show me our position, our route premarked on the chart, and retire.

And I'd sit up there in that big chair, the autopilot working the steering wheel back and forth, looking out at that wonderful panoply of brilliantly colored sky and water, feeling pretty great about how things had turned out for me.

Old Mick would usually come up with a hot mug of tea, maybe with a smell of rum to it, and we'd talk over the events of the day, and that kindly old man's thick hands would wander over the chart and those wonderfully rich stories would begin to tumble out again.

And so the pattern of the first half of the season evolved—three or four days out on the grounds—usually the straits and bays on the west side of Southeast Alaska, a 6- or 8-hour run to Metlakatla, and a busy couple of days at the cannery, unloading, taking fuel and water, and generally tending to the many tasks keeping a big boat like the *Sidney* with many systems up and operating smoothly entailed. As engineer, I was pretty busy, particularly in those first few weeks, making sure I thoroughly understood all the many systems and what they required for operation and maintenance, etc.

Today most canneries in Alaska use these big vacuum unloaders, essentially giant vacuum cleaners that suck the fish out of the holds of boats like ours and deposit them into big tanks where they are rinsed and moved on to the canning line. But in 1965, the *Sidney* and the Metlakatla cannery used the old method: fish elevators. Installed in our fish hold was a big galvanized steel structure containing an endless vertical chain of rectangular buckets that lifted the fish out of the hold and dumped them on a slanted chute on deck on which they slid into the mouth of another fish elevator installed between the pilings of the cannery dock. So to unload, first I would pump out most of the refrigerated seawater out of our holds, and then the noisy clanking process would start. For a full load—the *Sidney* could hold almost 200,000 pounds of salmon—it would take us most of the day to unload. During the peak of the salmon run in mid July, the cannery would be running essentially around the clock—two full canning shifts and the late night shift for clean up.

Asian cannery worker feeding fish into the 'Iron Chink,' the circular machine in the background, circa 1930.

The essential core of the canning process: gutting, cleaning, and cutting the fish, filling, weighing, sealing the cans, and then cooking them in big pressure cookers called retorts was essentially unchanged since the first canneries came to Alaska in 1879. In those early days Asian cannery workers cut the pieces to make the cans out of big flat sheets of tin and soldered them together. In 1965 the cans were shipped flat in the same big cardboard boxes that the filled cans were shipped south in. On the second floor of the cannery was the 'reforming' line—where the flat cans were opened up and one of the ends or lids put on and mechanically sealed. From there an endless line of ready cans ran through a chute down to the can line below.

Aside from pre-made cans, the other big advance in the salmon canning process was the invention of a big drum-shaped machine that cut off heads and tails, sliced open the belly, whisked out the internal organs and intestines, brushed and washed the cavity clean and delivered the salmon ready to be cut up and put into the can. As previously that same work had traditionally been done by Chinese contract labor, the machine was nicknamed the Iron Chink.

Dan Kowalski

A bag of fish comes aboard a purse seiner, already loaded heavily.

Our skipper had a wife and family in Ketchikan, the main town in that part of Alaska, and often as soon as we were back at the cannery, would jump on a float-plane and leave for the two days before it was time to head to the grounds again.

For myself, there were some very attractive native gals my age working in the cannery. On our second weekend in town, I invited one aboard for a beer. The next morning a thoroughly annoyed village elder came down to the boat and made it very clear that if I ever did anything like that again, I would be lucky to keep my job, much less my teeth. It was a sobering visit.

Luckily, on one of our stops in Ketchikan, I struck up an acquaintance with a gal whose dad operated a one man flying service with a float-plane tied up in front of their house. So on those cannery weekends when there was time, and all my chores were done, and it was calm, I'd put on a clean shirt and a warm jacket, jump in the outboard and buzz the 30 miles over to Ketchikan to hang out with Jackie.

The cove at Inian Islands was my favorite anchorage that summer. Icebergs from Glacier Bay would regularly wander in. Today, with the ice much farther up the Bay, such events are rare.

This was two decades before the cruise ship boom would put ten or twelve thousand passengers onto Ketchikan streets most summer days, doubling the population, and transforming the economy.

On summer weekends in 1965, Ketchikan was a rough and tumble frontier town, with logging and fishing crews roaming the streets, filling the rowdy bars and making their own fun. I was 19 and the drinking age was 21, but as far as I could tell, no one cared or even bothered to ask. One night after I ended up on someone's couch, I had a chance to see what the streets of town looked like on Sunday morning: like a war zone, with bodies here and there, though luckily just drunk rather than dead.

At Ketchikan's latitude in mid-June, if the sky is clear at all, it doesn't really get full dark. The sun sets after 9:30, rises again around 4 a.m., but sunset slowly becomes this pale twilight, which eventually becomes a long drawn out dawn. For myself, it meant that I could have a great time around that wild town, but jump into my outboard at 11 or midnight, and in just a few minutes be traveling through this exquisite seascape of blue-black islands and mountains silhouetted against the still pink-yellow sky and water. It was magic experience for a young man.

While the 1965 salmon season started out slow, with most boats delivering just a few tons a day and sometimes much less than that, by mid-July things were cooking, as the salmon, primarily the pinks, poured in from the ocean on their way to the streams where they would spawn and die (if they weren't caught by the five hundred seiners and gillnetters spread across Southeast Alaska.)

Most of the time we would be anchored in a protected cove out of sight of where the guys were fishing out in the wind and the ocean swell. For me it would always be a thrill to see them come around the point, deep in the water with their load of fish. They would tie up, two and three deep on either side of us with the crews excited and talking with each other as they waited their turn to unload.

With the run at its peak, instead of the nice mellow schedule of one round trip a week between the fishing grounds and the cannery, we were almost operating around the clock. Usually the first day's boats would fill us up, and we would head back to the cannery, unload as soon as we got there, and turn around and head right back out to the grounds for another load. The long hours were hard on all of us aboard, but for me at least, it was exhilarating as well—the sense of being part of something so exciting as a big fish run.

Plus so much of the media back then—remember I was from the East Coast—portrayed commercial fishing as an industry in decline, the participants sort of an historical anachronism, like the oyster fishermen in Chesapeake Bay still using their sailing oyster boats, and the lobster fishermen in Maine with their homemade wooden pots. Yet what I found in Alaska was a well regulated, successful fishery that was the core business of many of the region's towns, had been going strong for almost a century, and showed no signs of slowing down.

Plus, I knew that for the natives, the salmon tradition went back way farther than just the arrival of the white men and the first canneries. That it was the availability of salmon and the convenience of being able to smoke and dry the fish so that it became a year round food source that allowed them to create a culture with permanent village sites and relative prosperity as compared to the inland tribes who were more nomadic, having to follow game in its seasonal migrations.

So in that sense, I was part of a tradition that went back thousands of years, the boats and the cans just being the latest iteration of the deep, at times almost spiritual relationship between the salmon and the native peoples of Alaska.

For us on the *Sidney*, especially me, the peak of the run was a blur—meals snatched here and there, a list of little maintenance and repair jobs that never seemed to get shorter. For Mick, our cook, and our deckhand, Chris, they could basically take it easy once the boat was cleaned up at the end of an afternoon of fish buying. But for me, as often as not, I would be called down into the engine room of one of our boats to see if I could sort out some problem. At that time, most of the seiners were powered with either GM 6-71 diesels or Chrysler Royals, flathead eight cylinder gasoline engines. Fortunately, as engines go, these were pretty basic. The Royals usually needed just a set of points or plugs, or a fuel filter changed to get them good as new, and the GM's might need a filter change, a new injector, or perhaps the rack adjusted–the rack was the device that coordinates the fuel flow settings of the six injectors. As we had four separate 71-series GM diesels down in our own engine room, by mid season I was pretty dialed on how to keep them running smoothly. For a 19 year old, it was a pretty exciting and fulfilling time.

As the salmon follow their own cycle, so did our boats. The pink run peaked in mid-July and on the 2nd of August, we followed our fleet north, almost a 20-hour run, to Icy Strait. Our seiners fished the Strait for silvers and chums and we waited for them in this exquisite spot called Inian Cove. Steep hills around us rose to snowy peaks, and it was here that I had that first encounter with an iceberg.

With the advance that I had gotten from Lloyd down in Seattle I had purchased some used dive gear: wet suit, fins, mask, tank, and regulator. The tank, as it turned out, was an old fire extinguisher tank with a valve stuck on top. Can you tell this was way back when rules and regulations on diving equipment were pretty lax? I had used it once in July, just to get the feel for it in shallow water, used maybe a quarter of a tank.

Only luck brought me up alive from a 100' dive in the black of night to untangle our anchor. I had never taken any scuba lessons, it was only my second dive, and my tank was an old fire extinguisher.

Then one August night our anchor wouldn't come up; it had stuck or snagged onto something on the bottom. We tried pulling it from all directions but couldn't budge it, and finally Lloyd turned to me, "You want to try and go down there and try and see what the hell's holding it?"

"Sure," said I, without a second thought, without a clue that I was volunteering for something way, way above my knowledge and skill level.

Lloyd figured we might have to pull something off the anchor and pulled out a coil of 3/4 inch nylon line while I got my gear on, and found one of those rubberized waterproof flashlights to take down with me. They rigged a ladder over the side, and, excited to be using my new gear, I eagerly climbed down, gasped for a moment as the cold water slowly infiltrated into the wet suit, and worked my up to the bow and the anchor cable. Tying the nylon line around my waist, and turning on the flashlight I started working my way down the greasy wire.

We were in about a hundred feet of water, dangerously deep for a diver with no training or knowledge of how easy it is to get the bends.

The cheap "waterproof" flashlight died after a couple of minutes, but I was pretty focused on getting to the anchor and finding out what the deal was.

I reached it without a problem, and feeling around in the total Stygian blackness, found that there was what felt like a steel cable around the fluke, and working carefully and by feel through the neoprene gloves, untied the line from my waist and tied it around the cable.

Then I was slammed by blind, unreasoning panic. For after I tied the nylon line onto the cable, I let go of it and for too long a moment, was not connected to anything. And suddenly realized that I didn't know which way was up. Essentially weightless, and with no visual clues to where up and down lay, for a moment I flailed wildly, breathing rapidly and literally forcing myself not to take off my weight belt, as the only escape. Had I done that, I would have shot to the surface, and if I didn't knock myself out or break my neck on the bottom of the *Sidney*, I would have probably died from the bends. Divers at depths such as I had reached that night absorb nitrogen gas into their bodies, and if they ascend too quickly, the dissolved gas turns into bubbles, causing sometimes fatal nerve and joint damage.

The panic was on the verge of overwhelming me when I bumped into something and frantically grabbed it, and just hung on while my heart slowed down and I could again control my breathing. Eventually I calmed down, realized I had bumped into the anchor, found the chain and cable and started up but somehow remembering that I needed to ascend slowly.

Just then, I started having trouble getting the air I needed, but by that time was calm enough to reach around to the top of the tank behind my head and twist the valve that allowed me to use the reserve air remaining in the tank.

Mick's memory stretched almost back at least 50 years, back to when most smaller boats didn't even have engines, and the seiners pulled in their nets by hand.

From there to the top, I just had to keep my fear in check, forcing myself to ascend slowly, by breathing in enough to achieve slight positive buoyancy and feeling the steel cable sliding through my hands. I remembered that I had to do a safety stop at 20 feet for a few minutes to make sure I didn't get the bends. But when I finally started seeing a glow of the *Sidney's* deck lights in the water above me, it was all I could do to not just bolt to the surface.

As it was, it was an sobered and lucky young man that passed up his flippers and tank to his friends, and clambered slowly up the ladder to the deck.

Everyone was there, waiting.

"How'd it go down there?" Lloyd asked.

"Cable over the anchor . . . I tied the line onto it. But dark down there." I answered, trying to control the shivering that was coming over me in waves.

They worked the cable loose and the anchor up, and I took a long hot shower. But still, it was a long while before I stopped shivering. Part of it was the cold, sure—it was a thin wet suit and there were a few small icebergs in the cove. But a big part, I think, was the sobering realization of how close I had come to dying down there, and how lucky I had been. The panic had almost completely overwhelmed me and, if I'd had the additional burden of trying to remember how to turn on the reserve air valve when I was flailing around, not sure of where up was, I'm sure I would have dropped my weight belt and bolted to the surface and that would have been my end. Or even worse—passing out from running out of air and sinking slowly to the bottom. I never would have even been found. Plenty to shiver about . . .

Power scow Eigel B, *Inian Cove, 1965. Note the A&P red logo—this major grocery chain used to operate canneries in Alaska. She was still going strong in 2019!*

But for the most part, those weeks with the fleet fishing Icy Strait, and us anchored up in Inian Cove and making the long round trip back to the cannery once a week, were the best part of the season for me, especially when we'd finished unloading our boats, I'd wrapped up my engine room chores and had dinner and finally walked forward to take over steering.

The sun would have set by then, but the twilight would be bright enough for Old Mick to be OK steering for another hour, so I'd just sit up there with him talking. The automatic pilot would be doing the actual steering, so there would be plenty of time at the chart table, with those old knobby arthritic hands stabbing at places on the chart and telling stories.

Finally when it got good and dark, Old Mick would sigh, "OK, kid, here's where we're going," and spend a moment showing where we were on the line marked on the chart, make a last entry in the log book, and shuffle out the pilothouse door, and I would be alone.

View from our anchorage, Nakat Inlet. Remote, perhaps visited by a few dozen boats a year: this is the wonder of Southeast Alaska.

By then we would have made the turn south out of Icy Strait, and Chatham Strait, like a vast dark canyon, wide and empty, would stretch away to the south in front of us.

I'd turn all the instrument lights to their lowest setting, and just settle down in that big pilothouse chair, looking out at the dim outlines of the land and sea ahead of us.

Today's boats use VHF radios, which only have a range of 25-30 miles, but back in 1965, work boats used AM radios (though on a different frequency than radio stations). The AM signal would sometimes skip between atmospheric layers and travel for many hundreds of miles or even more. With the modern VHF sets, folks would call each other on Channel 16, then agree to do their talking on another channel, so unless you 'chased' a call to whatever channel they went to, you would only hear their initial call.

But in Alaska in those old AM days, most boats used two channels, 2638 and 2738 kilohertz (kHz). to talk on. On those night runs down Chatham Strait at the end of the fishing period, most of the seiners and gillnetters were anchored up for the night with radios off. So the conversations would be mostly between other tenders, like us, loaded with fish, and headed for their home cannery. One tender, buying fish south of Ketchikan was headed for Bellingham, some 500 miles south, and sounded like he was having a breezy buck across the open waters of Dixon Entrance, near the Alaska -Canada border. He'd have just enough time to get there, unload, take on fuel and water, and start steaming back to Alaska, arriving just as the next fishing period started, a hard schedule.

And now and again, we'd hear a conversation obviously from a very different part of the country, either by the accents, or what they were talking about.

"It's pretty bad out here, Dad," started one conversation, "it looks like they're breaking all the way across." The voice was anxious, strained.

"Just take your time, Son," came the reply, calm, reassuring, and measured, "I came across just an hour ago, and it was ebbing even harder then . . ."

The son started to say something else, in a voice that seemed a little calmer, and then he was gone as the layers in the atmosphere shifted and his signal bounced to land who knew where.

I figured they might be Oregon crabbers, off a coast where most of the harbors were river mouths guarded by bars that broke when the weather got bad; just when you needed to get in. I cocked an ear toward the radio and waited, but the callers were gone.

Lloyd had a lot of friends on boats, and I'd heard him talking to fish boats or tugboats way up or down the coast, coming in clear as anything, and then cut off in mid-sentence, not to reconnect again. It was just the way those old AM radios worked.

On work boats today there'd be a big GPS plotter, front and center, or set on the counter near the engine controls. The plotter would display a nice colored chart with a boat icon to show you where you were, as well as the contours of the land and the depth of the water. On more sophisticated setups, the plotter could be interfaced with the automatic pilot, so you could lay out a course with changes in direction around buoys or points, and the autopilot would make the course changes you had programmed into it. So navigation was just like a video game: just keep the boat icon in the blue away from the yellow land or black rocks (or whatever colors your particular set showed.)

But on the *Sidney* and the rest of the fleet back in 1965, it was navigation the old fashioned way: keep cross checking your position with all the information available. When we'd pass one of the few navigation lights, I'd open up the 1965 Light List, and check the light's characteristics against what I was seeing: one light might be three short flashes the next one down the line, two long ones, and so on. Our radar had this variable range ring thingy so that I could see how far off the land we were, so that I could compare it to the plotted line on the chart. Our fathometer constantly registered our depth; that too would be compared to the depths shown on the chart.

And so our season went—never a dull moment; always something interesting going on. For me, just 19 that summer, a pretty green kid, it was ALASKA in capital letters.

And more—as the weeks passed and the season progressed sometimes we'd be first back to Metlakatla from the distant grounds with our load of fish and you'd see the cannery crews ambling down the dirt road from town to the cannery, getting ready to work on our fish. That whole little native village centered around that cannery. All those lives wrapped up with the fish that we carried from hundreds of miles away.

Before the whites arrived with their diseases and their booze to wreck havoc on the native culture, this had all been going on too—at a different level, to be sure, but the same idea. Wherever the salmon had run and there had been people, there were fish camps along the rivers or on the shores of the bays. In western Alaska, up and down the great rivers, the natives dried the fish in big racks in the sun, putting them up for the long winter ahead. In rainy Southeast Alaska, where there really weren't enough long hot days to dry fish, they would be smoked; today's delicacy, yesterday's staple.

And so I felt part of this grand tradition, when each spring, thousands of men and boats would leave their home harbors to go "Up North," wanting to put that elusive winter money in their ass pockets.

The end of the season was bittersweet. After a rainy summer the weather at the end of August turned fine, and I was in just a t-shirt and shorts as we unloaded the big fuel tank, the scales and the fish elevator, and scrubbed and washed our fish hold in preparation for filling it with pallets of case salmon to take back to Seattle.

"Our greatest food from the sea," was printed on each case of cans that went into our big hold, along with the codes that identified the species, size of can, and the lot number. In those days, and even today to a certain extent, much of the canned pack was shipped south and warehoused before being labeled. Some would eventually get the Annette Island Packing labels, and others, from the same cannery, might be sold to some grocery chain that preferred to put on their own labels.

It was just somehow deeply satisfying to be involved directly in the production of such a great food like that, something so rewarding in the daily life that I had been living on the boat. Something that I knew that I would miss in the very different world that lay ahead of me after I got off the boat.

On the 650 mile trip back to Seattle, I took most of the night watches, and old Mick would sit up with me until he got tired, as was his custom, and we'd yarn for a bit as the silhouettes of dark hills and mountains against the starry sky marched past the windows and I wondered how long it would be before I had a experience like that again.

Lloyd saved his last trick for the very end. On that last day, as we steamed south down Puget Sound for Seattle after the three day run from the cannery, I cleaned up the engine room, the tools, and the workbench until they all shone, packed my sea bag, and couldn't wait to hit the dock, call my parents and make a plane reservation back to the east coast as soon as I got to a phone.

A Caddy was waiting for Lloyd when we got to our berth inside the locks.

"Hey, Lloyd, what about getting paid? School starts in a couple of days." I'd done my part, now I just wanted to get home; I hadn't seen my family in over a year.

He pulled a bunch of twenties out of his wallet, and jerked his chin over toward his beat up old pickup truck parked at the head of the dock. "Here, kid, take my truck downtown to the Millionaires Club, and hire some rummies to unload the cans. Call me when you're done, and I'll cut you a check."

Two days of hard work finally got the *Sidney* unloaded, and I said good-bye to old Mick, and headed East. After that amazing summer, all I wanted to do was to get back to Alaska with my own boat.

Mick and I, Southeast Alaska, 1965.

Denise, *Saltspring Island, B.C. After all my dreams, and talk, and Fish U., how did it end up like this?*

WOULD YOU GO TO ALASKA IN THIS?

IT TOOK A WHILE. AT FISH U. (actually the commercial fisheries program at the University of Rhode Island) we studied navigation, diesel engines, hydraulic and electrical systems. A squeaky voiced character from Newfoundland taught us the art of building and repairing trawl nets. We fished them with our own 50' boat, all of us taking turns to practice our boat handling.

When one of the guys in the program offered to lease me his salmon gillnetter, the *Denise*, to take and fish in Alaska, I was beyond thrilled: at long last, taking my own boat up north. In those pre-cell phone days he didn't have a photo, never actually told me how long it was.

And so in my mind it became this handsome 36 footer, and I envisioned my girlfriend and myself, sipping wine up on the flying bridge as we cruised up the winding channels of the Inside Passage.

ALASKA

CANADA

BERING SEA

SOUTHEAST
ALASKA

Kodiak Is.

To The Bering Sea:
Getting There Is Half the Fun

1 - Seattle: our shiny Marco 104 seemed soooo big at the dock..
2 - Heavy southerly gale with snow, violent tide rip blocks our route, had to pick our
    way through narrow channels in the black with no chart...
3 - The sheltered island waterways of SE Alaska tugs at my heartstrings...
4 - Iced up and turned around by northerly gale to huddle in Yakutat
5 - Iced up very badly at Cape St. Elias, all hands on deck to chip ice off
6 - Almost frozen into the "ice-free" port of Seward
7 - Huddled in Uyak Bay from violent norther - gravel blown off the beach
    sandblasts our hull. Iced up badly in Shelikof Strait each time we try to exit...
8 - The Weather Gods allow us a safe entry to the Bering Sea at Unimak Pass
9 - Dutch Harbor at last: we tie up next to a 50 year old wooden crabber, unloading
    crab and all iced up. And we thought we were soooo tough: very humbling.

King Crab was the biggest fishing bonanza in Alaska history and I was very fortunate to get in on it. This is my shipmate Walter Kuhr in 1971; he went on to own a fleet of large crab and groundfish boats.

And so when school was over, I flew out to Seattle from my East Coast home with my tools, boots, clothes, and rain gear, totally excited by the prospect of a season in Alaska in my own boat! Walked finally, down the dock at Seattle's Fishermen's Terminal to see my new command.

And stopped, dead in my tracks: could that piece of . . . shit be the *Denise*? But it was: instead of 36' it was 26', and all but derelict. The fly-bridge was quarter inch plywood; for show only; if two people climbed up there, the boat would capsize.

And though in Fish U. we had all those technical courses, there wasn't a single minute of discussion about how some boats could be unsafe: how to walk away from a bad boat. I should have; with Fish U. behind me, I could have gotten a great job.

But no. I was determined to go to ALASKA IN MY BOAT.

I tore into it: painted, rewired, hauled the engine out and rebuilt it in a friend's garage. Built new nets, and all the time thrilled to be part of that exciting group of young men at Fisherman's Terminal, getting their boats ready to head to Alaska for the salmon season.

Iceing up is wahat we feared most. In extreme conditions a vessel would accumulate enough ice, which if not removed, would capsize even the most seaworthy craft.

Finally I was ready to go; all I needed to do was to test drive the rebuilt engine, load groceries and head north!!

A hundred yards from the dock the engine threw a rod through the side of the block, ruining it. As we were waiting for someone to tow us back to the dock, the mechanic said, "Weird . . . that same thing happened to the last engine I rebuilt."

My money was almost gone. I threw in a used engine that would barely push the boat at 5 mph, rebuilt the nets (Washington State nets are deeper than Alaska nets), and tried to make a season in Washington State waters where the salmon runs are much smaller.

At the end of the season, I was broke and deeply discouraged. Only the new understanding that had I tried to reach Alaska in the unseaworthy *Denise,* I would have probably drowned in the first bad tide rip or storm made me feel a little better.

But meanwhile, in the distant reaches of the Bering Sea, the most remote and roughest of all Alaska's many commercial fishing areas, big things were happening. The king crab fishery, which was to become legendary four decades later with the widely popular *Deadliest Catch* TV series, was hitting critical mass.

With high catch volumes and rising prices, the first new steel crabbers were just appearing, a huge improvement over the wooden vessels that had been pressed into service for which they were never built or intended.

In an ironic turn of good fortune, George Fulton, the American whom I had met when I was fishing in Iquique in northern Chile seven years earlier, who had gotten me on the boat that I took up from Chile to Seattle to begin my Alaska fishing career, was in town. He was taking delivery of one of the first new big steel crabbers, the 104' *Flood Tide*, and needing one more man to fill out his crew, hired me on!

Our 104 footer was the toughest crabber that the best Northwest shipyard could build, but when the Bering Sea winds screamed, we ran and hid.

Loaded up with new crab pots—6'x6'x2.5' and each weighing around 700 pounds empty, more like giant cages—stacked on the back deck in two layers—we left Seattle for the Bering Sea in late February, 1971.

I just assumed our trip up to Dutch Harbor, the primary port in the Aleutian Islands, would be basically just driving the boat up to start work. Foolish me. The dangerous weather along the Alaska coast at that time of year wasted no time in humbling us. First a gale and a viscious tide rip in Hecate Straits had us picking our way through the islands to the shelter of the Inside Passage, on a snow thick night, without a chart, guided only by the hazy memory of our skipper's brother. A few nights later near lonely Cape St. Elias, we became so top-heavy from sea spray freezing on our boat—icing up—that we were in danger of capsizing. Only by going out on deck in the middle of the night with hammers, baseball bats, and shovels were we able to knock off the ice and save ourselves. A few days after that we were huddled behind a sandspit off of Shelikof Straits on Kodiak Island where the wind blew so hard that it was picking up sand and gravel off the beach and sand blasting the paint off our bow.

It was a mighty sobered crew that finally started their crab season.

There were some big trips from the Bering Sea that summer, but not from us. Though there was legendary crabbing somewhere, the grounds were thousands and thousands of square miles of almost featureless bottom, and as a newbie, George hadn't made a tight circle of friends who might share knowledge of where the mother load of crab might be.

One day in May this tug passed us towing a big barge stacked three layers high with 40' metal container vans. But on top there was half dozen nice looking gillnetters. They seemed a long ways from any fishery that I was familiar with, so I queried Russell, our mate, "Bristol Bay," he said, jerking his head toward the eastern horizon. "Getting to be a few more fish there now . . ."

Small boats, that you could run yourself maybe with a friend. Such had been my failed dream with the *Denise*. Crabbing was seeming more and more like a bad factory job, without yet any sign of the big paycheck that was supposed to make up for the dangerous and remote conditions. Seeing those nice seaworthy gillnetters got me dreaming again, hoping that there was a rainbow we hadn't yet seen at the end of the dark tunnel that the season was becoming.

But finally, in September and October, working our gear among the hidden underwater canyons south of Unalaska and Akutan Islands, where the bottom begins to drop off into the 18,000' depths of the Aleutian Trench, we found 'em. There was a 75 pot limit in that area, and we had our 75 as close together as we could without getting the buoy lines tangled with each other. And pot after pot they came so full of big male crab that the nylon meshes were bulging, the crab bunched in so tight that you couldn't possibly put them all back in without pushing and injuring them. 2,000 pounds or more, pot after pot and we'd look down into the dark thousand foot-deep water and wonder how many crabs we were crushing when the heavy pots crashed into the bottom after we had set them.

A big sea comes over the Flood Tide's *rail. Often when our skipper saw one coming, he would blow the horn alert us of the danger.*

Crab are hardy enough to survive out of water if you hose them down every little while. So when the fishing was hot we'd fill our holds full (about 170,000 pounds of crab) but then keep fishing, putting the rest on deck. I've seen a lot of science fiction movies, but nothing ever as weird as night-time fishing with 30,000 pounds of crab slowly sliding back and forth on deck in the swells.

And so, as the expression goes, we put our "winter money (and actually a lot more) in our ass pockets." With the great steaming volcanoes of the Alaska Peninsula in the distance, we loaded that boat, and loaded it, and loaded it again until the season was over.

George asked me to come back for the following season. Said I could be relief skipper. Said if I did good, he and his partners would help me get my own boat. But I turned him down. The Bering Sea was a hell hole; I'd seen where and how I wanted to fish that summer on the *Sidney*, six years earlier: for salmon in the protected waters of Southeast Alaska.

The full story of the crab fishery and our 1971 Bering Sea season may be found in my *Bering Sea Blues*, published by Epicenter Press in 2011.

A wonderful woman, a dog, a new boat, and all of Southeast Alaska to fish in: life was great!

MY OWN BOAT AT LAST

IT IS SUMMER, 1973. I am a young salmon gillnetter, working on my net on the float at Port Protection, a tiny roadless community lost in the vast wilderness archipelago that is Southeast Alaska. A dozen other fishermen, mostly older, have their small, one and two person boats tied to the float; most are working on their nets, 1200' long by 30' deep. This settlement of some 60 year round residents has no roads; everyone gets around by boat. But in the summer salmon season it is home to a dozen or so salmon gill-net boats from Puget Sound ports in addition to the local boats.

A fisherman from Gig Harbor, Washington, Ralphie Sulich, from a fishing family of Croatian immigrants, is walking slowly down the dock, kibitzing as he goes; the fishing community is small here; we all know one another. He stops at the guy next to me, John Bucich, another Croat; they talk for a bit about the three day fishing period past, compare notes and scores.

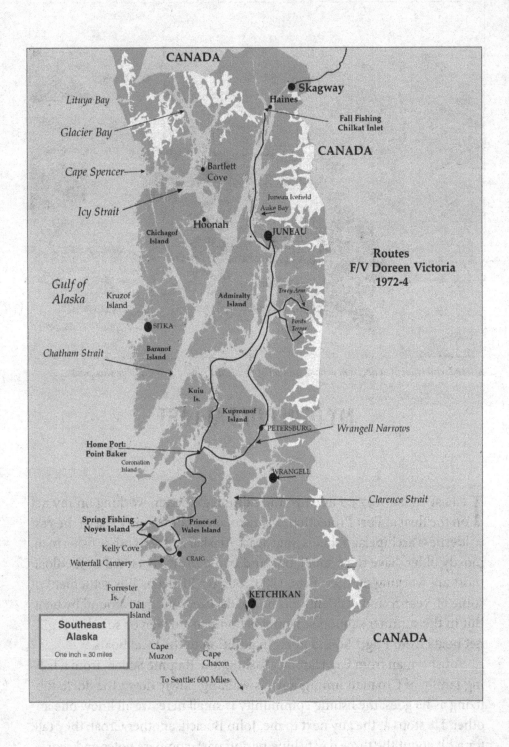

CANADA

Lituya Bay

Skagway

Haines

Glacier Bay

Fall Fishing
Chilkat Inlet

CANADA

Cape Spencer →

Bartlett
Cove

Icy Strait

Juneau Icefield

Auke Bay

Hoonah

JUNEAU

Chichagof
Island

**Routes
F/V Doreen Victoria
1972-4**

*Gulf of
Alaska*

Kruzof
Island

Admiralty
Island

Tracy Arm

SITKA

*Fords
Terror*

Chatham Strait

Baranof
Island

Kuiu
Is.

Kupreanof
Island

PETERSBURG

Wrangell Narrows

**Home Port:
Point Baker**

Coronation
Island

WRANGELL

Clarence Strait

**Spring Fishing
Noyes Island**

Prince of
Wales Island

Kelly Cove

Waterfall Cannery →

CRAIG

Forrester
Is.

Dall
Island

KETCHIKAN

**Southeast
Alaska**

One inch = 30 miles

CANADA

Cape
Muzon

Cape
Chacon

To Seattle: 600 Miles ↘

Doug Stokes, off Cape Addington in Anatevka, *spring 1973. Not a very nice place.*

Bruce Gore, another young gillnetter and a friend was working on his net next to mine, 'overhauling' it with his wife Kathy, on the net rack, two long poles set parallel to the ground at about hip height. She was pulling the cork line from one end to the other, he the lead line. When they came to a rip, they stopped to sew it up.

Ralphie came over to where we are working and started right out with:

"You guys should get a Bristol Bay permit. Limited Entry just started up there; you could get one for two grand."

John Bucich hears the conversation, answers for us. "Ah, c'mon Ralphie, everyone knows there's no fish up there, the Japanese fished the Bay all out."

"Yeah, but we're gonna get the 200 mile limit, there's gonna be fish, you'll see."

Our hands were pretty full already. We were still relative newcomers to fishing Sumner Strait and still had a lot to learn. The idea of trying a new fishing area, a thousand miles further west and north, where you had to put your boat on a barge to even get there, seemed way too big a step to make. But still, we all had heard stories about the Bay, and there was something fascinating about such a place: no trees; volcanoes and tundra. So alien to what we were used to.

I'd taken my king crab crew share the previous spring and bought a sweet fiberglass 32' combination boat (rigged to both troll and gill-net for salmon) and finally, in May of 1972, achieved the dream I'd had ever since that summer of 1965 on the *Sidney*: going to Alaska in my own boat.

It was everything I'd hoped for and more. Exploring and fishing in that vast wilderness with my wife in our new boat filled me up almost to bursting. We found other young couples, also fishing Alaska for the first time, traveled up the Inside Passage together: 8 days of winding through islands and channels almost without number. At night we'd drop the hook in some protected cove and wonder, once again, how many miles it was to the next nearest human.

Seeing your boat out your living room (actually our only room) window is a fisherman's dream.

We made the tiny community of Port Protection, and its equally tiny (50 folks) neighbor two miles away, roadless Point Baker, our home base for the season. We liked the community so much that we bought a tiny two acre island, on a private cove, with a gorgeous western exposure and view, for $17,000. It was more than a year before we even realized it was an island. The west side was waterfront, to the east was a marsh, with a winding path to a neighbors a hundred yards away. I'd headed over one fall afternoon to borrow something and came around a corner in the path to the marsh and stopped in my tracks: the marsh had been replaced by water with bits of grass sticking up here and there: the biggest tide of the fall had totally filled it.

After the '72 season, in our houseboat on Seattle's Lake Union, we made plans for a cabin on our island. But the boat needed a new radar, there were nets to buy, etc. So as our money dwindled, so did the size of our new-home-to-be until whatever roof we could get over our heads for $1,500 would have to be it. We settled on a 12-by-20-foot box with a half loft, 240 square-feet: an early tiny house.

With tight-fisted determination, we scoured garage sales and discount building suppliers. At a second-hand store we found a big oil range for $35; at another, all our windows and doors for $175. In my tiny floating shop— our winter home was a houseboat in Seattle's Lake Union—I prefabbed a Formica kitchen counter top, complete with sink and drawers. We got a wood stove, nails, and shingles, all on deep discount, and purchased a 16-foot cedar skiff with a 10-horsepower 1958 Evinrude outboard. Tool by tool, fitting by fitting, we packed the supplies aboard our 32-foot gill-net vessel and skiff to tow north.

Hand trolling family, 1973: in such little boats a season can be made.

Loaded deep with supplies, we had to pick our weather for the 750 mile trip up the Inside Passage. In every exposed passage I had to stop, have my wife Susanna steer the boat slowly into the seas and pick my moment to haul the skiff alongside, jump carefully aboard and pump it out.

Shortly after we arrived in Point Baker, the mail boat came in with our pickup truck-sized bundle of lumber. The plan had been to tow the tightly strapped bundle of lumber through the narrow back channel to our secluded cove and house site. But it was so green and dense,—locally called "pond dried"—it wouldn't even float. So we had to set it temporarily on the dock and then haul it in our skiff, load by load to our island.

End of the season and only the die hards are left: buying fish in October snowstorm, Chilkat Inlet, near Haines.

In the three weeks before the salmon season began we struggled. The wood was so wet it splashed when your hammer missed the nail. My one and only hand saw bent on the first beam we cut. It rained every day; every night we would take the skiff back to our boat at the Point Baker dock, heat up something quick, and fall, exhausted, shivering, into our sleeping bags.

And created something exquisite: out of every window was the water. As we ate at the driftwood table, we could see eagles swooping low over the cove. There were curious seals, and most marvelous of all, a pair of humpbacks that hung out in the tide rips by West Rock, off the mouth of our cove. On still nights, we could hear the sigh-like breathing of the whales as they surfaced and exchanged fresh air for stale.

We called our little cove Port Upton. With friends we dragged big logs off the beach, got more lumber from town to build a big float to work on our nets. Just us and our friends in that wild and remote cove.

When the first snow came one November evening, the fire in the wood stove crackled cheerily and our kerosene lamp shone out on the vast and wild world beyond the windows.

It was magic.

Exploring: a decade before the big cruise ships began coming to Alaska, we set out to discover South-east Alaska's special places. This is Fords Terror, a spectacular and difficult to enter inlet.

At Point Baker there was a floating store/bar, and across the harbor, a floating post office. The bartender was also the fish buyer; you could sell your fish for bar credit. The mail/freight boat came Thursday, usually after midnight. If you wanted ice cream, Friday morning was your moment as the freezer in the store didn't work very well. The big city, where we might take our boat every month/six weeks for major shopping, was Petersburg, fifty miles away, population maybe 2,000 if the salmon fleet was in.

Of course a floating bar had a few wrinkles. It was built on a raft of big cedar and spruce logs, with foam blocks shoved underneath here and there when the logs got waterlogged. And it didn't need one of those

"Maximum capacity" signs; on a Saturday night in fishing season you better be wearing your boots as when it got crowded, water would start to seep up through the floor, and it was time for a few folks to leave. It wasn't a place for fancy drinks either. Once a rare yacht tied up at the bar and a well dressed couple—not seen much in those parts—walked in. Asked what might be his pleasure, the gentleman asked for a whiskey sour for his wife and a Manhattan for himself.

"Look," said the burly bartender, putting a fist the size of a ham on the counter, "we got whiskey and water, whiskey and coke, and whiskey and Tang. And we save the ice for the fish." The couple settled for cold beer.

Getting to and from the bar/store had its own challenges. Most of the folks at Point Baker lived right in the harbor so they could row home easily if they had imbibed a little too much. But my wife and I and several other households lived on the back channel, accessed through a narrow passage which was almost dry at low tide. Stay a little late at the bar on a dropping tide? You might up wading, towing your skiff and hoping you could make it all the way through.

There was another way to the store for us back channel folks if the tide was way down: out into Sumner Straits and east a few hundred yards to the entrance to Point Baker harbor. One late fall morning, thinking ill of no one, needing milk when the tide was down, I jumped into our little cedar 16 footer and headed out into Sumner Strait. Daydreaming I putted along, not realizing how fast the was current was ebbing and how hard it was blowing up the Strait from the south. In an instant I was in a violent tide tip with steep breaking waves. Had the engine failed at that particular moment, which it regularly did, the seas would have come aboard and your author's epitaph might have been: "Lost at sea, going to get the milk."

What was special about Point Baker-Port Protection was this: there was land for sale and the fishing was good. Due to so much land being under Federal control as National Forests, parks and wildlife refuges, little was actually for sale, so it was really a rare situation. Plus, the fishing grounds were so protected and so close that you could make a good enough living trolling for salmon with a very small open boat. So a little fleet evolved that we called "puddle jumpers": wooden, usually less than 20', rigged with two trolling poles and usually powered with a Briggs and Stratton 15 h.p. inboard, fitted with a reduction gear made locally of belts and pulleys to slow the rpms enough for the propellor. The B&S engines were popular because you could order them from the Sears & Roebuck catalog, they would be delivered by the mailboat and were way cheaper and simpler than an outboard.

The hand trollers were a throwback to the days before small engines became widely available and fleets of rowing trollers would congregate in places where there was a store, good fishing, someone to buy their fish and a protected harbor. Whole little tent cities would appear seasonally in places like Port Alexander, at the south end of Baranof Island.

And like those traveling rowing trollers, the hardiest of the young Point Baker hand trollers with the most seaworthy boats would travel in the spring to the rugged ocean coast, set up their tents and fish in the big waters. It wasn't without risk; a friend told me about his close call:

"I was a mile offshore and was just thinking maybe I should head in and a big wave I didn't see came over the stern and killed the engine. I started bailing, but there were more seas coming and I figured I was done for. Then this big power troller came out of nowhere and threw me a line and started towing me really slowly giving me time to bail and get my engine going and then he followed me in to make sure I was O.K.

"But's what's weird is this: I had looked around earlier and remember thinking that I'd better be careful as I was all alone out there. It was a miracle."

The patriarch of the hand trollers was a older local nicknamed "Flea" who fished a single line out of his tired Briggs and Stratton powered puddle jumper. He was retired, had his monthly social security check and rarely missed the daily bite. At the end of the day you'd see him after selling his handful of fish, beer in hand, put-putting along the narrow back channel to his little cabin. Not a bad retirement.

A lot of the newcomer hand trollers were young folks with long hair— this was the '70s—and looked down up on by the older conservative power troll fishermen of the community. But not Flea—he welcomed them, showed them how to rig their gear, where to set the little gill-nets for bait herring. Often the newcomers would be down on their luck as they figured out how to fish and often, Flea might take them or one of their children out with him, even give them his fish money at the end of the day.

The Gores and ourselves were welcomed by the older fishermen of those communities. We had big, able boats, our hair was relatively short and we listened to their advice. But mostly we were young in a community that definitely needed new blood. And so, as Flea had been to the long haired hand trollers, the old timers mentored us: the right color of gill-net to use, how to avoid the "big meanie"—the violent tide rip that roared up the straits full of logs and kelp on big tides, where the streaks of fish were along the shore—stuff that would have taken us years to figure out on our own.

In the spring we would travel out to the wild ocean coast, often with weather so bad we'd have to lie two days on our anchor with the wind howling, for every day that we fished.

In the summer we would troll and gill-net in Sumner Strait, right in front of our cabin, our little fleet of friends laying at our float in Port Upton on the weekends.

This was all a decade before the big cruise ships started coming North and except for the Alaska State Ferries, and a occasional tugboat, we felt like we had that vast island wilderness all to ourselves.

Once we poked our way past the icebergs in narrow, steep sided, and winding Tracy Arm to the face of Dawes Glacier and just lay there in awe. The water rushing down the raw rock walls, the ice tumbling from the glacier face gave it a primeval, desolate, even frightening air. And yet the beauty was overwhelming, and we got in our tiny dingy with our dog and rowed among bergs the size of houses. Clueless to the dangers: that as the bergs melted and their center of gravity changed they could capsize without warning, literally falling on top of us. That a thousand ton piece of ice falling from the glacier into the bay would create a wave big enough to easily capsize our little craft.

The next day at high water slack, we transited the creek-like entrance to the gash in the mountain wall that was Ford's Terror and dropped the anchor. And looked up and around in wonder as the sun played on the tops of the mountains around that remote and steep sided basin. At dusk pairs of ducks settled into the creek that wound down from the hills, and when the day was gone we looked up in wonder and awe at the northern lights playing above us. Little known or visited in those days, I wondered how many years it might be before that remote basin even had another human visitor.

In the fall we would travel to the wind tunnel that was Lynn Canal, with Glacier Bay just on the other side of the mountains, to try to double our season gill-netting for the ten-dollar-a-fish dog salmon. We'd stay until the snow drove us out of there. I remember a trip back to our cabin that took three days, anchoring up each night, the only boat in lonely and wild anchorages. The last day we went through winding and narrow Rocky Pass just at dusk, with flights of ducks settling on the water in the shallows. Crossed Sumner Strait with the light failing to tie up at our own float after six weeks away. Pumped out the skiff and rowed ashore. Our dog ran off to try and find his old friends, while I built a fire and Susanna found the rum. The warmth of the fire finally filled the room as we looked out at the wild world outside, and our life seemed filled up in a way it never did in the south.

In later years, when many of my gill-netting friends and myself had moved our fishing operations to the bleak tundra and volcano-rimmed world of Western Alaska for more lucrative fishing, we would refer to our lives in Point Baker/Port Protection and in a larger sense, our lives in Southeast Alaska, as a "lifestyle fishery," It essentially meant we weren't making much money but were loving the experience. But if someone had told me that when we were trying to gill-net in the snow in the fall with our cork lines icing up, or the fall that it took us a month of hard traveling to just get our boat back down to Seattle, I probably would have disputed it.

But in reality the experience of fishing in the wilderness like that with just a few other boats around, of having our little cabin on the water, with a wonderful sunset view out over "Port Upton," fit in with what a friend pointed out once: "If you are a commercial fisherman and you can look out your window and see your boat on the mooring, you are living your dream." We could and we were.

More of those days can be found in my first book, the award-winning *Alaska Blues*, published by Alaska Northwest Books, 1975.

North Wind *in Grenville Channel.*

PART II—THE FISH BUYER'S TALE

IN THE SPRING OF 1975 MY life was at low tide. I'd split up with my wife, Susanna, and sold my gill-net permit to a friend; I just felt like I should try something else for a while. Maybe heading back east to fish; I had friends in Maine. Also I was trying to write a book about my Alaska experiences and it wasn't going very well. So at the same time, I wasn't really ready to put Alaska behind.

Then literally out of the blue, I got this call from John Enge Jr., a friend who was coordinating the tenders or fish buying operation at the Whitney-Fidalgo cannery in Petersburg, Alaska.

"Hey Joe," he said, "you want to run the *North Wind* for us this season?"

"Wow," I thought, "the *North Wind*, a 80' barge-shaped boat with a big comfortable pilothouse aft. They even had a little hot tub on the back deck.

It was a totally creamer boat."

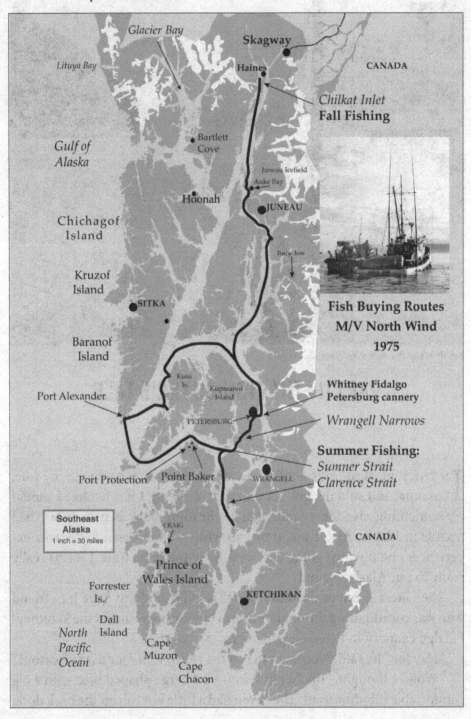

Glacier Bay

Skagway

Lituya Bay

Haines

CANADA

Chilkat Inlet
Fall Fishing

Gulf of
Alaska

Bartlett
Cove

Juneau Icefield

Auke Bay

Hoonah

JUNEAU

Chichagof
Island

Tracy Arm

Kruzof
Island

SITKA

Fish Buying Routes
M/V North Wind
1975

Baranof
Island

Kuiu
Is.

Kupreanof
Island

Port Alexander

Whitney Fidalgo
Petersburg cannery

PETERSBURG

Wrangell Narrows

Port Protection Point Baker

WRANGELL

Summer Fishing:
Sumner Strait
Clarence Strait

Southeast
Alaska
1 inch ≈ 30 miles

CRAIG

CANADA

Prince of
Wales Island

Forrester
Is.

KETCHIKAN

Dall
Island

North
Pacific
Ocean

Cape
Muzon

Cape
Chacon

The wilderness begins; in Sutil Channel, north of Yuculta Rapids.

I jumped at it. A few days later, I was in the office of John Lyons, who ran the Whitney Ketchikan cannery in the summer, and Whitney's Seattle shipyard in the winter.

"Hey, John," sez I, "Where's the *North Wind*, you know, that great power scow?"

"Look, kid," he said, "the only *North Wind* we got is that ferro-cement piece of shit, and the sooner it gets out of here the better."

My heart sank, I walked the docks, past the really nice *Eileen* and *Linda*, gorgeous steel 80-footers with two story pilothouses, the *Snow Mist*, *Quaker Maid*, and *Cypress*, nice one deck 70-foooters, the *Nautilus* and the *Sea Raider*, slightly funky 60-footers with portholes instead of windows in the pilothouses, but still pretty nice, and all at least with flying bridges.

And there at the end, like the ugly duckling of the whole fleet was my *North Wind*: a 55' homemade ferro-cement jobber that looked totally funky, and without a flying bridge. I stepped from the dock to the deck and even that felt different: a dead feeling instead of the nice spring of a wooden boat. The deck house was all one room except for the toilet—at least fairly roomy, but all pretty much a mess, like the previous crew had just walked off the boat in the fall, leaving dirty dishes in the sink and no one had been back since.

And so aboard the humble *North Wind* began my introduction to the world of being a gill-net tenderman. It was made clear to me in the very beginning that I and the *North Wind* were at the very bottom of the fish-buying food chain. Seiners (high producing 58 footers with 5 man crews) and the big seine tenders (like the old *Sidney*, that I'd had my first Alaska job on), which the yard was full of, were obviously at the top. Even the other workers in the yard gave me the cold shoulder as I tried to get the sad old *North Wind* ready to go north.

Kari delivers beer to our fleet!

So I started: one foot after the other; cajoling what I needed from the shipyard: paint, electrical and mechanical parts, all the myriad supplies needed to transform the semi-derelict *North Wind* into a little ship fully equipped for whatever a long season in Alaska might throw at us. Sometimes it got nasty. For instance we only had a hand crank anchor winch, totally unsuitable it if we were caught off a lee shore in a blow, or the engine failed and the anchor failed to catch. John Lyons turned my request for a hydraulic one down flat until I suggested that his fleet insurance might not even cover the *North Wind* if they knew she had a manual winch. And even then he would only give me the parts I needed to convert it; I had to do the all the plumbing and installing myself.

Fish buying: signing the fish ticket. Note hopper scale on right that dumps into open fish hold, and 55 gallon drum of gas or diesel that we can sell to our boats.

In the evenings I made a big effort on the cabin interior, covering the dirty pegboard walls with vinyl fabric, buying a nice rug, putting up pictures (screwed into the walls, not hung), painting the inside of the head (marine toilet), scrubbing the rusty stovetop until it shone. And on a fine early May afternoon, moved aboard.

It was an unexpected delight. After 5 p.m. I had the whole shipyard to myself. We were tied at the end of the dock, and so on those long warm evenings, as I fiddled on small projects, all manner of craft would pass on their way to the locks, just a hundred yards to the west. (Smack in the middle of Seattle are a series of connected freshwater lakes on the shores of which much of the Alaska salmon fleet winters. They are connected to Puget Sound by a set of locks.) If I wanted to go out, a short walk took me across the tops of the lock gates and to a pub. After a rocky winter as a single guy trying to write a book, life was good again.

I buy the first fish of the 1975 season from my neighbor, Flea, the oldest fisherman at Point Baker.

A big Northern Air Freight Hercules arrives at Petersburg with a full load of iced totes of dog salmon from remote villages up on the Yukon River.

Then one day this handsome woman walked through the yard, turning heads as she went, and came straight to the bow where I was installing the anchor winch hydraulics.

"I'm Kari. I heard you need a crew," she said, " I speak Norwegian. I've worked on gillnetters." I hired her on the spot.

Things switched around pretty quickly around the shipyard for me after that. Guys would chat me up when I was waiting for something at the parts window. Guys started coming over to our boat and chatting with Kari on their lunch break while she was painting. The *North Wind's* stock took a big jump up at the old Whitney Yard, believe me!

Once again I was in the thick of the pre-season excitement that sweeps along the Northwest waterfront every spring as boats of all sizes got ready to go to Alaska. But more—now, as a tenderman, working directly for a cannery, I felt part of that grand tradition of the Alaska salmon industry that started when the first square riggers headed up North to build canneries in 1878. In many Northwest families, children grew up listening to Alaska stories from fathers, brothers, uncles, and grandfathers. And then when they were old enough, they'd start heading up North every spring as well.

We would also buy the occasional halibut!

Once we all left Seattle, we'd spread out over thousands of miles of remote coast, catch fish in hundreds of different places, and return with pockets full of cash and heads full of stories.

We moved to the West Wall finally, the traditional place for loading Alaska-bound freight. At that time there were probably at least 40 different canneries operating up and down the Alaska coast. The bigger ones received the bulk of their freight aboard big barges in containers that had left Seattle a month earlier. But their tenders who mostly spend the winters in Seattle, all filled up with freight at the west wall of Fishermen's Terminal.

Here were the *Haida Queen*, the *Pacific Queen*, and the handsome *Victory*, all built for the California sardine fishery in the 1930s, now fitted with refrigeration, perfect cannery tenders. Down a little way were two blunt nosed so-called power scows, the *Muskrat* and the big *Sea Lion*, built during WWII for the Army, to haul freight in the battle to drive the Japanese out of the Aleutian Islands. Flat bottomed, they were perfect tenders for the shallow rivers of Bristol Bay.

And there was the little ferro-cement *North Wind*, not exactly the belle of the ball, but she was mine, for the season at least, and we were HEADED NORTH!

There's a day or two of traveling up Puget Sound and lower British Columbia, with lights on the shore at night and the always present distant humming of the great lumber mills. Then finally at Yuculta Rapids, 200 miles north of Seattle we plunged into the forested wilderness that is the core of The Inside Passage. From then on the trip is almost a catharsis: five days of steaming along winding waterways, barely seeing another boat, or, except for the occasional navigational aid, even a sign of man's existence. The steep hills on either side disappear into the low clouds, here and there lonely inlets wind back to bays that might see years without a human visitor.

For us smaller craft, after the intensity of the last several weeks of getting ready in Seattle: frazzled, running around, a list that seems to get longer instead of shorter, it's always a relief to finally leave, clean up the boat, and just settle into the rhythm of life aboard. After a long day of traveling we would slide into some remote and empty cove at the edge of night, let the anchor and chain run out, shut off the engine and let the darkness and the silence filter in around us: this was my bell, ringing, ringing, ringing.

Kari was competent, easy-going and fun. We were traveling in company with a smaller gillnetter with friends aboard. If the night was still, they would tie alongside, laying on our big anchor, come aboard for a gam (sailor's term for a visit between crews of different boats originally from whaling days). It was all the things I'd wanted the passage north to be.

And finally at 9:30 in the evening, on the seventh day after leaving Seattle, we tied to the Whitney Fidalgo cannery dock in Petersburg. Walked around town after dinner to catch up with friends a bit. Then through the silent cannery and out to the end of the dock to climb the ladder down to our boat tied to the pilings below.

It was 11:30 but the sky was still light. The tide rushed past like a river. Across the channel the trees rose into snow and clouds. Out in the channel the buoys started to flash, and beyond to the north, Frederick Sound stretched away, misty, silent, and mysterious. On the other side of the sound, 10,000' Kate's Needle and 9,000' Devil's Thumb, their tops still glowing pink loomed above the dark water below.

We traveled 750 miles to get here, through all that spectacular country, but that night, just laying at the cannery dock seems like the prettiest spot yet.

Our beat that summer was Sumner and Clarence Straits some 40 miles south. To get back and forth we had to transit Wrangell Narrows, a 22 mile channel winding among some 60 buoys and markers, through which the tidal currents swirled. Our base of operations away from Petersburg were the roadless settlements of Port Protection and Point Baker, where I'd built a cabin a few years earlier.

Of course the locals in Sumner Straits—my old stomping ground from my days as a gillnetter—didn't waste any time seeing if their new fish buyer really knew his stuff. On the second day we were buying fish, a guy came alongside and we pitched about a thousand pounds of fish into the scale hopper. I called out the weight to Kari:

"982 on dogs." (Dogs are another term for chums, a lesser valued salmon species.)

Instantly the fisherman was in my face.

"Dogs? Goddammit, those are reds!"

At the time reds or sockeyes were worth about four times what dogs were worth. The guy took me aback. I knew that in June, before dogs start to change color, they can look a lot like reds. I looked at the fish again. I was pretty sure that they were dogs, but not positive.

"Goddamn kid doesn't know a dog from a sockeye," the guy called to a boat beside him, also waiting to unload.

Then I remembered the trick Old Mick had taught me on the *Sidney*, years before. I asked Kari to pass me a fillet knife and made a small cut in the belly flap of one of the top fish. It was pale pink, not the bright red of a sockeye.

Lynn Canal: not a nice place to fish. Larry Buatt's gillnetter Lucien B *bucking past Glacier Point.*

I showed it to him. "If you think these are reds," I said, "you better find another buyer."

We didn't have any problems after that.

In those days free booze was an integral part of fish buying—with each delivery you gave a six pack of beer (or soda) to your fishermen. We had a LOT of beer; it seemed like we loaded five pallets of the stuff down in Seattle.

We were also generous with it. New boat in town? Send Kari over with a goodwill case. Seiners in Port P. for July 4th festivities? Throw in a couple of cases to the party. One of your boats have an extra good week? Pass along a case instead of a sixer for the last delivery.

However the competition, Icicle Seafoods, whose tender the *Rosalie*, also bought fish in Sumner Straits had better beer. Real Rainier instead of the off brand Columbia that we were giving out.

I kept complaining to John Enge, the cannery boss that Icicle's better beer was costing us business.

Finally he relented, and let me take one of the cannery forklifts to the liquor store which was conveniently located near the head of the dock. With a pallet load of nice cold Rainier, we were ready to be competitive again!

Salmon "fishing periods" are typically from noon Sunday to noon Wednesday, occasionally extended to Thursday if there were a lot of fish around. It is all managed around something called "escapement"—the term for the fish that make it past all the fishermen's nets and into the rivers to spawn. To determine that number, ADF&G (Alaska Department of Fish and Game) hires usually college biology students to camp out on a few representative rivers or large creeks, count fish and report back by radio every day.

A friend of mine was a bush pilot and often flew these stream watchers out to remote bays, and spun me quite a tale of this green young couple:

"It was a couple of kids, maybe 20, boyfriend-girlfriend, biology majors. Anyway I flew them out to Red Bay and helped them unload all their stuff: tents, food, radios, a white board for the creek (putting a white metal plank at the bottom of a stream makes it easier to count the fish passing over it). But I noticed they didn't have any guns.

"So, kids," I sez, "you didn't bring any guns?"

"G-g-guns," sez the kid, "no one said anything about guns."

See, this?" I kicked some bear shit on the beach with my rubber boots, "That's bear shit. Where's there's fish there's always bears."

"And oh my God, they headed back toward the plane: 'No one said anything about bears; we're quitting.'"

"Whoa now," sez I, "you guys signed a contract and even got some money up front. You're not going anywhere. But tell 'ya what. Here, take my gun, I pulled out a pistol I had in the plane, It's only a .22, it won't hurt a bear unless you get it in the eye or the throat, but if you get in a jam with a bear, you can shoot yourselves with it. Those kids, they turned just sheet white until they realized I was just funnin' them."

I liked being a tenderman. Actually more than gill-netting. I liked the pace of things—the hustle of unloading back in Peterburg, going through your list, and getting back out of town. Plus I was buying fish in my own neighborhood. A lot of times after the fishing period ended, I'd be giving friends a ride to town. We didn't have a fly bridge, but I had the autopilot control on a long cord, and when the weather was good, we'd just sit up on top of the pilothouse, take some cannery beer up there and enjoy the ride into town.

And if things were slow during the fishing period, I could just pick up the mooring in front of the cabin my first wife and I had built earlier, and have Kari take care of things if a boat came by to sell. I could work on the cabin, and keep an eye on the *North Wind* as well; if a bunch of boats came in to sell their fish, and it looked like she needed help, I could row out there and lend a hand. Kari was pretty social; sometimes boats would stop by just to visit.

There was just one little fly in the ointment: demon rum. In Petersburg, once we got the boat cleaned up after unloading and the groceries loaded for the week, (we also served as a floating grocery store for our boats) there was some free time, and Kari would head up to The Harbor Bar and after a few drinks become even friendlier than usual and often end up wrapping herself around a big crewman from one of the many purse seiners who were in town for the weekend. That didn't bother me—she was so great on the boat—getting boats to sell to me that would not have otherwise done so—that I didn't begrudge her kicking up her heels in town.

The wrinkle was this: often we would have to leave Petersburg late at night to catch the tide in The Narrows to get out to Point Baker to deliver groceries and fuel the guys up, etc. She'd be a no show, and I would have to go uptown and find her before I missed the tide and had to buck the current for six hours out to Baker.

Two drinks and she was Ms. Party, and wanting to keep the fun going, and whoever was with her was probably thinking that he was going to have a really good time that night as well.

So I'd have to explain to some really big belligerent guy that actually she was going out on the *North Wind* with me. Sometimes it was ugly.

Then one rare hot afternoon, we were heading up the Narrows for town with our fish, and Kari was sunbathing on the back deck with her top off.

Then here comes the big Alaska State ferry *Matanuska*, headed toward us, looking like we'd pass in the narrowest part of the channel.

I figured I'd better go out on deck and tell Kari to put her top on.

Fully loaded tender Apache *leaving the shelter of Sullivan Island. Shortly afterwards she took a sea over the bow that shattered her fish weighing machine and she was lucky not to have blown out her pilothouse windows!*

But then I thought about all those annoying evenings in Petersburg, when it would be time to go and Kari wouldn't have shown and I'd have to roam the bars and get into an ugly confrontation with some disappointed bruiser.

So I said nothing.

It was a gorgeous day and the ferry's decks were full of passengers. Someone with binoculars spotted our bare-chested beauty and by the time we passed, they were all on our side, and Kari woke suddenly to the ferry passing just 20 feet away and a hundred or so passengers waving and calling down to her!

But 1975 was a strange year for salmon in Southeast Alaska. We had a single sideband shortwave radio for long distance communication, and every night we would call in to the cannery with our fish totals for the day and listen to our cannery's other tenders giving their totals. And the numbers were grim. The season was so poor that ADF&G shut down all fishing in the region for 10 days at the end of July and I actually flew down to Seattle in the middle of the fishing season to hang out with friends in the sun.

But I felt odd, and out of place—the first time in four years I had been somewhere else in the summer except Alaska.

To get back to Petersburg from Seattle, you take Alaska Airlines' "Milk Run": first Ketchikan, then 20 minutes later, Wrangell, a small town at the mouth of the Stikine River, where you're sure your plane is going into the river. Then at the very last possible moment, the runway appears under the plane, the pilot hits the breaks really hard before you run off the other end, and you're there. Then 15 minutes after taking off again, I was pulling on a welcome sweatshirt as the 737 banked over the ice coming out of LeConte Glacier, passed over cannery row and came down hard and without a bounce on Petersburg's short gravel runway.

But meanwhile, other places in Alaska were having big runs.

"C'mon out to the airport with me, I want to show you something." John Enge said the day after I returned from Seattle, glad to be back.

When we got to the airstrip, a big Northern Air Cargo four-engined Hercules, a monster of a plane, was banking over The Narrows on final. It rumbled to a stop in a cloud of dust and flying gravel and the big doors in back opened to reveal tote (a big aluminum box) after tote filled with dog salmon and topped with flake ice. One of the cannery forklifts was already there, and started moving the totes out of the plane and onto a cannery truck.

"The Yukon's having a giant dog (chum salmon) run." Said John. "Luckily there's some ice machines up there and they're flying fish up and down the coast to anyone who'll take 'em."

All those little villages in the bleak and treeless northern river deltas: Eluktuk, Apoon Pass, Kusilvak, Andreafsky: just settlements really, were seeing more fish than they had in years.

I talked for a moment with the co-pilot, who was opening little access panels around the plane, looking in and writing numbers in his logbook. "How was it, getting in here?"

He jerked his head back toward the short gravel runway. "This is easy, compared to some of those strips up in the delta. . ."

In the 1970s the fall run of dog salmon (chums) into the Chilkat River on the west side of Lynn Canal near the town of Haines was a lifesaver for many gillnetters. The big ten pound fish were worth a buck a pound; it wasn't hard to get 5 or even 10,000 pounds in a good one-day fishing period: most who made the big effort to travel to rough and windy Lynn

Canal from their mellower summer fishing grounds doubled their season in a month, even though in that month you might only fish four or five days because of the large fleet.

But they usually paid for it. Lynn Canal is a notorious wind tunnel in the fall: rarely a nice day, the wind often switching 180° without warning and snow and often a blizzard usually by mid-September. A couple of entries from my journal gives the flavor of that windy fall:

Sept 8, 1975—Dropped hook at Glacier Point with five other tenders. Wind very strong with driving rain just as first boats come alongside. Dirty afternoon with rain horizontal at times, driving through oilskins, and dirty short chop in the anchorage. Busted three lines and drug out once with boats on both sides and more behind in vicious squall. Ran up and dropped anchor right on the beach. Clouds racing overhead and wind-spray in the anchorage. Jug out on the galley table, you bet; this country sure isn't giving an inch this year.

Sept 30, 1975—Inside Sullivan Island. Up anchor at three and out into the full force of the wind—an easy 40 and everything is white, even inside the island, and finally to S. anchorage where unloaded 3 boats, their last delivery for the season, with the rain driving horizontally and the wind just a howling off the beach. This is the worst yet. *Cypress* stops by, and wants us to run with them and *Apache*. Kari wants us to go too, but I told her not on a bet would I leave the anchorage in this kind of weather. They leave and in a few minutes are lost in the flying spray. They made it through the gut, but *Apache* called a few minutes later for me not to even think about trying it. Phil had taken them clean over his house, and *Apache* had taken one on deck that smashed his scales into three pieces.

So ends this last day of September, with 65 of us crowded into this little anchorage, with fresh snow very close to the water now, and squall after squall racing down on us, the gusts sometimes over 60. Hope the month to come sees the end to this and us all safely home.

Oct 7, 1975—First boat, the *Cape Chacon*, alongside at seven after fitful sleep with the northern lights very bright. Quiet morning with boats trickling in one by one. So the season ended with kind of a whimper: pretty slow fishing all around. Would have preferred a big week, but this way we can sit around and have a coffee with each boat, thank them for their fish this season, ask about their winter plans, etc. Ran down to the south end of Sullivan Island to pick up my last boat and so on a fine, fair, fall afternoon, with the shore a bright blaze of yellow alders, we bought our last fish and headed out the gut and out into the Canal for the last time, with *Kay II* behind us on the towline, to save them a little gas. Kari took the wheel and I went on deck to wash down. Ahead of us as far as I could see was a line of boats, the fleet headed south from Lynn Canal after six long weeks.

Nice way to end the season: with friends aboard for dinner, their boat on the towline as we put Lynn Canal finally behnd us.

Did anyone double their season by coming up for fall fishing this year, like we had gotten used to over the past three years? Probably not, but after a skinny summer, everyone needed every fish.

By Pt. Lena, the water rippled, the evening sky orange and red, we pulled the *Kay II* alongside for a moment and Bob and Kay Anderson and dog Tasha came on board for supper of fine baked salmon with soufflé, spuds, salad with homemade dressing, and washed down with plenty of wine while we ran full bore for Petersburg 14 hours away.

How's that for a fine way to end the season and how different from years past when the end of the season always meant just beating your way out of the Canal against the weather, or lying at the float day after day listening to the wind howl, and waiting for a chance to leave?

Dirty northerly chop at Taku Inlet, so cut Bob loose, and ran in the black around the point and into the anchorage in Taku Harbor with Paul and Nancy Maudslien on *Anna H* close behind as well. Found a quiet corner, down hook, they both came alongside, and what a time we all had, crowded in here with the northern lights just blazing outside.

> "Twenty boats in the lonely harbor
> miles from nowhere, asleep and waiting
> to run south at first light.
> The tender lays in one corner
> a boat on either side, portholes
> bright, music and laughter in the
> cold night. Outside the northern
> lights blaze, inside the jug's out
> and the stories fly.
> Season's over—running south!"

The North Wind *in Sumner Strait, taken from our Point Baker cabin.*

THE WINDING WAY SOUTH

MUCH IS SAID AND WRITTEN ABOUT the glories of the Inside Passage, especially by cruise lines that take some million plus passengers a year on parts of that route. Sadly, very few ships, primarily the Alaska State Ferries and small cruise ships take the traditional route inside of Vancouver Island, past Bella Bella and through Grenville Channel. Vancouver based ships pass through the scenic channels east of Vancouver Island, but then almost always go up wide and boring Hecate Strait out of sight of land. In the summer, especially the early summer with its long long days, the route is truly spectacular, even if you just do part of it as Seattle departing ships do—only transiting the true Inside Passage once they arrive in Alaskan waters.

But in the late fall it becomes a dark and moody place. For myself, heading back to Seattle after a long Alaska fishing season was always a bittersweet experience. First, the weather has always changed dramatically for the worse. Another side is this: Alaska fishing seasons are always intense and fast paced: living on board, long hours of daylight, close to nature and the always changing weather: life in capital letters; my bell, ringing, ringing, ringing. Compared to a long, full speed ahead fishing season, winter and its short dark days was always a let down for me. So the closer I got to Seattle and the end of the season, the slower I went, not really wanting to see it end.

On this Seattle bound trip, a friend, Laura Blevins, had taken time off from her job, flown up to Petersburg to travel south with me. She had never been North, nor spent much time on a boat before. We weren't in any hurry. A few excerpts:

A stormy night outside, a good friend and a jug of wine inside: so begins our journey.

Oct 18, 1975—Comes stormy with spits of rain and strong wind SE. Lines off from the Petersburg cannery at 7:30 a.m. and off we go without even the slightest trace of daylight in the sky. Out of the Narrows at 10:30 and so our trip starts on a blustery, dirty morning with driving rain, and strong SE wind right in our teeth.

Looking down at Butedale Cannery and the Inside Passage from the top of the penstock that feeds the powerhouse.

Gave up the idea of beating our way against it all day in wide Clarence Strait, so swung east to Chichagof Pass, and the back way through Zimovia Strait. Followed the chart to Canoe Pass, and as we entered, we both stood in awe; it is more like a creek opening up to a little steep-sided basin. All ashore for long, wet, walk with kitty mewing along. Last night's snowfall is only a few hundred feet above the water; another day or two and it will be right down on the deck.

L. rowed us back to the boat, her first real experience with one of them rowboats, and it went smoothly, meaning we got there without capsizing and it only took a rainy half hour.

With L. cooking dinner while kitty licked herself dry and the rain drumming hard on the roof, so ended the first day of our trip south: wind and driving rain, ugly seas, racing clouds, and then best of all, a lovely watch-pocket of a cove where we now lie, sheltered from any sea, most of the wind, and not another soul for maybe twenty or thirty miles.

Oct. 19, 1975—Comes cool, gray, and still here in the harbor with only the muted rush of a waterfall. With only 50 miles to go today, it was a lazy morning, lying in the bunk until nine, then up, yank the anchor, and out the creek-like entrance and into Ernest Sound on a raw cold morning with low scudding clouds, slate colored water, and flying spray. Winter is on our heels and even in a 50-footer we need to be cautious. Passed two little trollers just north of Guard Island, just wallowing in the rips. The channel narrows up, then the houses and streets of Ketchikan on the shore and just at 7:30 on another black, rainy, and windy evening, we tie to a float downtown, and found three seiners that have been waiting a week for a chance to run south.

Moon tonight back-lighting the cumulus clouds: very dramatic. But very black to the south and the wind from Dixon Entrance sweeps up the channel and heels us over at the dock. Report tomorrow is for SE 35 and 15 foot seas. Set alarm for 5 anyway, but without much hope.

Oct 20, 1975—Alarm off at 5 and up to black night with wind and seas hissing past on the outside, so gave it up and went back to sleep. So for fine, quiet, lazy, day spent reading and long visit with Snapper Carlson, aboard his fine tender, *Crane*, in his salon with cozy wood stove, and he brought out his collection of old fishing photos. The afternoon clearing with the evening fine and still and a good weather report to boot, so tied everything down with high hopes, then set the alarm for 3 a.m.

Oct 21, 1975—Lawson Bay, B.C.—Off at 4 on a glassy, black morning, so it looks like a chance. Running with those three big seiners, but they all soon outdistance the slow *North Wind* so we're pretty much on our own.

Pale fine dawn near Foggy Bay with Tree Pt. Light flashing ahead and the Canadian mountains pink and jagged to the east. Dropped the hook at 4 p.m. in Lawson Bay, Lewis Island, Canada, and all ashore in the skiff to walk the beach past the deserted and roomily laid out community with plenty of room between each of the houses spread out around the little cove and even sort of a community center. Wonder what brought all those people to this spot and what made them leave, after they had done so much. And what a tale of sadness these abandoned buildings tell.

The night very still, with the flasher out in the channel the only light in the whole panorama spread out around us. Moon-rise late and the snow on the mountains to the east eerie in its glow. We both feel the special charm of this place tonight. Weatherman speaks of 'Continued northwesterly flow,' but suspect southeast for the morning.

Oct 22, 1975—Butedale, B.C.—Hook up 4:30 a.m. to SE 25 with driving rain; glad to be traveling in protected channels. Radar even worked for a few minutes before dying in a dramatic display of bright lines all across the screen.

Day passes gray and dreary—the clouds pressing down on the hills and the water and mile after mile of steep, green, gloomy walls on both sides, opening here and there to inlets winding deep back into the interior, and at times we pass waterfalls so steep we could run by and have the water splashing right down on the deck.

Work Is. at 4, then the lights of Butedale cannery appear, eerie after so much gloomy total wilderness. We could go further, but I feel like a shower and a walk, even on this rainy afternoon and this is the only place in many miles for either, so we pull in and tie to the rotting float. Looked in the logbook from last year and that very long trip south and see that we are a week ahead of when three of us pulled in here, beating our way down the coast in the worst fall weather in years.

L. has never seen the likes of this—a ghost town with just a couple as caretakers totally in the middle of nowhere. We climbed the steps beside the thick wooden pen-stock that carries the water from the lake down to the turbines. On this quiet evening, we can hear the loud rush of water from inside.

At the top walked to the edge of the lake that winds far back into the hills and along it to abandoned cabins built on floating log rafts. The mountains rise up from the water up into the mists that swirl around their tops, and the snow lies on all the ledges. As we stood there this rainy evening, a pair of ducks flew over and splashed down out in the middle, quacking to each other as they passed. Then came a strange rush of noise like a faraway jet and a flight of scoters, perhaps 30, flew over and settled onto the lake. We waited and a third flight came with the same eerie rush of wings and muted calls back and forth. Miles from the nearest hunter they still come in low and fast, just at dusk, to this remote lake.

Down the steps in the deepening dusk with the lights of the all but deserted cannery on with Fraser Reach and the Inside Passage beyond like a still river and the gloomy mountains beyond stretching away into the mists.

Long, hot, shower tonight in the huge old bunkhouse bathroom, then down to the dock in the misty evening. Then just at 8 p.m., another tender, the Gulf of Mexico built *Robert Wayne,* slips in alongside. Owner sez he's going to change the name to *Cajun Rambler*. Aboard for a visit and a drink and when we went back to our own boat, I looked out to the blackest night and wondered how many miles it was to the next settlement, probably fifty. This place sure seems like the last outpost on a night like tonight with all the lights on but no one there except for a caretaker and two tired packers stopping in on their way down from Alaska after a long season.

Oct 23, 1975—Bella Bella, B.C.—Up at 8 to just the rush of the waterfall on another gray and still morning. Off down misty Fraser Reach with Khutze and Aaltanash and Greene Inlets opening up briefly on the eastern shore. The mountains high here and the channel like a long winding channel between them.

Ocean Mist, a big steel American crabber, passed us at noon, and is soon lost in the thin fog ahead. Milbanke Sound still, with a long oily SW swell, then Seaforth Channel on a clearing evening with a patch of blue sky to the east. At dusk we pass the lighthouse at Dryad Pt., and the lights of the native village of Bella Bella open up beyond. Stopped there and L.

called her Seattle job to tell them that she was still alive but that she was delayed by the weather and the trouble that I was having with one of the engines (What. . . we have two?) which is better than the truth which is just that we are in no hurry to get back.

Then across to tie up at the old cannery across the channel where we usually lie, disused now, except as a storage facility. Ahead was the *Skeena Prince,* the local north coast freighter and like a ghost from a Howard Pease novel, ending up her career, making runs from Vancouver to Prince Rupert and all the backwater communities in between. As we watched, the old direct drive diesel started up as she backed away, hissed and clanked into forward and thumped its way off into the night and down the back channel to Ocean Falls.

Still, still evening here tonight, and kitty frisks about on the float until after dark, and I have to go and chase her in.

A nasty afternoon in Queen Charlotte Strait. We were mighty glad to have gotten across before dark.

Oct 24, 1975—Lucan Is., West of God's Pocket, B.C.—This day begins at 4 on a still and peaceful morning and ends in the black of a windy night with violent winds and lashing rain battering the boat in a tiny and constricted anchorage.

Queen Charlotte Sound, always an anxious spot to get across, started out as flat as I had ever seen it: no swell and only a confused and leftover lump. By lonely and windswept Egg Island we were bucking into a light chop, but by Cape Caution, the last anchorage until we were across, it was wet going and steady SE 25.

An hour later we were in the thick of things, the wind a steady 35, and the sea a nasty short 8' chop and every now and then I'd have to pull the throttle back and let a particularly big one slide by. Laid in the partial lee of Storm Islands for a bit to pump the bilge, check things carefully in the engine room, and make sure things were secure on deck. Then we eased out into it again, for a very dirty go for the rest of the afternoon.

Just outside Storm Islands, there must have been a tide rip or something, as all we could do for a long half hour was just idle along and let the seas slip under us, pitching heavily. Lightly loaded, I couldn't lay the course to Pine Island without putting us in the trough of the seas, so we had to steer a zig zag course. Made Pine Island on the dirtiest kind of afternoon with 12 long miles to go. Reduced to half speed, slowing for the big ones. Even at Scarlett Pt., it was so nasty that we had run way up into the lee of the land below the lighthouse before we could get out of the seas enough to make our turn and then quarter down into the shelter of God's Pocket. Happy to get out of it, you bet. But then saw that the cove was full of Canadians with no room for another. Laid alongside a 45 footer just as our steering wheel went loose on the shaft, had to make repairs and leave. Even in the few minutes we were there we chewed through a 3/4" pretty new bow line. Canadian introduced himself as 'Nelson,' maybe 50, heavy set with wool shirt and pants. As we were tieing up, he asked Laura if it was just the two of us aboard. And when she said yes, he shook his head and said that we were braver than he was.

So I kind of wonder what he makes of us—pulling alongside of him, a young couple, headed down from Alaska in a big company boat. Said the best anchorage was across the channel and around the point, just snuggle right up into the trees. So off we went, the whole bay white, the wind an easy 45 and blowing the tops off of everything. Running with it wasn't so bad, but when we passed the point, the wind was blowing the spray maybe forty or fifty feet downwind from each wave.

Dropped hook in the 6 p.m. black in a narrow gut between two islands. The wind howled through the pass but there was no swell. Mighty kelpy bottom: took two tries to get a good bite with the anchor and we were uneasily close to the beach. Mighty glad we put in hydraulics on that anchor winch!

So for windy night. After supper three other boats came in, one big seiner with a plywood patch over a pilothouse window, and then the wind started up in earnest with accompaniment of driving rain and the blackest kind of night. Re-anchored further out with a bit more room in case we started to drag.

Fitful sleep, natch, then around midnight woke thinking, "Hmm, that sure is a curious sound," then WHAM! Jumped up to find the *Martha Marie*, a 40' troller, had dragged down on top of us; the sound was his anchor wire sliding over ours. Pulled on pants and oilskins and out into the night to get that squared away and all the time like someone with a powerful deck hose had it aimed at us, so powerful was the rain and the wind. L. looking out with big eyes at it all. Then up again an hour later to re-anchor in a squall and looked downwind and two of the three other boats were doing the same. So for uneasy night; from then until five, the wind shook the boat and the rain drove with such force that it even opened up a leak over our bunk...

Oct. 25. 1975—Growler Cove, B.C.—Woke up at 8 to find the anchorage empty, the sky blue, and the water flat: wow, what a change! So checked the oil, upped anchor and headed out quick to buck our way through a leftover chop to native village of Alert Bay where made grocery stop. Five o'clock of this day found us tied to a disused net float in a very protected corner of Growler Cove. On the shore a few rotting cabins are slowly returning to the forest, and in the shallows, a heron walked slowly through the still water. L. jigged for cod, kitty played on the float, and I rowed slowly around in the skiff. It is as lovely and as quiet an evening as we have had yet on this trip. The night comes very starry, and across the way are the high hills of Vancouver Island, topped even now with fresh snow, gleaming eerily in the starlight, and between us and them, lies Johnstone Strait. L. says she has never seen so many stars before.

Today and tonight are such a change from the violence of yesterday and last night. How good it felt just to sit and enjoy the starry stillness after dark, with hardly even the call of a bird.

Oct 26, 1975—Stuart Island, B. C. Up at 6 to gray skies with low racing clouds, and the floats moving in the surge from the seas, as another "Pacific Disturbance" moved in. Out at 9 to buck south in very wet going.

Passed Boat Pt. at 9:30, the wind and the swell making it a lee shore. Glad we didn't anchor there last night, as locals had suggested.

Finally at 11, made the turn to the east and passed into the very welcome sheltered waters of Chancellor Channel and the most protected of waterways for a day or two. This is my favorite part of the Inside Passage: Wellbore and Cordero Channels, all very narrow and winding with snow on the trees down to within a few hundred feet of the water. Through the slot at Green Pt. Rapids, and then Whirlpool Rapids with the tide just swirling and the shores close at hand. The light fading quick, but passed the usual stopping place at Shoal Bay, with Phillips Arm reaching away mistily to the north, down Nodales Channel, past Frederick Arm to catch slack water at Yuculta Rapids, where the steep hills were laced with bright yellow alders and maples in fall colors and here and there along the shore are the first summer places, all boarded up now for winter.

Just at 5:30 tied to the government wharf at Stuart Island and walked around the immaculately laid out and planned little resort just as a pink haze settled over the mysterious islands of Desolation Sound to the south, and the sun set somewhere far above the clouds.

Kitty had a friend on board, the resort caretaker opened the showers for us, and so for another fine evening after winding all afternoon through this empty and mysterious country.

Oct 27, 1975—The morning gray, raw, and windy, with rain and a dirty SE chop. Butte Inlet with fresh snow close to the water opened to the north, then Hole-in-the-Wall to the west. Through narrow Calm Channel with the hills close on either side and dotted with yellow birch and alder.

Desolation Sound opened up before us on a mean morning with not another boat in sight. Narrow Thulin Pass, past Bliss Landing, the very end of the coast road, and even in this narrow pass, the wind whistled and kicked up a short chop. Malaspina Strait by noon and the day settled into a long, wet buck into lead colored water, under gray low clouds like most of the trip. The big paper mill at Powell River, once the biggest in the world, on our left, then a little later it's all wilderness again as the rugged coast— Agamemnon Channel and Princess Louisa Inlet—opened up to the east, punching deep into the wild interior, with no roads for many miles.

At 5 slipped in behind the outer islands and tied up at Irving's Landing, Pender Harbor. A few houses scattered here and there, but little sign of life. Walked up a winding road (first actual walk on a road for months!) and along a hilly shore, enjoying the cool fall feeling of that evening with a stiff breeze off the water. Here and there are houses tucked in amongst the trees overlooking the water, with patches of lawn in between with leaves underfoot. Summer homes? Almost an eerie feeling with no one about. After almost five months on the boat up in a world of thick forests and rocky shores, it feels good indeed to walk the road here. The shores are so steep and the woods so thick in SE Alaska, that I almost can count on my fingers the walks I had this season and even those were on rough beaches.

Almost dark by the time we got back to the boat and on the hills around the little bay, the lights in the little houses were starting to come on.

Oct 28, 1975—Comes gray and rainy at 8 after a windy night—woke twice to gusts shaking the boat, even in that sheltered spot. Suspect dirty going this morning so took time for hot breakfast and tied everything down before taking off. Sure enough, the wind howled around the point, and off we go, making heavy going of it in the short 6' hop. Too bad to even think about traveling in the trough of those seas, so we quartered across for very dirty morning. Stopped halfway across to pump bilges and stood looking out the back door for a moment. Even throttled back to 800 turns, we were diving into them and throwing spray clear over the house. To the east the horizon was lost in the murk and flying spray. To the west were the Gulf Islands, a long gray line on the horizon 12 miles distant. These are inside waters and close to home, but Georgia Straits can be nasty indeed, and we were glad to be across and into the shelter of the land at 2. Rushed through the narrow gut at Dodd Narrows with a 5-knot tide pushing us on, with whirlpools and overfalls on all sides. Civilization here: on all sides were bright alders and maples marking the homes scattered along the shores.

At 6 on another gray and windy evening, we tied to a friend's float, Saltspring Island, B.C. and went for fine walk ashore amongst gardens and fresh smelling woods. Sat for a few hours by the fire and talked with the caretaker's wife in warm living room with beautiful varnished board and batten ceiling and walls. Weather very poor to south; will stay a day here, sure. Don't have much desire to go further south, really. Every fall the closer we get to the end of the line, the slower I go, reluctant to call an end to the simple life on the boat.

After the endless green of the north coast, it was a treat to begin to see fall colors as we got further south.

Oct 29, 1975—Comes windy with rain and a short chop, even in this sheltered bay. Seiners on the radio in the American San Juan Islands just 30 miles to the south talking about wind and breaking seas in Haro Strait, so we're sure not leaving this peaceful spot. There was a big fire in the fireplace, the Bensons, caretakers, made us welcome, L. took a long hot bath and so for lazy day. Especially beautiful spot here, with orchards and gardens, and all in fine fall foliage now.

Evening with slashing rain and wind laying us over at the dock. The radio crackled with a call for us and then two more and it felt like we are back in the fish buying mode again: *Cypress* from up in Grenville Channel, where he is running in the black to get to Seattle, and then the *Carol Louise*, one of my boats from the last season. He was crabbing in Gambier Bay, north of Petersburg, and maybe 500 miles away, heard us on and gave us a call. Came in strong for a bit and then faded out altogether.

Oct 30, 1975—Comes clearing and brisk; a fine fall morning, the storm blown away in the night by the northerly. Off at 9 after a walk to pick a bag of apples for the trip. Blue herons abundant here; we heard them screeching in the night, and now this morning, there were two wading in the shallows of this little cove.

Fog here and there as we wound through these exquisite channels, burning off to reveal beautiful orange and red and green hills on all sides. Crossed into the US at Boundary Pass, near Turn Pt. Then through the narrow channels and passes of the American San Juan Islands as the day sadly turns gray around us. Many summer homes on all the shores now, but most are shuttered and closed for the season.

Anacortes at 3 for customs and a short walk through that sleepy town with streets of small older homes set back with little lawns and here and there a touch of gingerbread trim. Then it's off again into the fading light, across Padilla Bay and up winding Swinomish Slough with a fine sunset to the west and flights of ducks and geese trading back and forth across the fields as dusk settles in. To the east were the barns and farmhouses of the Skagit valley. A few look out onto the narrow slough and I wonder what their inhabitants think as they look out their windows in the chilly dusk to see this tired Alaska packer working its way home. This has always been a beautiful part of the trip in the fall: to wind through this farm country with the shore close at hand after so many miles through the vast and empty country of the North Coast.

Just at very last light tied to the silent town float at La Conner, the sky pale red to the west. Tied on all sides are purse seiners, including the *Mary Louise B.*, who was in Port Protection this last July 4th, silent and empty, their season just about over too.

Uptown for dinner in sleepy tavern, with just a few people sitting around talking or shooting pool. Back to boat through windy and empty streets, the stars out now, and the Big Dipper lower in the sky than the last time I saw it, miles north of here.

Each fall it is a little bit the same. We wind up the season a thousand miles north of here, in amongst the steep, icy inlets, with cold glaciers on all sides and the fresh snow on the hills lower and lower each night until the morning when we wake up and our decks are dusted with it. Then it's tie everything down to wind our way south, bucking the fall gales, ducking into little holes each night. The British Columbia coast is pretty empty when we come through late in the fall like that, and we come all that way through all that empty country, only to get down to the San Juans and La Conner, only to find that they seem deserted and empty, too.

Oct 31, 1975—The last day of October, the last day of the season, the last miles. Started at 8. Off from the frosty float and out the narrow slough, loafers and fishermen on the docks watching us pass: almost November and still they trickle down from Alaska.

Tired and sad looking, tied to the New England Seafoods dock, was the old steel seiner, *Capella*, with Morgan City, LA, painted on her stern. Boom on deck, gear scattered all over and on the dock as well, they're taking off the shrimp gear and rigging her up for yet another fishery.

There's an old friend, I thought. I first saw her 10 years ago in Iquique, Chile, where she was fishing for Harvey Smith and I was just learning the business. And it looks like she's been through harder times since then than I.

Funny how that fleet keeps turning up. In 1970, I fished on *La Nina* in Rhode Island. This spring I saw the *La Pinta* in Seattle, and now, here is *Capella*.

The day gray with a half gale SE and it was a long dirty buck south all the way right up to the locks, and we went through alone on a chill evening with the last of the light fading from the sky.

How different from that bright fair day so many months ago, when we locked down into the salt water with a press of yacht traffic on all sides, decks and quarters piled high with freight and gear still to be stowed, and the whole season ahead of us. The Whitney Fidalgo Seafoods dock and the trip and the season are over. The boat, rusty and paint chipped, is ready for a layup and refit. And the crew too, ready to tie it up and do something different through the dreary winter until it all starts again in the spring.

With 110,000 pounds of fish aboard, the "EJ" was mighty low in the water!

ON THE GARNET POINT RUN
WITH THE EMILY JANE

AFTER THE DISAPPOINTING 1975 SEASON WITH the *North Wind*, when fishing got so slow I actually left Alaska to come back to Washington to take a mini-vacation in the middle of the fishing season, I was ready for something different.

Very different. I went to Maine, bought a 60-year-old boat, threw in a new used engine, new systems, and worked in the herring fishery for a few years, loading herring at night from seiners and selling it during the day as lobster bait. (And wrote a book, *Amaretto*, about the experience, reissued in 2015 with a new title, *Herring Nights, Remembering a Lost Fishery*.)

Compared to Alaska fisheries with limited entry, fish cops in boats and planes, fish tickets (delivery receipts) that were collected daily: lots of rules, the Maine herring fishery was a breath of fresh air. The rule (during the time I was in the fishery) was basically, "Go out and get 'em boys!" Did you even have to have a license to fish herring in the '70s? I don't think so. In any case, no one ever asked me how much herring I was getting from the seiners to sell as lobster bait, and most years it was over 3 million pounds!

My herring boat, a sardine carrier, Vinalhaven Island, Maine, 1977

My boat, a so-called sardine carrier, was essentially a herring or fish buyer. (Juvenile herring are canned with various oils and flavors and sold as sardines). On the sides of our fish holds were marks to show how much herring I had aboard, but the marks didn't make sense, certainly not tons or thousands of pounds. So I asked.

"Them's hogheads; that *Amaretto*'s a fifty hogshead boat." came the answer from a grizzled old timer.

"Ahhh, what's a hogshead?" Now I am getting odd looks from the fishermen listening to our conversation.

"Why, seventeen and a half bushels, 'ya dummy!"

Eventually I figured out that a full load was about 53,000 pounds.

It was an unusual fishery, so different from anything I had experienced before.

In those days, Vinalhaven Island, where we operated out of, was basically herring central. Most summer evenings four or five big sardine

carriers, including often boats from Canada, would tie up at the big granite wharf in the harbor, left over from sixty years earlier when rock from
the island's granite quarries was shipped all over the East Coast. We would
sit in the roomy foc's'le of the *Pauline*, a handsome 80 footer, sip rum and
coke out of paper cups and listen to herring radio: our spotter pilot in his
little fabric covered single engined Aeronca Champ.

We worked at night, out and among the islands and rockpiles called
ledges that make navigation so challenging on that coast. This was way
before GPS and plotters that made finding your position so easy; this was
navigation the old way: pencil, chart, compass, sounder, radar, good judg-
ment and a bit of luck. But for all that, it was a good solid business with lots
of colorful folks in it, and we prospered.

A fleet of large schooners takes passengers on week long trips along
the Maine coast, and one day the best of them, the *Mary Day*, anchored in
Carver's Harbor, Vinalhaven Island, where I was unloading herring. I went
aboard to visit, met Mary Lou, a remarkable young woman working as one
of the crew, and a year later we were married.

Tender unloading plastic totes full of iced troll caught fish from a remote buying station.

Alaska still beckoned, Mary Lou had never been, and so the spring of 1982 found us headed up to Alaska as captain and cook/bookkeeper aboard the 65' tender *Emily Jane:* fish buyers once again. Much more substantial than the funky *North Wind*, the *EJ* had a refrigerated seawater system for keeping the fish cold, and a fine young engineer to oversee it.

Our home cannery was again in Petersburg, but for Icicle Seafoods, a much larger operation than the Whitney Fidalgo cannery I had worked for before. Plus this was more like a real job—as skipper I was paid some $130 a day and Mary Lou $80, seven days a week, and all our groceries paid for. Whereas on the *North Wind*, I was paid fifteen cents a pound and had to pay my crew from that as well.

Tight Quarters—in places the dredged channel in Wrangell Narrows is only a hundred feet or so wide, so move over for the big boys!

In the seven years I'd been away from the salmon fishery, there were a lot of changes. It was all pretty much summed up by a big sign on the Icicle Seafoods cannery dock: **"Anyone Picking up a Salmon by the Tail Will be Fired!"** (Doing so bruises the flesh.) The days of throwing fish from fish boat to tender with peughs (essentially a one tined pitchfork—you stabbed the fish in the head and flipped it into the scale box) were over. Quality was the word as more and more salmon, even the lowly low priced pink or humpy were being frozen instead of canned.

Secrets of the Old Time Fish Buyers—take advantage of your brief time alongside the dock to use the hoist to lower groceries (and the cart!) laundry, etc. directly down to your boat. Better than the alternative: carrying them down a 30' ladder!

The much bigger *EJ* could put easily 110,000 pounds below her hatches in the refrigerated sea water that filled her hold, while a safe load for the *North Wind* topped out at about 45,000 pounds.

Even if we only had 30,000 pounds aboard, the *EJ* would always be heavy and deep in the water as we had to keep her holds full to the top with cold sea water to maintain stability. (Water sloshing around in a partially filled hold makes a vessel less stable.)

Plus at Icicle, the main unloading dock was at right angles to the strongly flowing tidal currents, whereas at Whitney, the dock had been parallel to the current, and as such, much easier to get into.

Bringing the fully loaded *EJ* into the dock at Icicle, with the current running at 4 or 5 knots either pushing you away from the dock or into it was very challenging. Additionally, the dock was always full of other boats so you were trying to 'land' your boat in a slot only slightly longer than the boat with other boats on either side.

The boats we bought salmon from were a dozen or so gillnetters, generally operated by older fishermen and their wives, fishing in the vicinity of Garnet Point, almost the very southern tip of the state, about 160 miles from Petersburg. The usual fishing period was Sunday noon until Wednesday noon. Typically we'd finish up offloading our boats by late afternoon on Wednesday, clean all up, and head north for the 18 hour or so run—depending on the tide—to Petersburg, usually arriving sometime Thursday morning. Unloading—Icicle used a vacuum unloader instead of the bucket at a time hoist at Whitey—usually took a 2-4 hours, depending on how much fish we had.

Those hours when we unloaded were also the only time we were tied directly to the dock with a ladder, as opposed to tied to another boat two or three out from the dock. So it behooved Mary Lou to get as many of her errands done then instead of having to clamber down the ladder and over two or three boats as well.

Although our Garnet boats were only a four or five hour run from Ketchikan, most preferred to stay out at Garnet during the 'closure' between fishing periods. So at the end of each fishing period, each boat would give us a list of items they needed from Petersburg, mostly groceries.

Fortunately, in the early 1980s the main grocery store in Petersburg was located on the same block as the cannery. So while we were unloading, ML would hustle over to the grocery store with her lists, load up two or sometimes even three carts with all the groceries and push them out of the store, down the street and right out onto the cannery dock. The trick was to get it all done while we were unloading, as there was a 'hoist' above us on the dock—an electric winch and a boom. So instead of taking the groceries down the slimy fish gut covered ladder one bag at a time, she would just hook the hook onto the shopping cart, and lower the whole cart down to the boat, groceries and all. We called this, "Secrets of the old time fish buyers."

Though salmon was the main game in town, Icicle also bought herring in the spring, halibut spring, summer, and fall, and even occasionally king crab, usually for a two or three week period in the early summer.

King crab fishing was open in the summer of 1982, and when Mary Lou and I walked through the processing area on the way out to our boat one week, the shift manager gave us a big grocery bag full of still warm king crab sections: WOW! But when we hoped for the same thing the following season, the price had gone way up and there were no more freebies. Bummer!

Husband and wife gillnet team, Garnet Point, 1982.

The 30 or so hours we spent in busy Petersburg each week was always a bit of a frazzle, with lists of stuff to get, laundry to do, boat chores to attend to, etc. So getting out of town was a relief.

Petersburg lay at the north end of 20 mile long twisting and constricted Wrangell Narrows, through which the tide ran rapidly. With some 60 markers and buoys, it was a place where I would prefer to go through in daylight. Sometimes if the cannery wasn't in a hurry for our fish, we'd anchor off the south end, so that we could go up the Narrows in daylight in the morning.

But one foggy night the cannery wanted the fish ASAP, so we had to go. Then right in the narrowest place, the radio blasted in my ear: "This is the Alaska ferry *Columbia*, southbound at marker 16. Northbound traffic please advise." A mile ahead, and him with the tide pushing him on? I called him right back, and I could hear the tension in that man's voice: "*Columbia* back to the *Emily Jane*. Yeah, I see you on my radar, but you'd better pull over and let us by. It's pretty damn tight here."

We were right below Burnt Island Reef, and I could see his target on the radar getting bigger all the time. So I slowed and pulled over into the shallows; I'd rather run into a mud bank than get T-boned by a 400-foot ferry!

"Are we there yet?" Mary Lou was pregnant the second season on the Emily Jane *and long passages in rough weather were hard on her.*

I slowed right down until I was just idling into the current, and looked out into the black, trying to see him. With the radar we had when something gets really close, it just disappears into the sea clutter in the middle of the screen and you can't really tell exactly where it is. Well, the ferry did that and I was just bracing myself to hit either the shore or him, when I saw him, just a glimpse: a row of brightly lit portholes rushing by fast in the night, the big tide pushing him on, and then he was gone. Black night, thick 'o fog, a 400' ferry, a twisting channel, with the push of the tide to boot, I was sure glad it was him up there in the ferry's pilothouse that night and not me.

While most of our fish buying was done in the evening, we would often take a loop around the fleet during the day, a two hour round trip across the bay between Garnet Point and Cape Fox to the east. Occasionally someone might have had a big score and want to unload so that they had room in case they scored big again.

The Hamar family had the smallest boat in our fleet, but were one of the highest producers.

On a particularly slow fishing day, we decided to stop and explore remote Lord Island. Landing our outboard boat on the east and protected side of the island, we hiked through the bushes and found this remote sandy beach on the ocean side.

There was a big fat mother seal on the beach with what we assumed were her pups, perhaps 30 pounders. It was a gorgeous breezy day and the seal and her pups made for a cute scene.

But then as we looked on in shock and amazement, totally unexpectedly, out of the surf comes this medium-sized killer whale, maybe 12 feet long. It slid in on a wave and gobbled up both pups, seemed to burp, yes burp, then wriggled back into the ocean when the next wave came rolling in. The mother seal was frantic but it was all over in a couple of seconds.

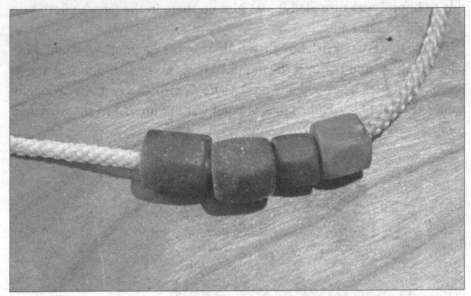

Octagonal Russian trading beads found on the beach below the old native village on Tongass Island.

In 1981-2, most of the boats fishing Garnet were older, with so called 'dry' holds, meaning they neither iced their fish or had mechanical refrigeration. So we encouraged them to deliver once at midday and once in the evening. Today, most gillnetters have insulated fiberglass fish holds where they hold their fish in an ice slurry, or RSW (refrigerated sea water) systems.

Though the area was open 24 hours a day during the fishing period, most boats would come in to sell and anchor up for the night. The salmon didn't seem to move much at night and second, during the day you could see the logs and debris in the water that could damage your net.

It was a colorful and salty group that sold their fish to us. Many had fished most of their lives, others had logged, worked on tugs, etc. before becoming gillnetters.

Booze could be a problem, as it was in many parts of Alaska. One of our boats was operated by a boozy ex-tugboat skipper and his wife, and we never knew what to expect when they came by to sell their fish.

Occasionally they would fish until dark, and if we were busy with boats on both sides when they came in to sell, they would go in and anchor up for the night, and just swing by in the morning to sell their fish on their way out. We called these "bathrobe deliveries," as usually they would be in pajamas, bathrobe, and the usual Extratuff rubber boots.

Sometimes, after nipping on Four Roses as they fished, one of our guys would forget to take his boat out of gear when he came for a landing, so we'd have to lasso him on the way by!

Our fishermen also knew that the cannery made sure we had a nice bottle of McNaughton's whiskey in the galley if they wanted a little nip when they came in to sign the fish tickets. So here's how it often went: the guys would come in, sit down, get their shot of whiskey and sit there complaining about fish prices while pounding down cannery whiskey!

Many of the guys also had dungeness crab pots aboard their boats which they would pull regularly on the long weekends between fishing periods. Catching more crab than they could eat, they often would have a bucket of cooked crab sections for us when we rolled back into Garnet Point from Petersburg, to thank us for bringing them their groceries.

Some of the fishermen from Puget Sound had wives who put up vegetables and fruit in mason jars and sent them north with their husbands, cases of them. And so as the season progressed, as they ate their way through the produce, they set up mason jar canning operations on the weekends, and the cases of jars that went north full of beans and peaches, returned south full of smoked salmon and dungeness crab.

Mary Lou was carrying our first child the second summer that we ran the *EJ*. I took longer wheel watches at night to give her a break, but there were some difficult jobs that she had to do, pregnant or not.

First was THE LADDER. There was almost a 25 foot tidal range in that part of Alaska which meant that at low tide, the climb up the slippery steel ladder to the top was always a long one. PLUS in those days all the fish guts went into the water which meant that most of the rungs had fish intestines, etc. hanging from them. So as Mary Lou climbed up the ladder, often with the cash/fish ticket box hanging from her mouth, her enlarged belly with our son-to-be would slide over each slippery rung in turn.

Tying up at the cannery, where you had to get a tie up line around the fish guts and creosote coated pilings was even worse. Our tall engineer would stand up in the bow, where his long arms gave him a good chance at grabbing the other end of the tie up line as he flipped it around the piling.

But ML was a shortie; the only way she could get a line around the piling was to fully lean onto it, belly and all. Against the barnacles, creosote and fish guts. Yuk!

One of the few families with children delivering their fish to us at Garnet were the Hamars: George and Ethel, with their two boys, Mike and Stormy.

They had the smallest boat in the Garnet fleet, but were some of the most consistently high producers. They had been coming to Garnet for many summers and had built a floating cabin with a fish smoker attached to it, which was anchored in a nearby cove. It was just one room with a wood stove but gave them all a needed break from the tight quarters of their small boat. At the end of the season, they would tow the cabin at high tide up to the beach of a protected cove, close it up, tie it to the trees and leave it for the 9 months until they came again the following June.

Ethel was a Haida native, from the tribe that had settled the Queen Charlotte Islands (now renamed Haida Gwaii) in northern British Columbia, and southern Alaska. George had been a logger before turning to fishing, and the rest of the year the little family lived in a floating home they had built on a protected cove on Prince of Wales, the largest island in Southeast Alaska.

Ethel was an expert at smoking fish; her arrangement with us and the other Garnet Point fishermen was that she would smoke fish "for halves," meaning that when you provided the fish, she would smoke it in exchange for keeping half the fish. In those days there was no market for white kings (most king salmon are red-fleshed; the much rarer white kings are today a prized delicacy) so our fishermen would just give them to us, and we would give them to Ethel, so we had a regular supply of the best smoked salmon one could get anywhere.

Ethel also knew, from years of experience, where the best places to explore were. She took us to Tongass Island, where her ancestors had lived a century before. In the woods, we found a rotting totem. She showed us the beach where before setting out on trading or hunting expeditions in their long cedar canoes, the natives would cast necklaces of trading beads into the sea as a good luck offering. On hands and knees we sifted the sand and the gravel, found tiny spheres of brightly colored glass, only the drilled holes in their centers showing what they had been. Beneath a boulder, still with the braided cedar line through the center, we found four octagonal purple trading beads from the days when Alaska was Russia.

Sometime in the 1920s Tongass Island natives came back from a hunting expedition to see a big yacht leaving the bay and when they pulled their canoes up to the village, discovered that one of their totems had been cut down and stolen. They jumped in their canoes to chase the yacht, but it was way faster and quickly was out of sight.

The Hamar's floathome on Coffman Cove, with bigger one under contruction.

The stolen totem was put up in Seattle's Pioneer Square. Decades later when the totem had rotted too much to be restored (made of weather resistant cedar, Northwest totems are good for about 50-60 years exposed to the weather) the city contacted the Tongass Islanders (who by then had moved to Saxman, nearer to Ketchikan) asking them the price of a new totem. The answer came back: 30 grand, but they would have to have the money up front. The money was sent and the city fathers got a curt message: "That thirty grand was for the totem you stole in 1920. If you want a new totem, that will be another thirty grand." So the city paid up, and the book was closed on the stolen totem.

When the seas and our schedule allowed, Ethel would take us to Garnet Point. In just an hour we could pick enough of the hexagonal dark purple crystals out of the rocky shore to fill a coffee can.

Ethel and George had two boys, Mike and Stormy. I asked her about Stormy's name and she told me:

Wanting her boys to understand her roots as a Haida native, Ethel's family built a dugout canoe the traditional way. They put a little outboard motor on it so that the two boys could use it to commute to school at the nearby logging camp.

"We were beach logging the winter Stormy was born. We were living in the boat then, we didn't have a house anywhere; times were tight. It was a hard way to make a winter's paycheck, but it was all we had then.

"Here's how it works: you lease a section of beach from the Forest Service and you get all the logs on that beach, mostly ones that had drifted ashore from log rafts that had broken up over the years. So one by one you get the logs off and make up your own log raft in a nearby sheltered cove, and then when you're all done, you have to call a tug to come and tow the logs into the sawmill in town. But you don't get paid until the logs get delivered.

"It was the hardest beach to get logs off of that I ever saw, and I was pregnant and almost due when we were finishing up. And I'd have to carry that heavy chainsaw and a hydraulic jack all that way to get to those logs. It was hard.

"It was blowing when I went into labor, no time to take our boat all the way across to Ketchikan, so we had to call a plane. The tug was already coming to take our logs to the pulp mill, and George had to stay to help hook up the raft. He said he'd ride over on the tug and meet me in town.

"It was so gusty that float plane had to make three tries before he could finally set down. Then I got to the hospital and you could hear the rain slashing at the windows and roaring through the trees all night long.

Look how excited they are in the dugout canoe they used to get across the cove to school (all the other kids at the logging camp used their dads' big shiny Lund outboard skiffs!)

"But I had my baby OK—he was a healthy little boy—around 10 in the morning, and I was just laying there nursing him when George came in.

"Right away I could tell something bad had happened; I could just tell by his face.

"'We lost them logs.' he told me right off, 'the raft broke up, coming across. The logs are all scattered. They're gone. We'll never get paid.'

"I just lay there a moment, then said, 'Here, don't you want to hold our baby?

"So George picked him up and asked me what I wanted to name him.

"I thought on it for a while, and finally came up with something:

"Let's name him Stormy, for the night he was born."

Land for settlers to purchase is actually quite limited, despite the vastness of Alaska and its small population, as so much is Federal: National Parks, National Forests, wildlife refuges, wilderness areas—it all adds up. Living on their boat before they had children, they found a harbor they liked—Coffman Cove on the east side of Prince of Wales Island. So they purchased a one room cabin on a log raft and towed it to their new home site. But then as their family grew they knew they had to build something bigger.

First they gathered logs off the nearby beaches—each log almost a day's work just to haul off the beach—and with cables and cross logs, they assembled it into a 40'x60' raft, just in itself a huge job. With the raft done, George set up his portable sawmill on the raft and he and Ethel began yarding heavy logs onto the machine to be sawn into rough boards to build a deck or floor on the raft. Then it was time to build the house. In hopes that at some point in the future some nearby land might become available to buy, the foundation of their new house was two huge spruce logs with the ends cut at an angle so that it could easily be pulled by a bulldozer off the raft, should the opportunity arise.

Of course life in a floating home has wrinkles that a normal homeowner might not encounter. For example, on nasty rainy windy days when the small cabin seemed way too small for Ethel and her two small boys, she would send them outside to fish. In the outhouse. (Which of course, was also floating!)

When the boys started school at the logging camp on the cove, Ethel or George would run them back and forth in their aluminum outboard powered skiff. But then as they got old enough to drive the boat across the cove by themselves, Ethel had an idea: build an authentic cedar canoe the traditional way and have the boys use that to commute to school with. Searching the surrounding shoreline until they found the perfect five foot diameter log, they brought it home and started carving it into a canoe the old way: building a fire where they wanted to carve it out, then putting the fire out and carving out the much softer charred wood, and then doing it again and again. And again. But the boys helped so it was a good family project. When it was finally done, they put a little 10 h.p. outboard motor on it, and it became their new school commuter.

But of course, their school buddies whose dads worked at the logging camp, all had their families' nice shiny Lund aluminum skiffs with big outboards to buzz around on. Somehow, for the Hamar boys, their own cedar canoe, hand crafted lovingly in the native way, didn't quite cut it with their school pals.

Years later, the Forest Service decided to start paving some of the logging roads on Prince of Wales Island, and Ethel got the job as flagger on the section near Coffman Cove, taking the outboard to the logging camp each morning and hiking up to the road.

By that time, Stormy was a married father, working at a log sorting yard on the west side of the island. There was no phone in the Hamar's float home, but Stormy found a way to pass along family news. Now and again one of the logging trucks would pass Ethel as she was flagging and the driver would slow, toot and point to the load of logs behind.

Where Stormy had put a message in spray paint on a big log, something like, "All OK here, Janie got her first tooth!"

With the improved road came regular ferry service from Ketchikan to Prince of Wales, and the State and the Forest Service decided to carve some of the land around Coffman Cove into lots and offer them for sale. And finally Ethel and George's idea to built their float home so that it could be easily moved to land paid off. Purchasing and clearing a lot, they beached the float on a big tide, hired a bulldozer, and dragged the float home off the raft and up the road to their lot overlooking the cove where the house had once floated.

A decade or so later, we got a card announcing the graduation of Stormy's son from Icy Bay High School.

"No way does Icy Bay have a high school." was my immediate reaction, as Icy Bay is a remote indentation on the outside coast some three hundred miles north of Juneau. I remember hearing something about a logging camp in there, or maybe some exploratory drilling for oil, but nothing big enough for a school. But the card even had the raised logo of the school on fancy paper.

I ran into Ethel's other son Mike later that year in Petersburg and asked him about that graduation card.

"What's up with Stormy in Icy Bay? I got a graduation card for their son. Is there a town there big enough for a school now?"

"Naw," Mike told me, "they're the only ones there, they're home school-ing the kids. There's a big logging camp there, but it's been shut down for a couple of years. Stormy's the caretaker, maintaining things. He gets to drive all that cool equipment around, and every couple of weeks a plane comes in with their groceries. They wanted their son to have some kind of a graduation, so Stormy's wife printed up those fancy announcements."

There were no licensing requirements to run a tender or fish buying boat, not even the most minimal "Six-pack" license that charter boat skip-pers have to have. Nor was there any kind of paperwork instructions from the cannery.

Instead I was lucky to have had some wonderful mentors along the way. Back in 1972, when I was a gillnetter out of Point Baker, our fish buy-er was this truly fine family, Peter and Sandra Schugren, operating their tender, Cypress, with their children, son Eric, 8, and Elena, 6, plus their dog and cat. Peter had been an artist, looking for a cheap place to live, when he ran across the Cypress in 1968. Sold as is with the engine stripped out, Peter transformed it into a fine living space for his family, complete with a skylight lit studio in the fish hold.

Thinking it might be fun to travel with it, he traded his big Ford pickup truck and a thousand bucks for a Caterpillar diesel engine reportedly hot from an Mexican sawmill, scrounged a well used reverse gear/transmis-sion from somewhere, and voilá, the family started spending their sum-mers tied to a piling in a harbor in the San Juan Islands and rowing to shore. Hearing that icicle Seafoods needed another tender, he arranged to get an advance against his charter fee for a radar, sideband radio, anchor winch, etc. And headed up to Southeast Alaska with his family to become a tenderman and my friend. Peter's art was all over his boat, both in the craftsmanship of his carpentry, and his small oil paintings. Eventually re-tiring from fish buying he became a well known musician.

Another mentor was Bob Holmstrand, one of those colorful guys Alaska seems to breed. Ex-king crabber, ex-processor, he settled into his 60s with his big *Frigidland*, buying fish for Icicle Seafoods, with his stepson, Russell, as engineer, and wife Anne as bookkeeper and cook. Theirs was a boisterous and happy boat, and when on those rare summer occasions our paths crossed, we would try to make time to anchor up together, turn off our radios for a rare few hours (Gasp...!), get out the rum bottle and catch up.

Peter Schugren (right) was also a talented carpenter.

Then there was Laland Daniels, another fish buying close friend and almost bigger than life. I met him when we had anchored the *Emily Jane* buying fish in a narrow channel and our radio crackled with a call:

"Hey Joe, isn't there a beach in that next cove? We got a bad leak and Dad needs to run 'er ashore?"

I looked quickly down the channel to see to see the big seventy-foot tender *Loon,* an old wooden Navy sub chaser steaming down the channel, dangerously low in the water. Just as they rushed past me, a lanky older guy came up though the engine-room door, as a thigh thick stream of water started blasting out of a port in the hull and raising his hands in victory like a prize fighter after a tough match. A moment late the radio spoke again:

Peter Schugren's fine tender Cypress, *buying fish at Point Baker, 1974.*

"Ahh, I guess he got the pump going."

This was Laland, in one of a series of boats he operated up and down the coast. In another of his ventures he operated a grocery boat. He had a grudge with the Ketchikan town fathers for firing his dad as police chief, so when the summer salmon season was over, he would load his boat with whatever he could get a good deal on in Seattle, and head north to Ketchikan. He'd tie up downtown, put an ad on the radio and undercut the local merchants with his load.

On one of his trips coming across the notoriously rough Queen Charlotte Sound, a nasty squall came up suddenly and a sea, coming over the bow, washed a dozen big pumpkins over the side.

He stopped and started to turn around.

"Hey Dad, it's getting bad, we gotta get out of here," cried one of his sons.

"Not until we git all them pumpkins," answered Laland, digging around for a dip net.

Hidden at the head of a remote inlet was the dock for an exquisite hot spring.

And so our season went: full speed ahead, day after day, just the way we liked it. I was again, as I had been in '75 on the beater *North Wind*, and in '65 on the fine big *Sidney*, part of a cannery's team. For a frenzied day or so between fishing periods, us and the dozen other big tenders working for Icicle would be tied three and four deep at the cannery, unloading fish, loading groceries, and supplies, fueling and icing, doing laundry, huddling with the fleet manager in his office overlooking the docks and the busy Narrows beyond. There was a big chart on his wall covering all of Southeast Alaska, with little flags here and there showing where all his boats were.

And then with the cash box refilled with fish tickets and greenbacks, a fresh bottle of McNaughton's for the boys, the tenders would head out. The *Frigidland*, and the *Lualda* and the *Apache* to the north, to Stephens Passage and Lynn Canal. The big seine tenders, the *Viking Queen*, the *Kupreanof* and the *Mitkof* out to Noyes Island, or immense Chatham Strait. And the other gill-net tenders, the *Marine View*, and us in the *Emily Jane*, to the south end, to Foggy Bay, and Garnet Point. For another busy week, to return to town deep in the water with our fish five days later. For another busy turnaround before we headed out to do it all over again.

By the end of that long season, we were beat, especially Mary Lou. The long days, the twenty hour runs back and forth to the cannery, the fewer hours of daylight had all taken their toll. Plus our first child had started to kick inside Mary Lou; a sign that it was time to be back in our cozy Maine home.

Lost in the vastness of the British Columbia coast was a hidden hot springs. On our way back to Seattle, we slid in there at dusk on a foggy rainy evening, tied up, stopped the engine and there was only the patter of the rain on the water and the distant rush of the falls across the bay.

We still had 500 miles to go. But as we soaked in that clear warm water, it felt like the cares of a long season in the North were just slipping away.

Luxuriating in the warmth of it all, we talked quietly of the season past, of the winter to come.

Then there was a noise that we didn't recognize. We stood up, looked out the openings in the cinder block wall.

A pair of humpbacks had come into the bay for some reason. Again and again they lifted their tales, blew loudly.

It was magic.

At the end of a long season: hot water up to our necks: magic!

Herring "skiffs" on tender Viva Yo. *Note 'SF' on registration number—these skiffs, probably among the ugliest craft to enter the Alaska fisheries, had started their season on San Francisco Bay, been trucked to a Puget Sound port, and put on the* Viva Yo *for a ride up to Alaska. Larger 'skiffs' can hold up to 20 TONS of herring.*

HERRING: HURRY UP AND WAIT

EARLY MARCH, 1982: "KAH SHAKE'S GONNA pop." The word, that the herring in a remote Alaska cove were about to spawn, spread like wildfire along the Northwest coast.

At truck stops up and down I-5, the north-south west coast corridor, Seattle-bound drivers with big rigs loaded with big ugly aluminum herring skiffs from San Francisco sleepily found pay phones for their daily check-in, jerked fully awake with the news, grabbed breakfast to go and headed out to their trucks.

The phone in our Seattle apartment rang with orders from Icicle Seafoods: load cannery freight aboard the *Emily Jane* and head north ASAP.

Norton Sound
Gillnet
May (if the ice is gone)

Bering Sea

Bristol Bay

Togiak
Seine and gillnet
April

Anchorage

Fairbanks

Homer

ALASKA

Seward

Kodiak Island

Prince William Sound
Never recovered from
1989 Exxon oil spill

Prince William Sound

Gulf of Alaska

The Herring Circuit

CANADA

Sitka
Seine
Late April - May

Juneau

Seymour Canal
Gillnet
April

_____
100 Miles

Ketchikan

**Southeast
Alaska**

*North Pacific
Ocean*

Kah Shakes
Gillnet
March

Small craft route

CANADA

San Francisco
Gillnet
Dec. to Feb.

**Vancouver
Island**

Seymour Narrows

**Vancouver
Seattle**

The big boys get ready: Kah Shakes Cove, 1982. The Bountiful *is a processor—she freezes the herring in blocks for export to Japan.*

The young man that was our engineer met me aboard, we started up and headed the hundred yards from our winter berth to the west wall, suddenly crowded with a dozen other tenders loading freight from trucks already parked alongside. As we squeezed into a space barely longer than our boat, a truck rumbled along the dock, trailer springs bottomed out with two layers of big herring skiffs stacked on top or each other, and still sporting SF herring registrations painted on their sides.

The 'San Francisco boys,' as we called them, were headed for a big change—from staying in nice hotels and motels in Sausalito, near the Golden Gate, being wined and dined in the hospitality suites of big herring buyers in downtown San Francisco high rises, to basically camping aboard their austere 'skiffs' in Southern Alaska, waiting for the herring to be ripe enough to fish for.

"It's not too bad down there, you know." A friend had described his San Francisco Bay herring season to me. "My girlfriend was staying with me and the room service in the hotel had about everything we ever needed. We could walk right down to the docks where we kept our skiffs and about every other night there'd be a shindig somewhere with booze and food hosted by some Japanese herring buyer to talk about when we might be able to fish. We were there a month and cleared 20 grand. Not a bad start to our season."

And so much for a nice mellow anchor-up-every-night 800 mile run up the Inside Passage to Petersburg. I loved that trip, and normally north and southbound from salmon seasons, we'd take our time, anchor up at night in little watch pocket coves, savor the magic and the vastness of The North, even spend an evening lounging in our favorite remote hot springs in Bishop Bay, BC.

But nooooo, not for herring. We loaded up with freight for the cannery, said our goodbyes to our wives, and joined the procession of fish boats of all sizes and descriptions headed for Alaska and the Great Herring Bonanza.

Day and night we steamed; just Eric, the engineer, and I, 80 hours of 4 on, 4 off. Definitely no fun. Ahead and behind were the shapes and lights of dozens of other boats.

In Petersburg, the word was: "Hurry, they might open it tomorrow," and the rush was on to unload the freight from us and the dozen other tenders fresh up from Seattle. As pallet loads of freight disappeared into the warehouse, the forklifts returned with the big herring pumps, hydraulic hoses, lengths of ungainly 10" aluminum pipe, weird looking dewatering elbows. (Sections of pipe made out of parallel lengths of aluminum rod so that the water drains out of the herring/water slurry pumped from the net.)

Yet all around us—along the shores of Wrangell Narrows, behind all the cannery buildings, the snow drifts were four and five feet high—winter was still very much there and it seemed odd that the herring should be arriving so early.

But winter or not, 7 hours after rolling into town, we were southbound though Wrangell Narrows. In the gathering dusk, the red, green, and white flashing lights on the 60-odd buoys and markers made the channel look like a pinball machine and the night, when it came, was very black.

By then we were basically running mostly on adrenalin—on the radio the tender channel was busy with excited talk about the coming rendezvous with a vast and silent body of herring, creeping in toward the shore of Kah Shakes Cove along the deep trenches from the North Pacific, guided by an amazing and powerful sixth sense.

And the mystery of the fishery was just this—the herring are only valuable during that brief interval when they rush in from the deeps to spawn on the beaches, the kelp, the rocks, anchor chains of boats and whatever else happens to be in the water. And yet with all the electronics, and biologists in the waiting fleet, no one could tell much in advance when that moment would actually be.

18 Hours of groggy steaming brought us to anchor at Kah Shakes Cove, near the Alaska/Canada border, and for 11 1/2 months a year a sleepy wilderness, but on that afternoon a frenzy of activity. All around us other tenders were unloading herring skiffs, trying out their noisy herring pumps, making all ready as a steady streams of skiffs and tenders steamed in from north and south.

And all the while to the south of us, a plane made lazy circles along the shore and out over the deeper water, looking for the herring that had brought us all there and finding none.

By four it was apparent that instead of the quick fishery that we had traveled almost a thousand miles non-stop for, we were in for a wait. So we picked up the anchor and followed our friend Bob Holmstrand on his big tender *Frigidland* around the corner and into the vast and winding reaches of the Boca de Quadra, seeking a quieter spot to wait.

We had the bad habit of anchoring up together, getting out the bottle, and turning the radios off. So for a few hours we did just that: set a jug on the table and just relaxed with our crews without the incessant chatter of the herring world on the radio.

While the rest of the fleet rolled in the long swell outside and listened to the whine of generators all night long, for us, surrounded by the vast and wild hills of the Misty Fjords National Monument, there was only the soft callings of ducks outside, and Emmy Lou Harris on the tape player.

Another friend was there, Larry Painter in his immaculate seiner *Alsec*. All winter Larry fished his shrimp and crab pots in the Boca and nearby fjords, a single boat working an area the size of some New England states.

We went alongside the next night to visit and the talk was mostly of The Mine: what was to be the largest open pit molybdenum mine in the world, soon to be built in the wilderness just a dozen or so miles from where we lay, with millions of tons of spoils—the crushed rock left after the moly was extracted—to be dumped into the pristine waters of The Boca.

When the plan was first announced, and it started going through the permitting process, the fishing and conservation community was stunned that such a project could be allowed. But the big pulp mill in Ketchikan was closing and the mine, potentially accessed by fast commuter boat from town promised good paying jobs for laid off workers and others.

At one of the many hearings the biologist paid by the mining company asserted that there was nothing of commercial value in the waters where the tailings would be dumped, the same waters where Larry made a very good living.

"Well," Larry countered, "If there's nothing on the bottom then there's sure a lot of shrimp and crab that crawl into my pots on the way up."

But the juggernaut of big money and big influence kept moving forward; the permits were in place, and the digging would start in less than a year.

A typical shrimp pot.

"I could have stopped it," Larry said, startling me, "I should have stopped it when I had the chance."

Side stripe shrimp.

That got my attention. How the hell could Larry have stopped it when the combined efforts of the United Fishermen of Alaska, the Southeast Alaska Conservation Council, the Sierra Club, and the Wilderness Society hadn't even been able to slow down the process.

"I met the guy." Larry explained. "The geologist, the guy who discovered the moly, who got the whole big ball rolling."

"Five years ago, I kept seeing this funky old boat anchored way up at the head of the Boca. Wintertime there's usually nobody ever there but me, so one night I took my skiff alongside, invited the guy over for a visit and a mess of shrimp.

"He'd just made the big strike. He showed me some of the samples he was getting ready to take to Ketchikan and fly out. He said it was the richest ore he'd ever seen. He was really excited about it. He was a nice enough guy just doing his job, but didn't know anything about the fishing here, what a special place the Boca was.

"If I'd known the shit that was going to happen, I would have taken care of it then." He paused, looked out the window at the landscape in the fading light: somber steep hills leading back to little visited valleys and lonely Hugh Smith Lake.

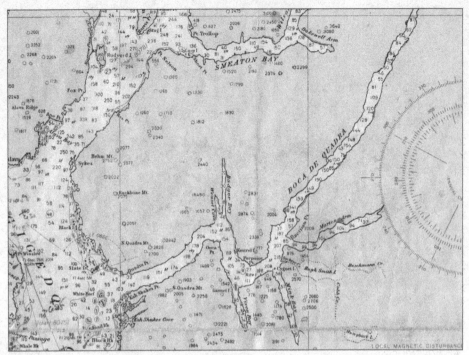

Boca de Quadra area: basically a steep sided many armed fjord. The depth notations are in fathoms. A fathom is six feet so in numerous places the narrow fjord is over 1,200 feet deep. Kah Shakes cove is at the very bottom of the chart.

I must have been obtuse; I still didn't get it, asked him.

"I could have sunk his boat; him in it. It's deep here. No one knew exactly where he was. No one would ever have known. I should have done it."

He waved out the window again toward the mine site.

"None of this shit would be happening."

But it had a different ending than what we were expecting. The cold war ended, the demand for moly (a major use is as an additive to harden the steel used to make turbine blades for the engines of fighter jets) collapsed, the mine was never built.

There's a lot of waiting in the herring business. For optimum value, the fish must be ready to spawn so that the roe sacs, the target of the whole fishery, are as large as possible, and the schools have a large percentage of females.

AF&G biologists sample the fish each day, announcing on the radio each night their findings. At the same time, they assess the size of the body of fish and come up with a quota—the amount of herring that can be taken without damaging the health of the overall resource.

From the quota and the number of boats waiting to fish, they establish the length of time the fleet will be allowed to fish. Sometimes a herring "opening" might only be 12 hours.

Finally after two days up in the Boca, with that hollow stillness every night and not another sign of man to be seen, we knew that we couldn't shirk our responsibilities any longer. But going back to Kah Shakes was almost like entering a scene from Star Wars.

Kah Shakes Cove. The fleet waits and waits and waits.

For laying in the 20 or so acres of the outer harbor was the greatest concentration of capital and technology to be seen yet this year in Southeast Alaska. Turning night into day with their brilliant crab lights were Trident Seafoods' big catcher processors *Bountiful* and *Billikin*, immense multi-million dollar floating freezers, their decks festooned with the thick hoses, pipes and odd paraphernalia of the fish pumps. Only slightly less impressive were the crabber tenders *Skipbladnir* and *Prowler*, anchored together, along with about thirty other tenders, with the black and silent wilderness stretching away on all sides.

But it was in the inner coves, Kah Shakes, and Bullhead to the north that the really strange boats lay. The herring roe fishery, a business that stretches from San Francisco Bay in the south to Norton Sound, up by the Arctic Circle, all targeting herring spawn, has itself spawned a very strange class of boats.

Some of the first were little more than big plywood boxes with an outboard on the back and a couple of posts to hold a shaker bar. (As opposed to salmon which become more entangled in a gill-net, herring are shaken out of the nets. The better equipped skiffs might have a hydraulically powered shaking device.)

Now, aluminum is the material of choice, and for the most part the boats are aluminum boxes with right angles everywhere and a straight sheer. They are as ugly a bunch of boats as ever came to Alaska. But form follows function, and the boats are ideal for carrying big loads in relatively sheltered waters, and loading—even stacking—aboard tenders for the long hauls between fisheries.

And at 8:00 on VHF Channel 10 comes the evening ritual of the area biologist talking about what is happening and asking for comments. So far they had not seen a big enough body of fish to justify opening the fishery.

A comment on the radio: "Ahh, go ahead and open it; we'll find 'em."

March 24, 1985—Same Spot: Awakened by 2 a.m. banging on the pilothouse: "They might open Sitka. We need your pump." The voice says.

So we unloaded our herring pump to another tender while outside all is light and noise as 10 or 15 tenders in the outer harbor started up their engines, hauled up their anchors, fired up their radars, and got underway.

But so many radars operating in so tight a spot just created interference and the radio was full of boats complaining about useless radars.

A reef, hidden by the tide lay waiting, and sure enough, a big Whitney Seafoods tender drove up on it, luckily without damage to be hauled off by the next tender behind him and sent on his way.

Then just two hours later, all was still again, with no sight or sign of the fleet driving through the night to Sitka, 32 hours away.

March 26, 1982—Kah Shakes—The day came with snow thick on the deck, obscuring the world outside for the second day in a row. But to the north, by Slate Islands, a ADF&G biologist in a skiff has found a bunch of ripe herring, ready to spawn. After a full week of waiting, a quota opening is announced for 11 this morning.

Form follows function; herring skiffs aren't things of beauty.

So for an hour the narrow channel out of the cove is filled with the dim shapes of skiffs, the skippers peering ahead into the snow, picking their way out. Finally the snow lifted and all at once the spotter planes were off with a roar.

But the main body of fish remained offshore and uncooperative, and the night produced few big scores.

March 27, 1982—Kah Shakes—Tonight as we were playing cards there was a noise outside and we stepped out on deck to find the cove full of herring, flipping on the surface, clearly visible in the water around us. On the sounder it was solid fish, all the way to the bottom.

At ten we threaded our way out the narrow entrance to a rendezvous with a boat outside. As our searchlight spotted the rocks, the herring, frightened by the light, boiled completely out of water, a dramatic sight. But oddly, the few gill-nets set in the cove produced little, even with a cove full of fish.

March 28, 1982—Slate Island anchorage—Herring vignettes: Half a dozen skiffs working the beach close to the island, the day fair. The boats, the men almost totally hidden by a cloud of gulls, and the water around them milky white with spawn and milt.

A single skiff slowly motored southbound across the mouth of the Boca, deep in the water with fish. In the slight ocean swell, it seemed at times to totally disappear, leaving only the figure of a man seeming to stand in the water with the vast canyon of the Boca yawning behind him.

Early "plywood box" style skiff heads out for an opening.

But these images on a rare fine day obscure what the fishery can be: an exhausting grind, out in raw and cold March Alaska weather, with no place to go and get out of it. Most of the boats here are little more than open skiffs. If they have cabins, they have only the most rudimentary facilities—an engine (probably not even covered,) a steering wheel, maybe a sheet of plywood to sleep on that flops down over the engine.

For many of the men, the only time they can really get warm is when they sell their fish. So we always have a pot of hearty stew or chowder waiting when our guys come in to deliver, sometimes standing by the diesel stove a long while just to stop shivering.

One of our fishermen, in an open skiff, straining to find his way into the cove through sleet, had his eyeballs abraded so badly that he had to be flown out to the hospital .

We went into Ketchikan for more groceries in the afternoon and returned in darkness, coming upon the support fleet again, all light and noise in that vast panorama of dark hills and water.

Then fishing got suddenly heavy again, with skiff after skiff deep in the water with their load, moving slowly through the fleet looking for their tender.

The roe content for these herring is high—some deliveries as high as 14-16% because of the predominance of females, which translates into a big price.

And Fish and Game announced that some 1,200 tons out of the 1,900 ton quota have been taken; at this rate few expect the opening to last more than another day.

Shaking herring out of the net as it comes aboard.

March 29, 1982—Kah Shakes—And just like that, it's all done, the quota filled, the fishery over. The fish came in a wave again at the end; the quota probably got over harvested by a few hundred tons. But it's the fish biz, not a manufacturing operation; exactitude is rarely possible. Besides these quotas are only best guesses, they could be high or low. But the stocks seem to be healthy year after year, despite a huge rise in demand from our only market: Japan.

Our top boat was a beat up open skiff that started in San Francisco, and will probably see the end of the season up in Norton Sound, by the Arctic Circle. By the end of the opening its owner, a friend, looked like something a raccoon had hauled out of a trash can. But he took a shower aboard us and sat for a bit at our galley table, his boat hanging off our stern while the rest of our boats delivered one by one. He'd brought a garbage bag of clean clothes and looked pretty good once he'd cleaned up. He asked us to tow his boat to town and after a while an air taxi float plane arrived to take him to the Ketchikan airport. He was headed for Hawaii for some R&R before the opening at Seymour Canal, the next stop on the herring circuit.

What with one thing and another, we were the last boat to leave Kah Shakes Cove. Likely as not, a good 11 months would pass before a boat went in there again.

Grant Thompson, in his state of the art 32 footer, around 1988. Grant was one of the Petersburg gillnetters who basically opened the eyes of other Southeast Alaska fisherman about the potential of Bristol Bay.

PART III—ALASKA'S GRAND PRIX: BRISTOL BAY

ALMOST MIDNIGHT, MAINE, FEBRUARY 1986:. THE phone rings, and I grab it and go downstairs, not wanting to wake our new baby, cradle the phone on my shoulder while I throw another couple of logs in the woodstove and open the draft. It's Bob Anderson, my old friend from Alaska gill-netting days in the early '70s.

"Hey, Joe, we've got a boat and a permit for you if you want to try the Bay."

12 years earlier, after a divorce and a slump in the Southeast Alaska salmon fisheries, I'd moved back to Maine. By then, Alaska had instituted a limited entry program for most salmon fisheries. I'd qualified for a permit,

but Bob, who started fishing a year later than I, did not. Permit prices were $10,000, a lot for Bob, with three young children. So I gave him mine, handshake deal: "Pay me when you can." It all worked out fine, and now, he was returning the favor, though in a much bigger way, as Bristol Bay permit prices were around $100,000.

Alaska calling again. I thanked Bob and told him I'd have to talk to Mary Lou and get back to him.

Nothing prepared me for the numbers of boats and the competitive nature of the Bristol Bay fishery.

After the *Emily Jane*, we'd settled back in Maine to begin our family. I started a mussel aquaculture project, with a friend, Michael Mesko, on Vinalhaven Island. But after five years I began to have doubts about mussels continuing to support us. So the opportunity to fish Bristol Bay came at the right time. Though it would mean leaving Mary Lou in an unfinished cabin with two young children (but finally with running water and a washing machine, though no dryer), Mary Lou told me to go ahead; she knew that Mike, and I had been talking about the Bay for a couple of years and that the opportunity presented was too good to turn down.

And so June, 1986, found me in the Anchorage airport and the very different crowd at the departure lounge for King Salmon and The Bay. In those days you got to King Salmon on Mark Air, a regional carrier servicing many of the more remote native communities in Western and Arctic Alaska. The clientele was pretty much commercial fishermen and natives. As I was to learn, both groups had a habit of partying hard in Anchorage before they headed out to the very different world to 'west'ard,' as it was known in the fish business, and the group in the airport looked like they had had a pretty rough night of it. Plus this was long before the heightened security measures instituted after 9/11 so many of the guys had pints of liquor in paper bags that they were sucking on as well.

Off to one side were three guys, very obviously not hung over and very alert and fit looking. Each had a big duffel, full of some sort of lumpy packages, each with a serious looking padlock. And if they weren't packing heat, they sure looked like it.

Breaking ice to get to the mussel beds, Maine, February 1988.

"Couriers," this bleary eyed fishermen from San Diego said, "You don't mess with 'em That's cash in them bags."

"Aren't there banks out there? What do they need to carry so much cash out there for."

Not your regular Alaska: after almost a decade of fishing among the thickly forested islands of Southeast Alaska, I was unprepared for the austere tundra landscape of Bristol Bay.

"Yeah, there's one little bank. Sometimes it's open, but it usually doesn't carry that much cash."

"But what do they need so much for?" I asked, realizing it probably showed that this was my first time up in The Bay.

"They're fish buyers. They got to have a lot of cash. We don't take checks up here from new buyers. We all tried it once a couple of years ago when the first new buyers showed up. One of my buddies spent the whole season down on the Ugashik; just a native village down there, no bank or nothing. Took checks from the buyer all season. Got back at the end of the season, the buyer had disappeared. He never got paid for those fish. All the cannery guys just take fish tickets and settle up at the end of the season. The big companies are good for it. It's just those small buyers, they're usually just starting up, hoping to buy fish cheap here and make a pile selling them somewhere else. But it ain't that easy, so sometimes they go tits up, and it's the fishermen that get the shaft."

Then the plane took off and I got a look at the very different world of Western Alaska, a landscape I hadn't seen since king crab fishing days fifteen years earlier.

It's not your regular Alaska with tall trees, eagles and glaciers. The first thing I saw as the plane crossed tide swept upper Cook Inlet were three almost perfectly cone shaped volcanoes rising from the rugged landscape: Iliamna and Redoubt to the south, and Spurr to the north. Spurr was smoking ominously and I knew that occasionally it puffed out enough fine ash to ruin car and truck engines whose owners hadn'd rigged a pre-filter made out of a nylon stocking over the air filter.

Though it was June, the landscape passing below was for the most part stark and austere: rock and snow, frozen lakes, jagged peaks and a bit later, another volcano: Katmai, or maybe Novarupta, whose 1912 eruption was the fiercest of the 20th century, burying Kodiak, 120 miles away with four feet of ash and creating the Valley of 10,000 Smokes (now Katmai National Park.)

Early days in Bristol Bay: 1905? Square rigger anchored with sailing gillnetters in front. At the end of the season the ship will be loaded with canned salmon, fishermen and cannery workers and sail back to San Francisco, leaving a caretaker and hopefully his wife to stay the winter.

Compared to the forest covered hills and low mountains of Southeast Alaska that I was used to, it was a sobering sight.

Bristol Bay is the eastern shore of the Bering Sea where it makes kind of a right angle turn to the north at the east end of the Alaska Peninsula. There are no trees, only low bushes, and wide stretches of tundra and thousands of small shallow ponds. It was settled by Siberian natives prob-ably following game across the Bering Sea Land Bridge during the last ice age 15,000 years ago. Their first contact with whites left a harsh legacy when Russia fur traders came to coastal Alaska in the 1750s to force na-tives to kill and skin sea otters, a single pelt of which was worth a year's wages for a laborer. Sometimes murdering villagers to encourage others to hunt otters, it was a brutal occupation. But a few decades later, sea otters were almost extinct and the Russians had sold Alaska to America, leaving behind bitter feelings among the natives, lots of Russian place names, and a few Russian Orthodox churches.

Five Rivers with Russian names—Nushagak, Kvichak, Naknek, Ugashik and Egegik—empty into the Bay, each the site of small native villages. The Bay is 300 plus miles from Anchorage and only accessible by water and air. If it weren't for a coincidence of nature—all the rivers begin in large lakes: perfect for the valuable red or sockeye salmon, The Bay would be an unremarkable and little visited Alaska backwater.

Instead, after early explorers reported an abundance of sockeyes, salm-on entrepreneurs wasted no time establishing first salteries—salting salm-on into barrels—and then canneries on the banks of the rivers. These were truly remarkable ventures: full rigged three masted sailing ships would depart San Francisco, Seattle, or Astoria, Oregon on the Columbia River in the early spring. Loaded with materials, carpenters, Norwegian fishermen and Chinese cannery workers, they'd reach Unimak Pass—the southern entrance to the Bering Sea—after 30 or 40 days—where a tug would be often be waiting to aid them through the tide swept passage. Finding a promising spot with strong salmon runs in Bristol Bay, they would anchor and build a cannery, complete with bunkhouses, docks, canning buildings and warehouses. In those early days the Chinese cannery workers would use tin snips to cut the tops and sides of the salmon cans out of big sheets of tin, and solder them together. When the fish started arriving toward the end of June, the 30 and 32 foot sailing gillnetters would be launched and fishing would begin. And six or seven weeks later, it would be all over, the fishing boats hauled and stored in the warehouse, the pack—cases of canned salmon—would be loaded into the ship that brought them all there, and leaving a just a caretaker (and hopefully his family) behind to watch over things until they returned 10 months later, sail south.

And all this without phone, internet, Fed Ex or UPS: truly a humbling achievement. And not just one, several **dozen** canneries were built on the banks of the Bay's five rivers.

Over time, salteries disappeared, canneries changed hands, shrank in number as more efficient ways of canning salmon were developed. But still, by the time I arrived in 1986, there were approximately 12 canneries operating in Bristol Bay. Delivering their fish to these processors were some 1,800 32' gill-net boats, each usually with three or four aboard, and some 1,000 setnetters, fishing anchored nets on the shore and living in fish camps nearby.

We flew further west and I got my first view of the tundra that encompasses much of the lowlands along the Bering Sea coast, including the immense flats where the mighty Yukon and Kuskokwim Rivers become multiple streams in their shallow deltas before they eventually empty into the Bering Sea. Low and green-brown, with uncounted and unnamed tundra ponds, it seemed to stetch away to the west and north without end.

On the approach to King Salmon—the airport that serves the Naknek area—the plane swung around over giant Lake Iliamna, and the brown and winding Kvichak River. The tide was down, and I glimpsed what seemed like thousands of acres of sand bars, which divided the river into many channels. Somewhere down there I knew, lay Deadman Sands, the desolate sand bar that had claimed so many lives in sailboat days. We passed over what looked like an abandoned town, which I remembered must be an old cannery, and then it was wheels down.

I'd expected a gravel strip in such a remote spot, but instead it was 10,000' of pavement and F-15 fighter jets parked in revetments—individual parking spots protected by high banked walls on three sides. The Cold War was still pretty hot, at least in Western Alaska, and it turned out that those fighters were scrambled regularly to intercept Soviet fighters and bombers probing US air defences.

For most of the year, King Salmon airport had one or two flights a day, mostly air force personnel or folks headed to the nearby Native villages of North and South Naknek. But for a few weeks in early June and again in mid-July, it was a chaotic, frantic place as 4,000 plus fishermen and cannery workers came and went for the short and intense salmon season. (and another 4,000 or so came and went out of Dillingham, the village on the West side of The Bay.) And I had arrived right in the thick of it—another 20 passenger turbo prop was at the rough terminal building ahead of us and a big Alaska Air 737 was right behind us, adding flights when Mark Air's fleet got overwhealmed.

Our bags were just dumped on the ground outside the terminal, where vans from the big canneries picked up their fishermen and workers. Right away I could see that in Bristol Bay, there were two kinds of fishermen: cannery and independents. The cannery guys had their regular rooms in the bunkhouses, the same rooms year after year, they ate in the messhall, their boats were stored inside the big warehouses, and were even worked on by cannery mechanics. Plus they had access to the cannery warehouse for parts, nets, etc. Need a little cash to get through the winter? Just call up the cannery and get an 'advance' to last you until salmon season.

The stickler, of course, is that you get what you pay for; the price the canneries paid for salmon reflected the services and infrastructure they provided to their fishermen. The independents, like what I was becoming, put up with a lot less convenience and comfort, paid for getting their boat stored outside in the weather, worked on their own boats, etc. in exchange for hopefully a higher price for their fish at the end of the season.

So, after the last of the cannery vans picked up their guys, a ragtag fleet of beater vehicles and their native drivers waited for us: a rough looking bunch of guys with toolboxes, bags of net, long engine mufflers—all the stuff that the cannery guys could just get from the canneries, instead of having to carry them up from Seattle, or wherever they were coming from. In earlier days the big canneries, many of whose cannery workers and fishermen were from the Monterey or San Diego/San Pedro area of California, would charter big four engined propellor driven DC-Sixes and -Sevens to get them all to Alaska, direct to King Salmon and Dillingham.

I piled into an old Ford Fairlane with three other guys, and told the driver "Lummi," as I had been told, trying not to appear too much like a greenhorn, and having no idea of what to expect other than Lummi was where my boat was. After a bit we pulled off the road, drove down a winding dusty lane with the low bushes scraping the sides. And came to a little riverbank settlement with a half dozen Bristol Bay gillnetters setting on top of vertical 55 gallon drums. It was a mellow, friendly scene—the river was just 20 or 30 yards wide; there was what looked like a cabin or community center, and a couple of guys working on their nets and chatting with each other, much like the little community we had back in Port Upton days when I was a gillnetter in Southeast Alaska. Two guys got out, and I followed, wondering what boat was to be mine, and looking forward to a mellow week or so of getting my boat together before my crew arrived, and it was time to go fishing.

Until the driver turned to me in a gutteral voice, informing me that this was Charlies, that we still had a ways to go. So back onto the road we went, me thinking shocks on cars probably didn't last that long there, as we wove back and forth down the road, trying unsuccessfully to stay out of the worst of the potholes. There were no actual trees in that part of Alaska, but the tundra bushes were high enough on either side so that there was nothing to see until we turned off onto another dirt road, came around a corner and a totally different river front came into view.

Naknek Marine Center boat storage yard, around 1993. Note how the fleet is dominated by aluminum boats and how large they are—though still 32'.

Two huge boat parking lots, each the size of several football fields had been carved out of the dirt of the sloping riverbank. Each was filled with rows of work battered aluminum and fiberglass 32 footers up on jackstands or 55 gallon drums, two lines of boats in each row, bow to bow, parked so close that you could jump from boat to boat, with battered pickups and cars parked helter sketer among the rows.

"Where you going, buddy?" the driver queried, after he had dropped the other guy and his gear.

"Ahhh, I'm supposed to go to the *Joe H.*" I stammered, a little over-whealmed at the scene, "Drive around slow, I'll look for it. " said I, not really knowing where to start.

"What kind of boat is it?" Again a question that I wasn't totally sure of the answer to.

"A Shore boat? I think that's what I was told," said I, glad that the others had all already gotten out, knowing that I was revealing myself as a total newbie greenhorn.

"Oh, yeah, I know where that is."

Fifteen years earlier, I'd been walking down one of the docks of Fishermen's Terminal in Seattle, toolbox in hand, again after a boat that I had leased sight unseen. That one turned out to be junk, that I never made it to Alaska with, that I was lucky didn't drown me and my brother or girlfiend in the first bad tide rip we came to. After I'd spent the last of my money replacing the engine that we'd rebuilt and had blown up afterwards. I was hoping the *Joe H.* would turn out a little better.

Another loop around the boat parking lot and I was standing with my seabag on the ground loooking up at the battered and dented *Joe H.*

But at least it was aluminum; the ill-fated *Denise* had been wood, and half rotten at that.

A few years after engines were allowed in Bristol Bay boats in 1951, Shore Boatbuilders, down on the Fraser River near Vancouver, B.C. started producing their aluminum 32 footers specifically designed for The Bay.

At the time 'Shores' were the Cadillacs of the Bay—roomy, comfort-able, with a galley, some even with a flying bridge, an almost miraculous change from the sailing double enders of just a few years earlier with a tiny kerosene stove and no real place to get out of the weather.

Now, she showed her 30 seasons in a hard fishery, her unpainted hull gouged and scraped from close encounters with other boats.

I found a rickety ladder, climbed up and threw my sea bag onto the sand and grit covered plywood hatch covers.

Battered and rough she might be, I realized, looking around at the deck layout, but at least she had been upgraded with a narrow reel.

For in a sense, what was happening in the last few years was a second gear revolution in the Bay, of which the narrow reel or net drum that sat in the forward part of the *Joe H*'s back deck was a symbol.

For the first 65 years or so of the fishery, it had been wooden boats with no power but sails and oars and the strong backs of the predominantly Native and Norwegian and Italian fishermen. As the expression went, "You pulla da net to catcha da fish to maka da money." The gill-nets were about 10' deep and 900' feet long, made of linen thead, with wooden corks along the top, and small tubes of lead crimped onto a line—the Lead line—along the bottom of the net, so that it was like a long fence in the water.

The Alaska Packers Association, operated the last fleet of square riggers in commercial operation, sending the boats north until just before the start of World War II. The big steel ships could be had cheaply, packed a lot, and could be operated by the same men that built the canneries, caught and canned the fish as well. This is the Star of Shetland, *northbound for Bristol Bay.*

In the early days, fishermen were only allowed to fish four or five days a week, with the two days off to give fish a chance to get up the river to provide for the next generation, and also for the fishermen to repair the damage that the fish had done to the relatively fragile linen nets.

Author's collection

Early cannery (Koggiung?) with gillnetters, scows, monkey boats, and tug on the mud. Suspect at the end or beginning of the season as all the boats are without their masts and sails.

Of course, as there were no engines in the boats the nets had to be pulled by hand—most boats had just two men aboard, the second man called the 'puller.' It was hard, hard work.

But, once power—engines—were allowed in Bristol Bay boats in 1951, it changed everything. First, obviously it allowed the fishermen to fish where they wanted without being dependent on the wind or their oars. But also, having an engine allowed them to have what was called a power roller, which, mounted on the stern and rotated by hydraulic power or chain and sprockets, made the hauling of the nets much easier.

Of course not everyone welcomed engines. As one fishermen at the time put it:

"The reason I was against power boats was because every Tom, Dick and Harry might fish. After legalization of power and the establishment of limited entry, it seems there are now twice as many fishermen. These include doctors, lawyers and other professionals; it seemed all the pencil pushers started fishing. During sailboat days, they wouldn't have been able to fish, because they might have been afraid to sail. The rigors of sailing and living in an open boat would have been overwhelming. I may be old fashioned, but I still feel that it's only those guys who know how to harness the wind who really know how to fish."

Of course a whole fleet of almost two thousand sailing gillnetters couldn't be replaced in a single season. Kits were prefabbed in Seattle, and all winter and spring mechanics and carpenters worked on the existing boats, cutting out a section of the stern to put in the engine and propellor, "BB Conversions," they were called. No cabin—there hadn't been time to do other than slap a little gas engine in—but still a huge improvement.

That same winter, while the mechanics in Alaska were working in cold warehouses putting in the conversion kits, Puget Sound boat builders like Bryant Boats in Seattle were building plywood Bristol Bay 32 footers as fast as they could. These and models from other builders were the first truly modern Bay Boats, with . . . gasp . . . a place to cook, eat, and sleep, a true transformation from the traditional Bay way of fishing: you don't sleep in your boat, you go back to the cannery and sleep in your room, and eat at the messhall.

Author's collection

Very early power boats at Red Salmon cannery on the Naknek River, probably around 1956. Note the tiny 'telephone booth' style protected steering stations and the small diameter exhaust pipes.

Each season after 1952 saw ships and barges loaded with new Bristol Bay power boats with power rollers, cabins, etc. Within a few years the sails were gone except for a few diehard holdouts, and the sloughs and flats were full of the old wooden double enders rotting away. Of course, except until more recently with the advent of the independents, most guys still preferred to sleep in their rooms and eat in the mess hall instead of moving aboard their boats for the season and traveling to whatever river offered the best fishing

Sternview of BB traditional wooden sailing double ender after installation of a conversion kit. In that most of the boats at any one cannery were identical, an engine/transmission/propeller/rudder kit could be prefabbed in Seattle and shipped to Bristol Bay on a barge. Part of the stern was sawn away and the new assembly fitted and bolted into place.

Traditionally Bristol Bay fishermen had come from the local native villages, California, where the Alaska Packers Association based their fleet of square riggers, and the Columbia River area in Oregon., Then starting in the early 1980s gillnetters from Puget Sound, Washington and other parts of Alaska, who were used to fishing gill-nets with reels or drums, a much more convenient way of handling the nets, started entering the fishery. Putting reels on their boats as well as power rollers allowed them to haul the net faster when fishing was light, but also having the option of using the power roller when fishing was heavy. A hydraulic motor rotates the reel, pulling the net in, while the skipper and puller work in the stern to pick the fish out of the net before they get to the reel. But in heavy fishing, when it might be critical to get the net out of the water fast, fish and all, they could use the power roller and just pile everything in the stern, fish, net, corks, and all. So as time went by, more and more new Bay boats were fitted with reels or drums as well as power rollers.

But Bristol Bay nets, at 30 meshes deep (about ten feet) were half the size of Southeast Alaska nets and a quarter the size of Puget Sound nets that were at least 120 meshes deep. Smaller net meant a smaller reel and it didn't take long for some of the new entrants to the bay in the late '70s to realise that if you made an extremely narrow drum with a large diameter core, you could set the net at full speed, and haul it back very rapidly if circumstances required.

The traditional drums used by gillnetters in Puget Sound and Southeast Alaska were wide with small diameter cores in order to handle the larger nets.

Abandoned monkeyboats and barge at the old Red Salmon cannery at Ugashik Village. These power-boats were used to tow the sailing gillnetters to and from the fishing grounds.

At 22" wide with a 15" core, the *Joe H*'s reel was narrow but not as extreme as some of the others I'd noticed as we bumped around the boatyard.

The door was unlocked and I stepped into the cabin. Compared to the 32' gillnetter I had had in Southeast Alaska in the early '70s, the *Joe H* interior was spartan: double decker v-berths up in the bow, small sink and minimal counter space to port (left), table with bench seating to starboard, cast iron diesel fueled stove centered on the back bulkhead. No fridge, no toilet, no shower: roughing it. The floorboards were half pulled off revealing a rusty big block gasoline V-8, with what looked like a new fuel pump in a box sitting on top.

I threw my seabag on a berth, pulled out my coveralls and got to work: putting together yet another boat for yet another fishery. Most of the boats in the yard, I had noticed, still had five gallon buckets tied over their exhaust pipe; their owners and crews not yet arrived for the season. I was glad that I had come on the early side; I could see that there was probably a lot to do and learn before we launched.

Bob Anderson pulling in a small gillnet to catch herring to use as bait for trolling for salmon, Port Upton, 1974.

I got the new fuel pump bolted down and the gas hoses all hooked up when there was the rattle of someone coming up the ladder and then my old friend Bob Anderson was in the doorway.

He waved at the boat, the engine, the tools, and parts spread all out. "What d'ya think?"

"Fixing old boats," I laughed, "Ain't it the essence of fishing?"

I'd first met Bob 13 years earlier, in 1973, when he, his wife Kay, and their dog Tasha had arrived in Point Baker in their gillnetter, which Bob had converted from a 30' steel pleasure boat, by just adding a 8' steel box onto the stern to hold the net reel, fish hold, etc. Bob was from Everett, WA, the home of the big Boeing Aircraft plant 20 miles north of Seattle, but his uncle was a well known Petersburg, Alaska, fisherman.

Bristol Bay canneries were basically whole little towns out in the wilderness, so there was plenty of maintenance chores for a winter watchman to do.

Tiring of his day job working in a boatshop, and having cousins and friends that always seemed to come back from summer salmon fishing in Alaska with good stories and even better money, Bob rebuilt the *Kay II* on weekends, then he and his wife Kay left their three girls with her parents, and headed North.

In those days, fishing licenses were but a few hundred dollars, so a person could basically get into Alaska commercial salmon gill-netting for the price of a modest boat and a few seven hundred dollar nets.

Having been built as a pleasure boat, the *Kay II* had the biggest cabin of any in the whole Point Baker-Port Protection fleet, so it was instantly the party boat.

Bob was quiet, an extremely talented mechanic and fisherman; Kay was just the opposite: funny, outgoing; the life of the party. Many the time Bob, Kay, myself, and other friends crowded into the cabin of the *Kay II*, drinking, while Kay was as funny as a standup comic. More than once I staggered out into the night after a long fun evening aboard with way too much to drink, and had to just lean against a piling for a few minutes to clear my head enough to climb into my skiff and pick my way through the rockpiles in the twisting narrow channel back to our cabin.

Inside the *Joe H*, Bob gave me the lay of the land: they'd ordered new nets for me, found a crew who'd be there in a few days, so I had some time to get the boat figured out.

"Come around to the *Pinnacle* later on, we'll have a drink and go out to get a bite." Bob headed out to keep working on his list of boat jobs, and I dug around until I found some sandpaper and cooking oil and attacked the cast iron diesel fueled cook and heating stove. Even though it was June, this was Western Alaska, the sky was clouded over and there was a chill wind off the water. I scoured the rust off the cooktop, sanded it until it shone, found the fuel valve on the oil tank on the back of the cabin, lit a bit of paper towel, set it on the bottom of the burner chamber, put the lid on, and after a few minutes could see the flame through the little viewing port. Leaving the stove to heat up, I climbed down the ladder, found a water hose and filled our water tank.

Next was the big block Chrysler 440 V-8: I put in the plugs and points that Bob had brought, changed the oil, changed the filters, cleaned the battery terminals, hit the starter and Yes! The big monster roared into smoky, noisy life. I just let it run a minute or two to get everything circulating again, then shut it down before it could overheat.

OK!! I could put the floorboards on, be able to move about in the cabin! By then it was late afternoon, but the stove had heated up the cabin nicely, and with water, I could wipe the table and counter down, lay out my sleeping bag in the fo'c's'le, stuff my clothes into the gear hammock above my bunk, set the binoculars I'd brought on the dashboard and generally make things shipshape. I rummaged around, found some tea and honey, made myself a cup, and just settled into the bench seat close to the welcome warmth of the stove to just sit and take stock of things.

Just 48 hours earlier, I'd been in the bosom of our little family in our Maine island home. We'd just finished up our mussel dragging season and our boat lay peacefully on the mooring out the front window. Ahead had been a busy summer of working on the cabin, taking outboard trips with Mary Lou, and our children, Matthew, 3, and Kate, just a year old, taking advantage of the summer that most folks on that coast wait 9 long months to enjoy.

Yet Alaska had called, and I'd put all that I so enjoyed, the best part of our year, behind. To come instead to this gritty, end-of-the-world, unfriendly place, to see what I could make of it. Southeast Alaska had been challenging, of course, but there had been big trees, cozy protected coves to anchor up in.

But Bristol Bay, from what I had seen, had this austere, almost bleak feeling. On all sides the vast tundra stretched away to the distant mountains. Once, on the way down from King Salmon, I thought I'd glimpsed a steaming volcano. Instead of hundred foot tall spruce, hemlock, and cedars, there were just head high dusty tundra bushes, just high enough so you couldn't see over, just enough to hide a bear, of which there were plenty. I was mighty glad I had friends in this strange country, so different from any Alaska that I had known, to show me the way.

The Pinnacle: *state of the art, 1986: refrigerated fish hold, diesel power, shower and toilet and many radios.*

I washed up, pulled on a heavy fleece against the cold wind, and started down the row of boats, half closing my eyes to keep from getting sandbasted from the dirt and sand.that the wind was picking up and whirling around.

As the *Joe H* had been state of the art, a Cadillac of boats when she first arrived in The Bay in 1964, the *Pinnacle* was the Cadillac now. Bob and his partner Paul Maudslien had Curry Boatworks build the hull, then trucked it, as was their custom, to a different outfit, Petrzelka Brothers, who finished off the bare aluminum hull, putting a fine teak interior, big GM 8-92 diesel engine, refrigerated sea water system to keep the fish cold, nice flying bridge, and full electronics.

I climbed the ladder and stepped into their cozy cabin. The stove was on, the rum bottle was out and the stories were flowing. Paul was sitting in the captain's chair behind the steering wheel, and their crewman, Dan Leech, was sitting at the table with Bob, along with some other friends whom I knew. Someone had brought in a mess of fresh halibut and it sizzled and popped in the beer batter, accenting the talk in the crowded pilothouse. The talk was mostly about which river to fish, as the Bay had five major rivers, each a separate fishing area with its own characteristics, and prediction of how many fish would return to be caught.

". . . .yeah, Egegik'll be the place to be this year, if you want to play the line game." The line game was a reference to the very aggressive fishing tactics used along the Egegik River's district boundaries where fish tended to pour across the line when the tide ebbed.

A big gust of wind and sand roared up over the dunes from the river, blotted out the sun like in a dust bowl movie, and hissed against the glass and aluminum, shaking the boat with its power.

"Better forget about the Kvichak," someone else said, "that place'll be lucky to get an opening at all until they get five million fish up the river."

"Who knows," said Paul, "the Noosh (Nushagak) might be a good bet if they don't get too many dogs."

Another gust of sand and dirt and wind filled the sky outside. One of the guys jerked his head out at the whirling gray: "We taped up our door with duct tape when we left here last year, some of the guys who didn't will have a surprise when they open up their boats."

"Ugashik looks good on paper, if you want to put up with the rotten weather." The speaker stood up, looked out at the hundred or so silent and waiting aluminum and glass boats around us, at another hundred fifty in the Leader Creek yard beyond, and shook his head slowly, "I tell ya' boys, if these predictions are anywhere near right, it's going to be a survival year."

"We called Southeast a 'lifestyle' fishery," laughed Paul, changing to a more pleasant subject, "We all fished with our girlfriends or wives, some even with children back in the early '70s. It was a long long season; the

Puget Sound guys would leave in April, sometimes not to get back until well into November. "We didn't make a lot of money, but we sure had fun doing it."

Alaska steamship Tanana *with a load of boats headed for Bristol Bay. In those few years right after 1952, hundreds of new power boats were constructed to replace the old sailboats, and all sorts of craft were enlisted to take them the 2200 miles from Seattle to Bristol Bay. Of course there were always a few boats that missed the last steamer, barge, or tender to get a ride on, and so if they wanted to get up to the bay in time, they had to load several hundred gallons of extra fuel in 55 gallon drums and start plodding along. At 8 knots (9 mph) the typical speed of early Bay power boats that was almost two weeks of running 15 hours a day!*

After fishing Southeast and its long season, the appeal of The Bay was obvious: a very short season with a good chance of making some serious money.

"I was pretty happy in Southeast," Paul said, "fishing McNamara was pretty fun. But now look," he waved out the window at the fleet of serious looking gray aluminum 32 footers on all sides of us, "Most of the guys I fished McNamara with are here."

It was true. A lot of the young guys that I had fished around back in what I call 'Alaska Blues Days,' (Alaska Blues was my first book, a photo/text journal of a long season in the Southeast Alaska troll and gill-net salmon fishery) had migrated up to The Bay over the years.

"But then Menish and Grant, (other young Petersburg fishermen who also fished Point McNamara with Paul and others) built new boats and went up to The Bay, and started coming back with these amazing stories about all the fish up there and how easy it was to catch them: 200,000 pound plus seasons—at sixty or eighty cents, and in just six weeks. Think about it: we used to think we were doing pretty well if we spent six months catching 50 grand worth of fish."

"Plus Nancy and I were wanting to start a family, and the Bay season was just five or six weeks. It was a no brainer."

That was another thing I noticed right off the bat: this ,was definitely a guys only program as far as I could see so far. Very different from the gillnet fishery in Southeast Alaska where most of the boats were operated by couples, and the docks and net floats were always very social places. Except for a gal who worked in the boatyard store, I hadn't see a woman since I got there.

Anchored fleet off Naknek River mouth with barge. The river, with a 26 foot tidal range, is too shallow to enter at low tide. The barge, full of empty containers is tied to a big mooring buoy. At the end of the season, it will get towed into the river, tie up alongside a cannery, where the empty containers will be replaced with ones full of canned and frozen salmon.

"Hey, watch this." said one of the guys, sliding back his window, and fitting a seal bomb into a pistol-like device. Seals were a constant annoyance to salmon fishermen and before it was prohibited, we used these seal bombs, essentially cherry bomb-like firecrackers that could be launched from a gun to scare them away from our nets.

A big fuel truck had just rattled around the end of the line of the boats in our row, and slowly made its way down the alley between the boats and stopped two boats away.

"I never liked this guy," the shooter said, and leaned out the window and aimed the seal bomb thrower/pistol in the air. His window was on the side away from where the truck was parked, so the bomb would have to make a long arching loop to land anywhere near the fuel truck; I figured it was a total long shot.

But noooo! He must have done it before, because just as the driver was getting out of the truck, the seal bomb landed at his feet and went off. He jumped about a mile and started looking around to see who had done it and probably heard us laughing.

Sailing gillnetters getting a tow in to the cannery at the end of the day. The fleets were cannery owned and usually painted the same color to help the tenders and monkey boats find theirs amongst the 1,400 plus boats scattered across The Bay.

Yelling, "I'll fix you assholes," he climbed back into the fuel truck, backed up 25 five feet or so and started rumbling forward toward the *Pinnacle*. For a frightening moment, I thought he was going to knock the supports out from under the boat, which would have been very ugly. But then we heard a big crunching smash and looked down and realized that he had rammed the old Ford Fairlane 500 that was parked under the *Pinnacle*'s bow, thinking logically that it must belong to one of us.

But it didn't. Instead it belonged to Harold, our electronics technician, who had been working on one of Bob and Paul's radios, and had just left to go to the boatyard store for something. There's no road connection from King Salmon or Naknek to anywhere else, so all vehicles come in by barge, and are pretty much beaters within a few months from the wind and all the sand in the air. Harold's car had been a beater to start with.

The fuel truck rammed Harold's car a few more times, and finally backed away down the row of boats with just a slightly bent bumper to show for the effort.

Harold's car wasn't so lucky; we looked down and you could see that the impact had partially buckled the hood and there was anti freeze leaking all over the ground, so he had probably gotten the radiator as well.

Bob was a cracker jack mechanic so it looked like he might have a bit of work ahead. If we could ever stop laughing.

Dinner was moosemeat, instant mashed, and canned green beans at a friend's house high on a bluff. Below us the sand bar choked Naknek River, probably a quarter of a mile wide here, wound its muddy way down from Naknek Lake, 40 miles to the east, to its mouth in Bristol Bay, just out of sight, four miles west. A handful of boats were rafted out from the boatyard's small float, the tidal current tugging hard at them.

Across the river was the Royal Red Seafoods cannery, a collection of metal sided and roofed buildings, a whole little town in itself sprawled along the bank. Behind it a red wind pennant waved at the cannery air strip. A few gillnetters sat on the mud in front of the cannery, another hung from the slings of the dock crane ready for the morning.

Finally after way too much wine, weed, and rum, I wound my unsteady way down the bluff in that odd high latitude twilight that in June lingers all night before becoming brighter in the pre-dawn at 3 a.m. Along a twisting path through the tundra bushes, past two rows of storage lockers, a couple of open doors banging back and forth in the breeze that has sprung up, blowing in from the Bering Sea, drawn up the narrow river valley by the warmer land to the east. Down to the rows of silent, dark boats, my head down against the whirling wind, sand, and dirt. Finally to the *Joe H*, looking in the grim light like the battle scarred veteran that she was. Inside it was cozy; once you light your stove in Bristol Bay, you rarely let it go out. I lit a candle, and sat for a bit looking out at the almost night. Except for a light by the boatyard bathrooms and another boat's cabin light two rows over, it was just that gray half light revealing row after row of dark and silent boats, as the gritty wind hummed in the rigging and rocked the *Joe H*. against the jackstands.

Just 48 hours earlier, I'd been in Maine. The journey, the boat, the big block Chrysler 440 rumbling into life. Assault by fuel truck, moosemeat overlooking the river. The walk back with the gritty wind swirling around the silent rows of aluminum gillnetters. The wind, the wind, the wind. I pulled off my clothes and got into my sleeping bag. The wind seemed to be clawing at us, moving the boat back and forth. Not a friendly place, and sleep came hard.

The Joe H: state of the art when built in the early '70s. Notice the narrow reel. Aluminum was a much better material than fiberglass in the rough and tumble nature of Bristol Bay where boats often smacked into each other in the close quarters fishing. The fly bridge (such as it was) was added shortly after I began operating it. She was pretty basic: gas engine. dry hold, no toilet.

I'm an early riser. To me, on all the Alaska fishboats that I've had, there was always something special about climbing out of the dark and cool fo'c's'le and up and into the stove warmth of the little cabin, making a coffee while the day starts to play around the edges of the sky. (Though in June, that far north, the sun was always up way earlier than I . . .) Sitting and spending a bit of time reflecting, putting something down in my journal and looking at The List on the galley table.

For commercial fishermen and mariners in general, pre-season work usually centers around The List—a column of tasks to be done before you are ready to start your season.

Even on a boat as relatively simple as the *Joe H*, and especially a boat that had been sitting outside and unused for the last ten and a half months in the harsh climate of Western Alaska, there are enough systems and things that need fixing that I learned to give me a good week to get ready, preferably before the crew comes, in a remote place like Bristol Bay.

Everything that had been out in the weather all winter like the reel drive and the anchor winch needed plenty of WD-40, grease, and TLC at the beginning of the season. That June the steel chain that ran between a hydraulic motor and the net reel had essentially frozen solid, and even soaking overnight in solvent didn't get the kinks out. I bought a stainless chain at the boatyard, and to be doubly sure, took it off at the end of the season, sprayed it thoroughly with WD-40, and put it in a plastic bag, inside the boat.

The old days: iron men, wooden boats, and 14' oars when the wind didn't blow.

The anchor winch was also frozen solid, not having been thoroughly washed with fresh water at the end of the season. The winch was a critical part of our equipment; once we launched we would be anchoring every day, and sometimes reanchoring in the middle of the night if the wind blew hard enough. The old wooden boats usually didn't have anchor winches, but most modern boats did, with typically a 33 pound Bruce anchor, fifty feet of chain and a couple of hundred feet of wire or braided nylon rode (anchor lines are called rodes). That was a lot of anchor gear for a 32 footer in such shallow water—rarely were we in more than 30 feet, but the tidal currents were strong.

Also the bilge pump wasn't working, the Clutchmaster for the hydraulic pump seemed to be having problems engaging, a fresh water line was split, several running lights were out: you get the picture. And those of you who have boats know that working on one system often means working on another as well. Plus we were in a remote area of Western Alaska with no roads that connected to anywhere else so finding that part that you absolutely needed had its own challenges. Our boatyard, Naknek Marine Center, more commonly called 'Lummi,' had showers, living quarters above for staff, and a store with a good supply of parts and equipment. If they didn't have what you wanted, you could hike down the hill to Leader Creek Boatyard, another big storage yard; maybe they would have it. If you struck out in both places, maybe a buddy would have what you needed. If you struck out there, you might try one of the canneries; they had warehouses full of stuff. But if you weren't one of their fishermen, they might not even talk to you. Worst came to worst, you could call down to Seattle and get it flown up, Bluestreak on Alaska Airlines but that always took at least a day and was pretty pricey.

Same thing with mechanics and welders: there were guys around with vans full of tools, supplies, and parts, but a lot of times fishermen had already contracted with them to get things done on their boat before they arrived. So, the more a fisherman was able to do on his own, the better his chances of a successful season.

Most of the guys who been in the Bay for a few seasons built a big box out of plywood, 4'x4'x4' filled it with groceries, boat equipment that maybe they had shipped south to have worked on, booze, etc. And delivered it either to a cannery facility in Seattle, (almost all Alaska canneries had some sort of facility in Seattle to work on their boats, forward freight, etc.) or, for the independent fishermen, directly to Northland Barge Services. It would go into a 40' container, and loaded onto a barge for the 2,500 mile trip across the Gulf of Alaska, through Unimak Pass, and finally northeast along the Alaska Peninsula to Naknek, eventually getting delivered by forklift and plopped down in the boatyard right next to their boat. Very handy!

I hadn't been that organized, plus I was living in Maine, so the day after I arrived, luckily a couple of other guys in our code group needed to make a run to the only store, The Naknek Trading Company.

Now, you have to realize that for about 10 months a year, the population of Naknek is about 600 folks, about half Alaskan Natives and half whites. Then suddenly June brings the arrival of about 5,000 cannery and processing workers, fishermen, mechanics, etc. The canneries obviously with their own onsite stores and messhalls ship up their own containers of food and supplies.

But many of the rest of those folks, especially the independent fisher-men, rely on what the Naknek Trading Co has on its shelves.

Not to mention that just getting to Naknek from Lummi was an adven-ture in itself. Our code group was six other fishermen who elected to work together to find and catch fish in Bristol Bay, specifically sharing the costs of a spotter pilot, and having radios specially adapted so that the conversa-tions between the group would hopefully be secure.

The group also shared an old beater Chevy Apache pickup with a vinyl sofa in the bed of the truck. So when the word went out that there was going to be a run to the Trading Company, members of the group showed up, beer was brought and the trip was friends in the front, friends in the back, beer all around, swerving around potholes on the 7 mile drive to 'downtown' Naknek.

By then, I'd worked as a fish buyer for four years up and down the Alaska coast, gill-netted a year in Puget Sound and four in Southeast Alaska, and worked a year as a king crab crewman in the Bering Sea. So it seemed like every day that week in Naknek, I'd bump into a couple of old acquaintances and do some catching up.

Of course, you'd go to the Trading Co. with your list, but you better be ready to improvise and substitute as the chances of finding everything or even most of what you wanted weren't high. No Crisco . . . hmmm . . . would lard work? No Honey Nut Cheerios. Would the guys go for Bran Flakes? You get the idea. Plus the *Joe H* had neither a fridge nor much storage space. You had to just get the basics, and plan on getting the rest of what you wanted from the tenders that bought your fish, because once we launched, getting to the store would be even harder. And eating a lot of salmon.

At night sometimes I'd go over to the *Pinnacle* after I'd made supper for myself on the *Joe H* and strategize with Bob and Paul about what might be the best plan for our season. The way the fishing was managed in Bristol Bay was different from any that I had encountered. In Southeast Alaska, I usually fished Sumner Straits in the summer, as that was where our cab-in had been. The we'd go to Lynn Canal in the fall for the dog salmon run, along with a couple of hundred other boats, and that was our regular circuit.

The Bay was different. As each of the five rivers was a separate fishing district, with different size salmon runs and timing, each was individually managed. Plus the amount of fishing horsepower in The Bay—some 1800 individual gill-net boats plus some 1,000 setnetters (setnets are fished off a beach, most setnetters have a cabin where they spend the season tending their nets) makes it very challenging for the biologists to manage the fishery. So a rule was made: you have to register and fish in one district at a time, all your fish must be delivered to tenders within that district, and the killer: if you transfer to another district you must wait 48 hours before fishing there. In a fishery where the peak of the run only lasts a week or so, and you can make the bulk of your season in four or five days, having to sit out 48 hours is not a decision made lightly.

Marvin Huguinen works on our net off the stern of the Joe H. Note that the net has three different colors, each a 50 fathom (300') long panel. The idea is that if the fish see the net, they will travel along it until they come to the color change, think that the net has ended, make a turn and end up gilled. It is very common to catch fish in the color change between panels. The three boats in the row directly behind Marvin are all Shore boats, built by Shore Boatbuilders near Vancouver, Canada.

We decided the best choice for someone not familiar with the sometimes intense style of fishing in the Bay was for me to head for the Ugashik River, the most remote of the major districts and typically the least crowded. Before the regulated fishing season starts at the end of June, there is what it is known as free week, when all the rivers are open 24/7. After free week, fishing is limited to openings, typically 12 hours, announced by radio and depending on the number of fish entering the upper river, past the areas where they are caught.

A couple of days before we were ready, my crew joined me: Chris, Paul's cousin, around 20, and Marvin, probably 35, a friend of Pauls. Marvin had been crew on Bay boats for years, and he and would be co-skippers on the *Joe H.* Chris was new to fishing, but friendly and eager. With three of us aboard, the cabin was suddenly much smaller.

Finally the big green tractor came for us on the morning of June 20th and a few minutes later we were floating on the swift and muddy Naknek River, whose banks seemed to be lined with one cannery after another. It wasn't like Cannery Row in California in the 1940s with sardine canneries cheek to jowl along the street. Here each cannery was a whole little town unto itself, with its own power plant, water supply, even air strip sometimes. Then a hundred yards down the beach would be another whole cannery/town. As we traveled along the river I counted 8 canneries that seemed to be operating, or at least had boats tied to their docks and two or three that seemed abandoned, and the ruins of a few more. Wow: I'd known that there was a lot of processing horsepower in the Bay, but seeing 8 plants each with substantial fleets tied to the dock was humbling, and at I knew at least three of the other rivers had operating canneries and fleets of gillnetters.

But by noon, we were all alone, bucking into a hard westerly with no other boat in sight, or even any sign of man's existence in any direction. The shore was distinctly unfriendly: low bluffs rising back to tundra ponds and distant volcanoes. It was odd, after hearing so much about how crowded it got in Bristol Bay, I expected any move we made would be in the company of at least a dozen other boats.

Once I saw what looked like a bear on the shore, got the binoculars and slowed down. It was clamming, digging big clams then smashing one into his mouth and spitting out the shells. Then it got up on its back feet and clawed the air for a moment at a chopper that was buzzing along the beach about fifty feet up.

We had no chart of the bay, only a coffee stained hand-drawn sketch of the Ugashik River, our destination.

The only directions we had were: "Just head sou'west along the Peninsula, Ugashik's the second river on the left." After being used to having a chart to look at, buoys and such to check my position with, "just go into the second river on the left" made me more than an little uneasy.

And so the edge of night found us off a wide and shallow river mouth, unmarked by lights, buoys, breakwaters, or any aids to navigation. There were no other boats to be seen, nor houses on the distant shore. The bars on the sketch map seemed to have no relation to what I was seeing ahead of us. Luckily there was an onshore wind and a short chop that showed the bars as masses of dirty-white breakers. But still, having always relied on a chart before, I really had to screw on my courage pretty tight to enter that lonely river, coming on dark, with no chart, masses of breakers everywhere, and no obvious channel through them. The little voice in my head said, "Careful, you could get in trouble here, and who's going to come and help?"

But the rising tide gave us confidence and though we bumped on occasion, around midnight, the sky still lit with the lingering sunset, we scoured the sand with our propellor and made the shelter of Dago Creek, the only anchorage for small craft in many miles, where we were relieved to find a dozen other boats.

But what looked like ample shelter at high tide was reduced to but a narrow stream surrounded by mudflats when the tide dropped 20' or so. We'd missed the channel and lay over in the mud; my bunk was on the high side. So much for a good sleep.

The next day at 10 a.m. we threw our big orange end buoy off the stern and let its drag pull our shallow 150 fathom (900') long net off the reel (also called a drum) for the first time. After so much talk and planning and anticipation, the results were disheartening. The main body of the fish run was still apparently far to the west, and the few that wandered into ours were just stragglers. But it was a good chance to get our three-man team together and learn the ropes of fishing in shallow rough water amongst sand bars.

Each morning we'd chow down on instant oatmeal, put on our damp rain gear, motor out of the river with a handful of other boats and lay out our 900' net in the muddy chop to begin another long, cold, and nasty day. If it was summer, you'd never know it; some days it barely made it into the 50s. Let the net soak for an hour or so, roll it in, pick out the dozen or two handsome sockeye salmon, run back toward the outside line, set it out again, and huddle by the stove until it was time to do it all over again.

Usually by five or six at night, we'd have had enough and run into the river, stop at the tender to unload our sad thousand pounds or so, and anchor back in Dago Creek for a dinner of baked salmon, instant mashed, and green beans cooked in the can.

Repeat, repeat, you get the idea

And yet for all the grimness of the place, the constant cold and rough seas, it was a content trio that sat down together each night to talk about the day. There is something about putting in a hard and cold day on the water and returning to the shelter of a cozy, if remote and desperately bleak harbor, that is deeply satisfying.

Then after a week of fishing every day, though not for much, fishing was closed while we and the biologists waited for more fish to arrive.

All of Bristol Bay rivers are managed by counting escapement—the number of fish entering the upper river, beyond the limit of the fishing districts. By comparing that number to previous year's escapement on that date and taking into consideration the prediction of the size of the run, fishing dates and times are set. But before any fishing is allowed (past "free Week") a minimum number of fish must have entered the upper river.

And so we waited. Every couple of days, we'd run the boat up on the mudbank and go for a walk—with no docks and no skiff, if you wanted to go ashore, your drove your boat up onto the muddy beach and let the tide go out. Then you had to get across the deep mud without losing a boot.

Down the shore to the south was the immense old Diamond U cannery—all Alaska Packers Canneries were designated with "Diamond" and an initial. In the spring of 1918 with snow still on the ground in places, an Alaska Packers Association (the biggest salmon cannery operator at the time) square rigger arrived after a 35 day trip up from San Francisco, launched the pile driver and sent the crew ashore. By the time the salmon arrived, the brand new cannery was waiting for them.

But the next year brought tragedy: when the ships arrived, bringing Chinese cannery workers and fishermen of all nationalities, the Spanish Flu was there before them, probably come with the mail or freight a month or so earlier. The flu swept like wildfire through the Yu'pik and Aleut villagers. In many villages, most of the adults were dying or dead, and instead of starting fishing operations, the cannery staff found themselves burying bodies, shooting dogs that were feasting on the bodies and making arrangements for the village orphans.

By 1986 it was a ghost town, essentially abandoned; I walked through it, the wind rattling loose corrugated sheets of rusty steel on the roofs. It was an immense facility, one of the biggest in The Bay, set up so that in the glory days, three lines could be canning salmon at the same time, probably two producing half pound cans and the third one pound talls. Here and there in the tall grass along the shore were old wooden 32 footers left over from sailboat days. Eventually, we heard, the river channel shifted, the dock silted in, and the cannery was abandoned. On that gray chilly day with spits of rain, it was a grim scene and it was a pleasure to finally make it back to our boat and its warm cabin.

With all that time anchored, we got a good look at the fleet in Dago Creek. Initially coming to The Bay, where boats are only in the water for 4-6 weeks a year, I figured it would be a pretty well kept up bunch of boats. But boy was I wrong: everything looked so beat. The fleet was probably 40-60 fiberglass to aluminum, with here and there an old woodie, left over from earlier days in The Bay. But talk about battle scars! Rarely would you see a boat, especially glass ones, without a patch or at the minimum a nasty long gouge. Same thing with the aluminum boats, though as they were tougher, instead of patches there would be long dents or scrapes. As I was to learn, boat to boat contact, accidental or on purpose was pretty much expected.

And there were some very odd boats. One Shore boat had all its windows covered with plywood, presumably having been blown out, and a phonebooth-sized totally enclosed flybridge that looked more like a giant periscope. We immediately nicknamed it the mushroom boat, as in "It's so dark in there the guys must be like mushrooms."

At that time we were doing something called "fishing on an open ticket." Basically this meant that when you sold your fish, called making a delivery, your receipt, called a fish ticket, showed the species and the pounds, but not the price. With fishing already going on in the other rivers, some of the guys waiting to fish at Ugashik wanted some sort of reassurance from their market, Trident Seafoods, that they were going to get a good price for their fish. A meeting was arranged by radio and one blustery morning a helicopter set down on the beach and a big guy stepped out.

This was Chuck Bundrant, who was expanding his fishing and fish processing company, Trident Seafods, into Bristol Bay, bringing up a floating processor and trying to get independent fishermen to deliver to him.

Bundrant, like myself and many others had started his career by walking up and down the docks, looking for a job on a fishboat. Starting as a crewman just as the king crab fishery was just beginning to yield big returns, he worked his way up to skipper, became a boat owner, and taking a big risk, built the first big crabber/processor. His timing was good, the gamble paid off and with some other fishermen, founded Trident Seafoods which quickly expanded from king crab into buying salmon as well.

After 1952, as power rapidly replaced power, the old sailboats that had been so carefully tended for years, stored inside, painted each spring were unceremoniously pulled up on the beaches and left to rot. With length limited to 32', Bristol Bay fishermen who wanted to go bigger only had one option—go wider and higher, with bigger engines. But remember, both boats fish the same size net so bigger allows you a bigger fish hold and a more comfortable cabin, probably refrigeration, but not necessarily more fish.

That he was at heart a fisherman gave him a lot of credibility with the fisherman that were selling to his company. Additionally it was common knowledge that once the salmon season was over, Chuck went over to Tokyo personally, parked himself in a hotel and started negociating to get the best price for his salmon. As one fisherman put it, "You don't see the head of Icicle (Icicle Seafoods, another major salmon buyer) choppering in to talk to his guys . . ."

Nevertheless it was an akward meeting. It was looking like the run was going to be weaker than the forecast and already some smaller processors, anxious about being able to fill their markets, were bumping the price up.

"*Polar Bear*'s paying a buck and a quarter." said one fisherman, the *Polar Bear* being the smallest floating salmon processor, actually just a 110' barge crowded with plate freezers, generators, workers, and everything else needed to process and freeze fish in a remote location.

"But the *Polar Bear* doesn't have a net barge, or a chopper, or groceries on the tenders," answered Bundrant. "Ask yourself how important it is to have access to a chopper when you break down at the peak of the season and need a part flown in."

"You get what you pay for in the fish biz," Bundrant went on, "Ask some of the guys that have been selling me their crab for a decade if they feel I treated them fairly."

In the end it essentially came down to this: you either trusted Bundrant to do his best for you or you decided to go with a market you thought could do better for you. Most of the guys on the beach that day already knew Bundrant and Trident by reputation and took him at his word.

Before we came to the Bay, we'd heard about the big money, the filling-your-boat days, the chaos of the huge fleets, boats getting rammed just trying to get their net out. But no one had ever talked about the waiting. If we were waiting in the Naknek River, you could go to town, actually get a drink, a pizza. But in Ugashik there was essentially nothing. Once we walked an hour, heads down against the cold wind, to the village of Pilot Point on the bluff—a few dozen tired looking houses overlooking the bay, a closed store that didn't look like it had much, and a gravel airstrip with a sign, "Watch out for bears." We didn't go back.

When the tide was down it was mudbanks in every direction, boats laying on their sides. When it was up, it was featureless tundra stretching back to austere snow covered volcanoes. It was hard to imagine a grimmer place to be stuck. Once we'd worked our way down through the food we'd brought from town, we were limited to whatever our tender had, which seemed to be chili and spagetti. Some of the crews in the anchorage were eating salmon jigged off their boats, but aboard the *Joe H*, no one had brought a rod, and it was illegal anyway.

On about the 7th day of waiting, I looked over and noticed that one of the crew was doing a bit of intense scratching on his chest and groin. Then he picked something off his chest and squinted to see what it was.

"Shit," he said, "it's a crab."

Shit was right; I knew this could get ugly—all three of us were sleeping in very close quarters, plus I knew that if I came back from Alaska with crabs, I would have a lot of explaining to do to my wife. So I knew I had to get the kerosene-like shampoo and nip it in the bud.

Luckily our market had a processor anchored in the river, the *Bristol Monarch*, with a lot of rough characters on board as the processing crew. Surely, I thought, they would have some of that shampoo stuff on board. If we struck out there, we'd be reduced to washing ourselves with diesel fuel. And remember: we have no shower and only limited fresh water, and no water heater.

So we motored over to the *Monarch*, a boxy looking 140-footer set up to freeze salmon. We tied up, and I climbed the rope ladder up the steep steel sides. Made my way up to the wheelhouse, where the Captain and a couple of pretty rough looking guys were listening on the radio for whatever they could glean about when the biologists might open the Ugashik River for gill-netting.

"Uhhh, could I speak to you in private?" said I to the burly skipper, not wanting to advertise our situation.

He flashed me an annoyed look and jerked a thumb towards his stateroom.

"Uhhh, you got any of that shampoo stuff? I think one of my guys has the crabs."

His reaction was violent and immediate, recoiling from me as if I had The Plague, and pointing to the door to the outside deck. "Get out right now! Do you know how many guys we have here? Jesus, that's all we need—a fucking infestation of crabs. Just get back aboard your boat and we'll lower a bottle of that shampoo to you, and then get the hell away from my ship! "

That was probably the low point of our season, that and trying to shampoo ourselves with cold water in the *Joe H*'s tight quarters, boiling our pillow cases, shaking out our sleeping bags and hoping for the best.

The worst part of waiting was the wondering if we had made the right choice about where to fish. For, on the 10th! day of waiting; yes, that's **ten days of sitting on the anchor in Dago Creek**, two other rivers were opened for short but profitable 12 hour fishing periods. Of course the radio news was that the fishing had been great.

The 48 hour rule makes switching to one or another rivers a gamble. The fishing periods are only announced 12 hours or so in advance, so if you transferred out of Ugashik, you could very well be doing it on the eve of some huge fishing. It looked like it was going to be a short and intense season; missing an opening might mean missing 20% of your whole season.

So we waited, the radio always tuned to the only radio station on the dial: KDLG in King Salmon. After the fishing announcements were given in English, they were repeated in Yupik, the local Native language. And we learned that the fish came to the great Yukon and the Kuskokwim Rivers, to Goodnews and Security Bays, districts further north along the Bering Sea coast, then to the other Bristol Bay districts, but there was still nothing in Ugashik.

Floater Bristol Monarch: when I explained our embarrassing problem, the skipper backed away from me as if I had the plague.

Unfortunately we were the only one of our code group in Ugashik and our VHF radio couldn't reach the other rivers and the little *Joe H.* didn't have a sideband, the long range radio that most of the other guys in the code group had. Every other day or so our spotter plane would orbit overhead and relay messages—mostly about how many fish the other guys were catching—and we're paying for that? But it was a floatplane so at least he brought us a bottle of rum to take the sting out of the long wait.

But for the most part it was sleep, eat, read, and wait for the fishing announcements on the radio. To say life was tedious was a huge understatement.

Want to get into the fishery on a tight budget? If you can make an older wood boat work for you, there may be still a few being stored inside at the canneries.

I was an early riser, the other guys slept late, so each morning around six, I'd get up quietly, make a coffee and sit looking out the window at the grim scene, and think of Mary Lou and the kids, in our wonderful little waterfront cabin back in Maine and wonder what the hell I was doing stuck in Ugashik.

Finally, on the third of July, the day before the traditional peak of the run, Ugashik opened for 12 hours at 9 a.m. and we and about 300 other boats got a taste of that famous Bristol Bay action. Bristol Bay boats, limited by law to 32', are largely fish hold. Ours would carry around 15,000 pounds below her plywood hatch covers. I had wondered how we would fill it, but after the first two sets of the net, I didn't wonder any longer. Instead I worried about filling the boat before the 12 hour period was over, and about losing fishing time by having to unload when the period was still open. It was stunning—in just 12 hours we came close to filling the boat with those gorgeous 8-buck-a-whack sockeyes, and it wasn't even big fishing by Bay standards.

Getting your net in front of the fish was just part of it. The other part was getting the fish out of the net as quickly as possible so that you can get your net back into the water. And that means being able to pick fish fast. To aid in this, each of us used a fish pick, essentially a small device—about the size of a gas cigarette lighter, made of wood or plastic—I prefer wood—with a steel hook at one end and a small rectangular knife blade sticking out on the other.

As soon as we begin hauling the net back, I join the guys in the stern to help get the fish out. So all three of us are back there working in an area maybe 12' wide and 8' long. The rotating reel, controlled by a pedal at my feet, pulls the net out of the water and past the three of us at about chest height. The fish are caught by the gills in the net and hang down from the corkline. In heavy fishing there might be 40-50 fish hanging from the net in that space. Each fish essentially presents a puzzle. An experienced picker will be able to read the net and with a few deft flicks of the wrist, have the fish hanging vertically, tail down, and be able to clear the net from behind the gill plates quickly, and once freed, flip the fish forward into one of the open hatches.

Usually you can free the fish from the net quickly. But sometimes it requires you to cut a single mesh of the net—made of very light but very strong nylon. The reason for the knife blade is that it is much better to cut a single mesh to free the fish than just ripping the fish free, which would make a bigger hole.

The crew is just working heads down, focusing on the fish and the net. I am picking as fast as I can, but also monitoring the situation around us. In tight fishing conditions there are usually other nets all around us. Occasionally when nets are really close together fish will hit a net hard, get gilled in one net, keep swiming and if another net is right next to it—a not uncommon situation—it will gill in that one as well. So then when that fish comes over the roller, it brings the other net with it. So we have to untangle that mess and throw the other net back in the water.

Somtimes when I see that if we keep picking we are going to get into a real mess—several nets all tangled together—I'll call out to the guys: "Let's roll it!" and engage the power roller and we will work together to pull the rest of the net back into the cockpit, lines, corks, fish and all. Then I'll go back inside and carefully maneuver us out of the tangle of nets and boats into clear water while the guys clear the mess in the cockpit and get ready to set again. Often Eric and Marvin will just clear the net until they get to a shackle break—remember that the 900' net is made out of three 300' pieces connected together top and bottom with quick release snaps—unshackle the piece with the fish still in it and prepare the set the remaining 600' (or

300') out after which they will continue working to clear the remaining fish out of the net.

The *Joe H.* did not have a flybridge so maneuvering in tight quarters was a challenge.

Power scows Excursion *and* Rolphy *at Egegik, 1995, originally built for the U.S.Army to support World War II operations in the Aleutian Islands. Their flat bottoms and great carrying capacity made them perfect tenders or fish buyers in The Bay.*

Some 24 hours later another 100 boats had transferred into Ugashik and grrrr: these were guys who had already put in some good pounds in another river. We got another opening, this one at 10 p.m. under a windy cloud deck that pressed down close to the water. In the last hour before the opening, some 450 boats churned around looking for jumpers. In the air above, almost at masthead height, a dozen planes and a couple of choppers did the same. And all this with the empty tundra to the south and the vast Bering Sea to the north. We'd found a promising looking spot, but as the moment to set aproached, it got more and more crowded. But it was pretty much the same wherever you looked, so right on the dot, we started setting our net along with everyone else.

And the amazing thing was this: as soon as the first meshes hit the water, they had fish in them. Before the net was even half out it was "smoking"—throwing white water all along the corkline as the fish hit the net and struggled. We slowed as the last of the net ran off the drum, snapped on a buoy and did a quick 180 degree turn to run back close and parallel to the net, frightening hundreds of more fish into it. Seeing the fish hit like that got us good and pumped up!

By then the word was out that Ugashik was the place to be. More boats arrived literally by the hour, until the river was choked with more than 700 gillnetters, guys who had creamed it in the Kvichak or the Naknek and now were trying to get in on our action. Plus there was the support fleet; we called it "Star Wars"—a city of light and noise out in that wilderness river—everything from 65' wooden power scows to 100' net barges with helicopter landing plaforms to 600' Japanese trampers.

But for drama and power, for all the things that I hoped the Bay would be, from bleak depression that soared into intoxicating euphoria, give me that third opening and its windy, black night.

Author's collection

Early 'floater,' the Alaska Reefer, putting its boats in the water, circa 1955. In that the canneries owned all the fishing boats, a floater, trying to break into Bristol Bay, before limited entry (1973) had to bring its own fleet of 32' gillnetters.

At 3 p.m. on the afternoon before the opening, while we were sleeping, still catching up from the last intense night opening, our anchored boat grounded out on the dropping tide. I felt it as soon as we did, but for some reason we couldn't start the engine to pull off. Flooded, we figured, and climbed down off the boat to take a long tundra walk, heads down against the cold wind, lost in gloomy thoughts about the balky engine.

At 9 p.m. the tide floated us but the big block Chrysler V-8 still refused to start. The fleet poured out of Dago Creek around us, as our batteries ground down toward exhaustion. Words fail to describe the change in our feelings when on the very, very, last gasp of the battery bank, the engine caught, falterered, sputtered, and finally kept going.

When the short subarctic night, still twilight really, began, we lay with hundreds of other gillnetters on our anchors, behind the shelter of a nameless point near the mouth of the river, with the wind starting to moan through our rigging. Outside, the bars were all breaking white. It was a mean night, the kind when the prudent sailor would have double-checked his anchor rode for chafe, and thanked his good fortune to be in a safe harbor.

Yet a little before midnight, we got up, carefully stowed everything, and tied the cabinet doors shut. We got our dry socks and gloves off the line over the oil stove, pulled on our sweatshirts, hauled the anchor, and headed out. All around us were running lights, boats throwing spray clear over their houses: the fleet was underway.

When 1 a.m. came, we set, somewhere off the mouth of the river, in a place only marked by little glowing red Loran numbers. Once again the net smoked and boiled with fish as the onshore wind and the flooding tide pushed us rapidly into the river and toward the lights of the ships in "Processor Row."

We picked fish with our heads down, the chop slamming into the stern, the spray exploding over us, the three of us working as fast as we could. We'd pick two or three fathoms; I'd step on the pedal and another 40-50 fish would flop over the roller and we'd pick some more. All around us were the lights of other boats, their sterns rising and falling, their long corklines heavy with fish.

The flooding tide's current was awesome, pushing us swiftly up the river. One moment it seemed that we were headed right for the lights of the anchored ships. Once I looked up just in time to see the steel wall of a processor's hull rushing by, his anchor chain stretched out tight, and then they were far behind and the tidal current was running like an express train into the darkess of the river and the wild, wild country of the interior to the south.

The Pinnacle *setting full speed while a slow wooden boat is setting parallel and outside of him. In this situation the faster he sets, the more time he will have before his net is covered up by that of the much slower older wooden boat.*

To get out and into another set sooner, we pulled the last 50 fathoms aboard in a big pile of fish and corks and net. Chris and Marvin picked, while I steered out of the river to find another set. Back in the stern, it was wild. Bracing themselves against the violent motion of the boat, they overhauled the net, throwing the fish forward and laying it out to set again. With the drawstrings of their hoods pulled tight against the flying spray, their vision was cut to a small circle. But through it on both sides were other boats pounding heavily into the seas, boats picking, boats setting.

In most fisheries, when the fishing is over, the unloading is a fairly relaxed time. At Ugashik, though, in that weather, the unloading was probably the most physically hazardous part of the whole business. First of all, there was little shelter anywhere for the deeper draft tenders. A 4' chop with wind against tide, was fairly typical. The tenders all had booms rigged out from their hulls forward, so that when you were unloading, your bow line was holding you parallel to the tender rather than pulling you into it. Even so, and even with heavy 3/4" tie up lines and big fenders, lines parted and occasionally even cleats broke their welds and shot into the air.

To speed unloading Bristol Bay fish holds have individual bags or brailers, holding about a ton of fish each. (In later years processors asked their fisherment to limit individal bag weights to around 1,000 pounds to improve fish quality.) Once alongside, the tender lowered a steel quick release hook from a boom rigged high over our boat to clear our antennas. You had to make the hookup to the brailer straps as the boat was jerking sideways and lungeing up and down two or three feet and still have 10 fingers left when you were done.

Plus, with a boat like the *Joe H*, with no fridge and limited storage space, the tender was also our grocery store during the season if we wanted to eat anything else besides fish. So as two of us worked to hook up the brailers, the third would have to make the risky leap over to the tender, forage quickly for food, often just a jumble of opened cases of canned goods and cereal, etc., in a dark fo'c's'le, and then throw what you found over to the *Joe H*. Some days you'd be lucky and there might be frozen steaks, on others, there might be just a case or two of assorted candy bars.

Why we sometimes called gillnetting in Southeast Alaska a 'lifestyle fishery:' it was mellow, relatively uncrowded, with sweet places to anchor up at night.

There was a real big 32 footer ahead of us at the tender that day, the *Clyde*. Not only was she really deep in the water with her load, she had full brailers in her stern cockpit and in another brailer tied next to the reel, a wide, wide, boat with a big, big, load. It was really impressive to see her maneuver once it was her turn to unload, as there was a noticeable lag between hearing the engine throttle up and seeing the boat actually move.

In Southeast, many guys fished with their wives or girlfriends. The actual fishing was typically only 3–4 days a week so there was plenty of time off to explore, and just enjoy the country.

Bristol Bay history: Greg Koetje and his big Rozema, Clyde at the tender, Ugashik, 1986. Their spotter plane, operating with a low ceiling, and in semi-darkness, kept Greg on the fish for their record delivery of 30,000# plus. Paralyzed by an accident from the waist down, Greg's crew hoists him in a special chair up to the flying bridge with an electric winch, slides the chair on the tracks and up to the steering station for the fishing period.

As was often the case, one of the crew went aboard the tender and wrote down the numbers as each bag came up and the weight was called out. The guys on the *Clyde* had basically stopped everything they were doing as they listened to the numbers. When they had weighed the last brailer and called it out, the entire crew cheered and slapped themselves on the back.

When we finally got alongside the tender, we got the story: the *Clyde's* delivery, some 30,000 pounds plus, broke the Bristol Bay record for the biggest single delivery. And this from a 32—footer!

It had been their spotter who'd been flying at masthead height the night before, staying up through the opening, flying in conditions that had driven all the other spotters back to the beach. By watching other nets, the spotter had been able to keep them on good fishing the whole opening.

Later we learned that the *Clyde*'s owner and skipper, Greg Koetje, had been paralyzed fom the waist down a few years earlier, when at the end of the season, with his boat hauled for the winter and sitting up on 55 gallon drums he had tripped and fallen 14' to the ground, and broken his spine. Surgery and physical therapy didn't return strength or movement in his legs, and, an excellent gillnetter before the accident, he decided to keep fishing. His family and crew modified the boat with a short boom and an electric winch on the mast, along with a specially made chair with tracks on the flying bridge.

Small floater Polar Bear *at Egegik, 1988. The introduction of the Limited Entry law in 1973 meant that the canneries no longer held all the cards and that all a new floating processor needed to attract boats was to pay a higher price than the canneries did.* **Note:** *not only did the* Polar Bear *process the fish, but she had to house and feed the crew. Think it was a little crowded in there?*

So when he'd eaten and been helped to the toilet, his crew would use the electric winch to hoist him in the chair up to the flying bridge where the chair would fit into tracks and be pushed forward by the steering wheel, and locked down. Greg would put in the whole fishing period up there, with snacks delivered as needed as he kept his crew and his boat on the fish, and made the biggest catch in Bristol Bay history!

Like a number of other code groups, we shared the cost of a spotter plane, a small single engine plane either with floats or big fat tires for landing on the tundra. Spotter pilots had to be hardy. If they were lucky, the boats they spotted for fished the Naknek and Kvicak Rivers and they could base out of the tiny Naknek airport, and if they could find accomodations, maybe even sleep in a bed at night and eat in the one restaurant in town. If their group chose to spend the season on the Ugashik River, comfort would be more elusive: tenting on a remote beach.

Most spotter pilots preferred Piper Cubs and Super Cubs, fabric over aluminum frames two seaters, often equipped with the STOL (Short Take Off and Landing) kits. These are a set of modifications to the wing and control surfaces that allow the plane to take off and land at around 40 mph, perfect for short sandbar runways. The fishing districts are big places and the spotter's value is that he or she can quickly cover a large area and report on who seems to have active nets with fish hitting. Also before the opening of a fishing period, the pilot can cover the whole area looking for jumpers—female salmon jumping into the air to loosen their eggs.

Sometimes the planes had another purpose: watching out for fish cops. Each day of the season huge numbers of sockeyes are caught at the fishing district boundaries, particularly the Johnson Hill line in the Naknet district on the flooding tide and the north line of the Egegik district on the ebb. During those tides, each line, two or three miles long is just a seething, churning mass of boats. Absent a helicopter that could hoover over boats fishing illegally to record their position, and vessel name/number, the only way enforcement can keep the fishery under control is for fish cops to patrol the line in their outboards, a challenging, thankless, and occasionally dangerous task as they try to maneuver among much bigger boats, many setting their nets out at full speed. In this situation a spotter, orbiting over the line and watching the enforcement outboards can allow aggressive fishermen to set their nets out in illegal waters with much less risk of getting caught. Remember that the tidal current runs swiftly in each place, and an illegal set becomes a legal one in just a few minutes. But those minutes can be critical: a "front row seat" i.e. a set with no one in front of you for a minute or so can mean a thousand fish: a huge set!

At Ugashik, the spotter "airport" was located on the sandy north shore of Dago Creek, basically a big sand bar where a few weeks earlier a landing craft style of boat had beached, allowing the crew to roll 8 or 9 55 gallon drums of avgas onto the sand bar to supply the spotter pilots. Seeing as the westerlies typically blew at 25–30 knots in off the Bering Sea, and the approach was right over Dago Creek, these planes would seem to float over our antennas on final to the strip. Sometimes when it was blowing especially hard it seemed that they actually had to to speed up to land!

Rick Magill stops by Ugashik with rum, and news from the rest of our group. We did not have a side-band (long distance radio) so we had no communication with the rest of our group up in the Egegik River. So sometimes Rick would just orbit over Ugashik and with his added height relay messages to the rest of the group.

By the next opening, a total of 750 boats were fishing, and the radio announcer giving the daily fishing reports began to speak of Ugashik as "The Combat Zone." It was no joke. One we noticed a big commotion on the shore a hundred yards or so from where we were fishing. What looked like a police chopper flew in from who the hell knows where. Later the word came down through the fleet—a setnetter had murdered his neighbor for putting his net too close.

The big crowd of boats meant that each opening was kind of a first set deal; often you would get most of your fish for the period in the first set. After that most boats would migrate to the outer boundaries of the district to catch the reds that the tide was pushing down the shore into the district.

One day after we had unloaded and finally got the hook down and some food on the table, I noticed Marvin flexing his wrists and hands; I had noticed that they seemed to be bothering him. I asked about it.

"I blew my hands out four years ago up here; I had to get flown out in the middle of the season. They still hurt. I just hope I don't blow them out again."

'Blow your hands out?' I'd never heard of that, didn't ask; the information was conveyed in a tone that indicated that I should have know what he was talking about. So I just nodded and didn't say anything.

My hands hurt too; whose wouldn't after pulling four or five tons of fish out of a tangled gill-net in windy cold weather? Was I going to blow my hands out too?

A few days later he elaborated: it was carpal tunnel syndrome. It occurs when repetitive activity irritates a nerve where it passes though a tunnel in your wrist bones, along with some tendons. In severe cases like he had had, you can barely move your hands the pain is so bad. There is a surgical remedy where the tunnel is enlarged. Most folks that have it in both hands elect to just do the surgery on one hand at a time. But Marvin had both done at once just to get it over with; he said he had had just enough flexability in recovery to wipe his bum in the bathroom; it would have been too embarassing to ask his girlfriend for help.

As the season began to wind down around the 15th of July, it was obvious that we weren't going to make the 100,000 pound mark that we had been hoping for. But something else was very much in our favor: the price.

Much of the frozen sockeye that our processor was freezing went to Japan instead of the traditional markets for canned salmon: mainly Europe and the US. Bristol Bay sockeye is a prized commodity in Japan and when it appeared that the run at the least was going to be late and probably less than had been forecast, a bit of a price war started among the buyers. We started seeing gas station-like signs with the sliding numbers so that the buyers could easily make the changes. One buyer would anchor in front of the rest of the tender fleet with big illuminated signs showing the price that day. Each day when we slid past him, the price was another nickel higher: very exciting for us fishermen, as when the cash buyers raised their price, the other markets generally had to follow

Once, when we were laying on a set, having a candy bar lunch before we started picking again, this tender with the gas station style price signs— at a buck and a half a pound—a record and unheard of price for Bristol Bay—swung over towards us and lay there in the swell and a guy came out on deck with a bullhorn:

Usual Ugashik weather: Chris and Marvin picking a few out during "Free week."

"Hey Cap, if you sell to us, we'll do your laundry, throw in a free bag of groceries, and pay you in fresh hundred dollar bills."

I looked at the guys and they gave me the thumbs up. It wasn't the money so much—I knew that our market would probably come close to matching whatever the cash buyers were paying, but our clothes were definitely starting to smell, and our regular tender's food supply was down to candy bars and cans of chili. So we got our dirty clothes together in a big duffel bag, and went alongside after we'd picked up. Wow: great groceries: he had a whole freezer of steaks and frozen veggies to choose from, and good to his word, tracked us down the following day with our clean clothes, still warm from his dryer!

With the big price, but still a ways from our 100,000 pound goal, we figured we'd just stay as long as we could. After the peak was over around July 8, the fleet thinned out on each opening. The weather was shitty—typically SW 25–30, blowing all the way from Siberia up the Aleutian Chain and across the Bering Sea to us. But with three mouths to feed back in Maine, I knew that even a thousand bucks looks good in January so we just kept plugging away, some days just getting a couple of thousand pounds.

Then one day we woke up in Dago Creek, aching and tired from a particularly rough day for just half a bag (1,000 pounds) and realized we'd beat ourselves up enough. A nasty cold rain was blasting into the anchorage from the Bering Sea outside; it looked like half the remaining fleet had decided to leave after unloading the night before and only a diehard 20 or 30 boats were left.

Two boats had been chatting on the radio the night before about how to salvage their season. One had had a major breakdown at the peak of the run and Ugashik, so far from anything, is a really, really bad place to break down. And the other guy had gotten into the breakers, blown out a window, lost all his electronics, filled his boat with water, and lost four days just trying to put his boat back together enough to get fishing again.

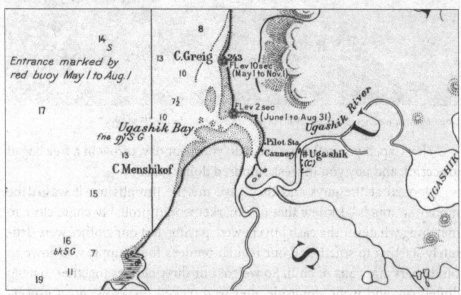

Ugashik—most remote and windiest of the five Bristol Bay districts. Both canneries marked on the chart—'C' denotes cannery—are no longer used for fish processing and are essentially big warehouses for fishermen to store gear, etc. The fishing district actually ends near where the river divides, but we would often steam up the river to Ugashik Village, home to a half dozen families, if it looked like fishing wouldn't open for a day or two. Dago Creek is the little indentation just inside the River on the right.

They'd been talking about going down to the Cinder River and fishing for silvers or coho salmon for another month or so. For us, after spending a month at Ugashik, the bleakest spot in that grim corner of Western Alaska, the thought of traveling further west, to a place with literally nothing except a barely protected anchorage, a place where you had to plead and beg a tender to even come down to take your fish, was unimaginable.

Faced with the prospect of that unspeakably depressing future if we wanted to keep plugging away, all of a sudden our modest pounds looked pretty good and in just a few minutes we had totally changed from the fishing mode: getting ready for the next opening in our minds, to the getting the hell out of town and going home mode. Very exciting stuff!

But first we had to get back to Naknek. It had been so rough when we unloaded the night before that I just wanted to get away from the tender before someone got hurt or the boat got smashed up. So we hadn't gotten filled up on gas. At the time, I wasn't concerned; we had enough for another opening, but now that we had going home fever, we didn't have enough to get all the 90 miles back to the Naknek River. What the hell, I figured, if we couldn't get gas out in the river on the way out, we could probably get some from a tender in the Egegik River, halfway to Naknek.

Drying out—the bars in the Ugashik river were in some cases several miles from their charted position. In the thick of heavy fishing, blowing SW 25 with driving spray, several boats ended up on the bars and took a beating before the tide left them high and dry. In a situation like that there's not much you can do but hibernate in the cabin and hope that your windows don't get blown out.

So it was pound down some instant oatmeal, batten down the hatches and head out. Once we got out of the shelter of Dago Creek, it was obvious that getting gas at Ugashik was out of the question: the tide was ebbing hard against the usual SW blow, creating a nasty, short 4-5' chop so there was no way that we were going to get alongside a tender for gas. Plus I looked around and our tender and processor had both also gone in the night. The forty boat support fleet that had turned the river into a city of lights at night a week earlier had dwindled to a couple of tenders bucking heavily at anchor.

It was so rough coming out of the river that we had to slow way down and just let the current push us along; faster than that and we could have taken out a window. The gray sky pressed down almost to the water, and in a moment the shapes and lights of the tenders were lost in the murk. With the tide almost down the bars on either side of the channel were breaking heavily, and we were mighty glad to finally get out by the sea buoy, and make our turn east and for home. We timed our turn for the bottom of the tide, and with the turn, the flooding current began to push east, and the seas, now running with the wind, eased considerably.

Home! Back to Mary Lou and the kids, what an exciting thought! Once we'd made our turn, Eric and Marvin hit the sack, I poured some coffee and just settled in for the ride, just now and again getting enough of a glimpse of an austere and lonely shore through the gloom to keep me safely in deeper water.

When we arrived off the Egegik River, there was no sign of any tenders; it looked as if they were all done there as well and just a single floater, the big blue *Ultra Processor*, a giant high-sided barge, still lay in the channel. I hailed them on the radio and explained my situation; they said they usually didn't service boats like us; they left that to their tenders. Their season was over anyway; they were just waiting for the tug that would tow them down to Southeast Alaska for the rest of the pink salmon season down there. But they did have a couple of drums of gas and found enough hose to lower down their high steel side.

Except . . . that try as they might, the hose and nozzle was only just long enough to reach down to the tank fill and no more. But there was a swell running which meant that at the bottom half of the swell, the nozzle would pull out of the tank, and I'd have to shut it off and wait to jam it into the fill again when the boat rose, pump another gallon or so.

Finally we pumped enough to see us home and got the hell out of there before all the spilled gas blew up and cooked us.

Never was a crew so glad to see the big tractor at Lummi shove the trailer down into the swirling current of the Naknek River and wave us in. I jammed the *Joe H* between the heavy steel pipe guides, the tractor started up the slope to the boatyard, I shut off the noisy V-8, and just like that, our season was done.

As soon as I knew the boatyard was going to be able to haul us, I called a taxi on the VHF (This was before cell phone service in the Bay, but the 'cabs' all monitored VHF) And perfect timing—he arrived with the piping hot pizza and a cold case of beer just as the tractor parked us. After a season with almost no booze, and basically nothing but salmon, instant mashed and canned veggies to eat, hot pizza and cold beer were exquisite beyond words.

One of the few modern boats fishing without a reel, north of Ugashik, 1986. The skipper puts the boat in reverse, the crew turns on the power roller and roll fish and net into the cockpit, to be sorted out while they are steaming for the next set.

Plus, by the looks of the boatyard—the boats all in neat rows and hardly anyone around, it looked as if we were almost the last one in. Once we got blocked up on 55 gallon drums, all that was left was to clean up the boat, arrange to have our extra nets delivered to our locker and get the hell out of town. The one upside to being one of the last boats in is that you could actually get out of town. If we'd come in five days earlier, we'd have been trying to fly out with two or three thousand others and might have had to wait a couple of days just to find a plane with a seat.

But first I had to get my settlement, our end of the season check less all the gas and groceries that we'd charged. I had the guys start to clean up the boat, found our group truck, someone to jump it (it seemed to have a perpetual dead battery), and headed into Naknek and the trailer where our market had its office.

Only no one was there, even the sign was gone.

And then it hit me: I'd done the classic Bristol Bay newbie mistake:

trust a new market. All season we'd delivered our fish to a new fish buyer becaused he promised a big price, figuring to pick up a check for the balance at the end of the season. And even with our modest pounds, the big price meant that would be well over a hundred thousand dollars.

Except that they were gone, gone, gone. My chest tightened—had we been taken for suckers, like I knew others had when fish buyers went bust or disappeared without paying their fishermen? How was I going to explain that to the guys?

"Never was a crew so glad to see the big tractor at Lummi shove the trailer down into the swirling current of the Naknek River and wave us in."

Just then a gal came out of the other office in the trailer, another tiny, one small floater fish buying company.

"Hey," I said, "Whatever happened to Ocean Pacific?"

We didn't have one of those monster Bay seasons that the hot shots like to brag about. But we kept our boat together, put in a season without anyone getting injured, learned to work together as a team, faced some hard challenges, and caught our share. For greenhorns (except for Marvin) I figured that was good enough for our first year.

"They all left," she shrugged and headed back into the small office, and my heart sank even further. Maybe they had an office down in Seattle, but it was Saturday, and my return ticket to Maine was via Anchorage and Chicago; we were fu--ed. But then she turned around again and looked at me. "Aren't you Upton?" said she, "I think they left something for you."

I followed into her office as she rummaged around in her desk, finally came up with a smudged envelope with my name on it. I ripped it open: checks for me and Marvin and Eric, totaling over a hundred thousand dollars: YES!

And 24 hours, three planes, a long bus ride, and ferry later, I walked off the boat at the lobster fishing town of Carvers Harbor, Maine, and there was my little family waiting to wrap their arms around me. That night, sitting at the dinner table, with Mary Lou next to me, Kate and Matthew chatting away, and the panoply of the sunset islands and Hurricane Sound in pinks and greys outside the window, Ugashik and the salmon world seemed far, far away. And it struck me: in all those grim weeks on the Ugashik River, we didn't see the sun once.

EARLY THAT NEXT SPRING BOB AND PAUL called me up to talk about the season ahead. They were happy with my first Bristol Bay season, the way that I had treated their boat, satisfied with their share of the proceeds and were wondering if I wanted to join them in their next very big step: buying a floater that would freeze our fish so that we could market them ourselves.

I'd been around Alaska fishing long enough to know that floaters—small ships and even barges converted into processing facilities that could be moved from place to place as markets and fishing required—had been part of the scene since before I was born. Most salmon still, even then in 1986, went into the can. But there was always an entrepreneur who would find a frozen market somewhere, find some investors or fishermen to fund buying and converting a ship, suffer through the considerable hassles of running a floater in the remote reaches of Alaska, and at the end usually sell their product at a price that justified it all.

The first floater in Bristol Bay was in 1894 when twenty guys in a schooner dropped the hook in the Nushagak and started buying salmon and salting them down in barrels.

Another notable floater was the *Pacific Queen* in the 1940s, a 173' ex-Navy rescue and salvage ship. She had a complete canning line putting up reds in the popular 1/2 pound cans. Then around 1955, after power boats had pretty much replaced sail in the Bay, the *Pacific Reefer*, set up to freeze salmon, sailed into town.

But because the actual fishing boats were owned by the canneries, these two early floaters had to bring their own fleets with them: ten boats each. Additionally, the *Pacific Queen*, operating before engines were allowed in the Bay had to pack a small power boat, known as a monkey boat as well to tow its sailboats when there was no wind.

Larger floaters like this strive to be as busy at they can, processing herring the spring, salmon in the summer, and sometimes crab in the winter. To achieve this, they might travel as far as Norton Sound near the Arctic Circle in May for herring, then move south to process Bristol Bay Salmon, and finally the almost thousand mile journey further south and east to process salmon in Southeast Alaska.

Then the limited entry system came along in 1975 and totally changed the balance of power. All of a sudden, the fishermen owned the production side of the business, and the canneries had to upgrade both their prices and the services that they provided to fishermen, to attract and keep boats.

However, most guys, with their own room in the bunkhouse that they'd had for years, their circle of friends at the cannery, with whom they'd fished for years, were understandably very reluctant to change markets: they had a comfortable deal already where they were, and if another market was paying a little bit more money, it didn't justify moving to another cannery, or even more inconvenient: moving away totally from being connected to a cannery at all.

Another early floater, the Pacific Queen, *around 1950, loading her sailing gillnetters and monkey boat. From the looks of things she probably loaded the two little tugs and maybe 10 sailing gillnetters. One wonders—if the* Pacific Queen *got overwhelmed by a big run, would the canneries, who had a chokehold on Bay fishermen, buy from the* Pacific Queen *gillnetters?*

But the coming of the 'independents' like myself, and the construction of the big boat storage and service yards at Lummi, Leader Creek and Dillingham created a sizeable fleet of guys who were not beholden to any cannery, and could fish for whomever they choose.

In more recent times, a bunch of Petersburg fishermen, had formed a little company, pooled their assets and bought . . . this big ship. We're not talking small barge like the *Polar Bear*, or a hundred and sixty footer like the *Bristol Monarch*, they bought a Knot Ship, an old C1-M, originally built for the Navy in 1944 to move supplies around the South Pacific. Some 338 feet long, the partners had a freezer plant installed aboard that could handle almost million pounds a day. Their timing was perfect—it came on line just as the Japanese marker for both herring and salmon was growing in leaps and bounds, and the word around the docks was that ship, the *Yardarm Knot*, was a money making proposition for the owners, who benefitted in two ways: a better price for their fish on the grounds and a slice of the profiits after the fish were sold.

My friends and partners had their eye on a more modest venture: buying the old *Nichole N*, an old YF—a Navy freighter—just 160 feet long, but already converted and operating as a floater, so that basically it was a 'turn key' operation or as turn key as a 1940s ship converted into a processor twenty years later could be.

If I wanted in as a partner, I would have had to invest a chunk of money (I think a share was $50,000) and get a share of the profits at the end of the season as well as a good price for my fish. I was excited at the idea of being in on the ground floor of something like that. But at the same time, I was saving for my own boat instead the leased *Joe H*. And I knew that the downside of such a venture was the dreaded cash call—if for some reason things didn't go as planned, and more capital was needed, then the partners would have to pony up.

Spotter planes on Dago Creek spit, Ugashik, 1986. The pilots would have to arrange for a barge to bring in barrels of AvGas (center of photo) before the season. Many spotters were fabric Piper Super Cubs, adapted with tundra tires and short takeoff and landing packages. With STOL packages, the approach speed for a short field landing could be almost as low as 25 mph. As the wind over the spit was often close to that, we would watch the planes actually accelerate to land, and from wheels down to full stop might be less than 200'!

And of course in the Bay, changing markets is a little like getting divorced and married again: not to be done hastily. So I needed to to ask a few questions. Like about the last processing venture one of the partners had been invoved in, when, rumor had it, he'd had his drivers shuffling freezer vans with his frozen salmon from place to place, trying to rendevous with a tramp freighter before the state caught up with him.

"Oh," he guilelessly answered, "that was just a technicality, and it was my daughter's deal anyway . . ."

"Yeah, but what exactly was the technicality about?" said I, a little uneasy about the kind of technicality that would have the state trying to impound a processor's entire production.

"Ah . . . we were using tundra water to process the fish with. I mean, no biggie. Those fish were fine."

"And how old was you daughter?" I wanted to dig a little deeper.

"Ah . . . She was sixteen then, but . . ."

I finally decided that at least for me, I wasn't ready to be a partner. But in that the guys that had set me up in Bristol Bay with no money up front were partners, I agreed to change markets and deliver my fish to them for the season.

Earlier in the spring my partners had paid a welder to create a flying bridge on the *Joe H*. Actually it was just a set of railings up on the roof of the cabin leading up to a little alumium podium-like stand that held the steering wheel and the engine controls.

But it was a truly immense improvement. I had discovered in the few times we had been in crowded conditions at Ugashik that you simply could not be competitive without it—your vision was too limited inside the cabin. It was also a measure of the changes in the Bay: higher fish prices meant more new boats with hungry owners which meant the traditional places where fishing was hot—the district lines—got more and more crowded.

But my biggest worry was gas.

I flew up to Naknek and the first night there had been a meeting in the back room of the one restaurant in town. I looked around the table; all the guys were heavy hitters, in many cases second or third generation Alaska fishermen with big new diesel boats: players. I was the only non partner in the room; really sort of an afterthought: "Well, we oughta invite Joe to this . . ."

"So, how many of you guys have gas boats?" was my only question . . .

"Hey, no prob, Joe," Paul, the owner of the *Joe H*, assured me with a man-to-man whack on the shoulder, "Plenty of gas on all the tenders, plenty of gas . . ."

But I noticed that no one else in the room had answered my question. I suspected that I was the only gas boat in the fleet. So in a cash starved start-up, with just one gas boat fishing for them, they would have plenty of gas?

But the next day I had other problems and forgot about the gas issue. Bob Anderson showed me a jar of light brown nasty looking stuff: "Lookit the weird color your oil turned over the winter."

Under the valve covers of our Chrysler 440 was a depressing sight: water droplets laying in all the low spots, and rust and scale all over the rocker arm, spring, and valve assemblies.

It didn't make sense; we'd added plenty of antifreeze at the end of last season. But maybe it hadn't been enough, maybe the record fifty and sixty below of the winter had cracked the block anyway. The options were discouraging; we'd swapped out engines the year before and hadn't gotten the old one rebuilt yet. But the odd part was this: we pressure tested the oil and gear coolers, even pressurized the whole cooling system overnight without being able to force more water into the oil. We racked our brains: where did that water come from? Changing the head gaskets seemed the next logical step, until Mark Premazitch, a veteran 440 operator, stopped by.

"Hold on now, boys," he cannily advised. "Better not start ripping things apart until you know for sure that you got a problem."

And then another veteran 440 owner, the winter watchman at the Leader Creek boatyard, suggested a possible cause: "Oh, yeah, I seen that lots of times in my boat, you get a winter of fifty, sixty below, the whole inside of the block gets so much condensation from the air, she'll make a quart of water easy over the course of a winter. And another thing, you get that engine sitting nine, ten months without draining the cooling system, that antifreeze'll go through gaskets water never would."

So we flushed out the engine again and again, until the oil stayed clean and set out for Egegik, but not really knowing if we'd solved the problem or if it lay hidden, waiting for the worst possible moment to burst out again.

As we slid down the Naknek River on the 14th of June a litttle past midnight, I gazed longingly at the gas scow in front of the freshy painted Trident Seafoods cannery, at the big bulk gas tanks on half a dozen sleek tenders flying the Trident flag.

But "plenty of gas," was the reassuring answer I'd been given when I'd radioed ahead to the Egegik River a few hours later. Yet when we pulled alongside the tender to unload our extra nets and gas up, instead of a nice clean bulk tank, a bunch of rusty 55 gallon drums was chained to the stern of the beat-up ex-Gulf of Mexico shrimper. All had water pooled on their tops, right to the rims, covering the bungs.

"They're all sealed, right?" I asked the skipper; I wasn't big on drum gas, unless they were sealed drums from the oil dock.

He gave me a funny look as he deftly kicked some dog poop off the deck into the scuppers, grabbed a bung wrench and started tapping each of the drums.

After ten empties, he finally came to a full one, rigged up his electric barrel pump and passed me the hose.

We were just finishing up our second barrel, when Eric called out to me, alarmed. "Hey, Joe, this doesn't smell like gas . . ."

He drew up the nozzle. It dripped an opaque, syrupy fluid: hydraulic oil.

"Son of a bitch. Has the whole drum been like that?"

He shrugged. "I just noticed it. It looked weird so I smelled it."

I confronted the tender skipper.

"Nah," he said, "Maybe you got a little in the bottom or sumpthing,' but no way could it have been all hydraulic oil, no way. I tell the boys to clean out them barrels good, but what can you do?"

"Fer crissake," I buttonholed one of the crew when the skipper was inside writing up the slip, "your skipper said he had plenty of gas. I still need another 100 gallons. what happened to the rest?"

He shrugged and nodded his head toward the pilothouse, "He musta' forgot that we traded most of that gas to the natives in Norton Sound."

Meanwhile, 75 miles to the west, near Pilot Point in the Ugashik RIver, a surprised tender skipper was watching a boat that looked more like a big speedboat than a gillnetter, roar in from the Bering Sea, do a couple of doughuts around the tender, and roar off again, before returning. From the speed and size of the gillnetter, the tender skipper assumed it was one of the new boats from the "Russian" fleet from Homer in Cook Inlet, 600 miles away. Finally he flagged the speeding boat down.

"Nik Nik," the bearded fisherman yelled from his flying bridge over to the tender in a heavily accented voice, "Nik Nik. Vere iss Nik-Nik?"

The tenderman waved his arms to show the way to the Naknek-Kvichak District, some hundred miles further east. The big bearded guy waved back, throttled up, and quickly disappeared. This was the big Russian gillnetter *Cruiser* and when she and her sisterships appeared in the Bay, we were awed by their speed and size, and assumed that they would set the standard by which all fast Bay boats would be measured.

In the fall boat shows, there'd been reports of groups of heavy, full-bearded men talking in hushed foreign voices at the M.A.N. diesel engine display. I'd heard it was almost impossible to even get a glimpse of the giant 800 and 1,000-horse monsters because of all the Russians crowding around.

Deja Vu—the Joe H *unloading to the Marco crabber* Sea Venture. *As I sat in the galley while my fish ticket was being filled out, I kept thinking, "This looks mighty familiar." Then I asked the skipper if it wasn't the old* Flood Tide, *that I'd crewed on in the Bering Sea king crab season 15 years earlier. I was right: it was! The fish are in a brailer made out of netting. Within a few years these would be obsolete as the fleet went to so called NoMar brailers, made of a heavy nylon so that the fish wouldn't have its flesh marred by the net meshes pressing into it.*

The Russians were actually a sect called the Old Believers who broke with the Russian Orthodox Church in the 17th century, and eventually settled outside Russia in a few dozen small tight communities scattered around the world. They followed a very traditional way of life, most notably in their dress: bright blouses and baggy pants for the men and full length dresses for the women. These Old Believers came from several communities near Homer, Alaska, and another one in central Oregon. The Homer Old Believers built a boatyard to construct their very large 32 footers—roomy as they took their large families fishing with them.

By then, my second year in the Bay, I'd started to see a few more women working on the boats, and especially on the setnet crews, whenever we were close enough to observe them. But the Russian gals with their kids trailing behind and in bright bouses, skirts and dresses were a real presence.

That spring after the boat show, the first of the big new engines arrived in the bay in a fleet of brightly colored boats from the Homer area yard with names like *Cruiser*, *Aquarium*, *Dynamic*, and *Destination*, huge high-sided 32 footers. When they idled by you, it sounded like a locomotive going by, and got up on a plane faster and traveled more level than the usual bow high Bay speedboats.

That the survivors of a record smolt outmigration of almost 350 million fish were headed to the Kvichak River was not lost on the Russians or the rest of the Bay fishermen. ADF&G's cautious forcast of 16 million harvest was buoyed by this hopeful note: "Because this is larger than any outmigration ever recorded, there is a good possibility that The Kvichak will come in stronger than forecast."

So naturally when we worked the Egegik south line on June 15, we were hoping for a repeat of the westerlies that had brought in so many fish the year before. Instead we found a crowd that was pushing way over the line, and three and four skunk sets in a row. Yet despite all that, the test fishing results at Port Moller, 200 miles west showed a huge run was headed our way.

The guys in our group had told me that in a Kvichak year, you had to be there, told me about the 2,000 and 3,000 fish sets when a big run poured in. But they also said that now, with no plane—they hadn't been able to find a spotter—it was a huge district, and maybe with a huge run there would also be a huge fleet. Maybe, it would be better to stay at Egegik, a much smaller district where our group of four boats would be effective at finding and communicating where the fish were. Also we still viewed the Kvichak as a bit of a crap shoot. Legendary fishing tales aside, in recent years the predictions of big runs had not materialised.

Our first set on the legendary north line at Egegik was a sobering kick in the pants. The line fishery is a totally chaotic, adrenalin fueled environment. Up on the flying bridge, the skipper's job is to find a set that is within district waters and be open (i.e. without someone setting directly in front of you) for at least 10 or 15 seconds after you get your net out. Such legal sets are basically impossible to find, as boats go further and further over the line into closed (illegal) waters to get their net out.

The fish cops are also there, zooming back and forth along the line in big outboards and occasionally overhead in planes, though in the fast moving fishery planes are less effective at identifying offending boats. Not knowing where you are is never an excuse as all Bristol Bay gillnetters with flying bridges vessels have (or better have) Loran displays on the flying bridge. The northern edge of the Egegik district runs along the 32570 microsecond line. If your Loran reads 32569.1, that's "one click" (roughly a hundred feet) over. But as you probably wouldn't get a ticket for going 62 in a 60 mph zone, you're probably safe there.

And here's where your personal risk tolerance comes in: how brave do you feel? Where are the cops? For some groups a key function of a spotter plane was inform group members where, on the crowded 2 mile line (shrinks to a mile or so at low tide) the fish cops were.

To save time we often roll the last third of the net into the cockpit, fish and all, to be picked out and readied while the skipper is running up to find another set.

And remember, the tide is ebbing, the current running hard into the district. So, if you set at say, 32569.8 (if you can even find room there to get your net out), within a very few minutes, the current will have pushed you back into legal waters. But there is rarely room at 32569.8 unless you go out near the district corner marker, where there are much fewer fish. Sooo . . . you go out to 32569.7 or even .6. A bit more room there, but how good is your information about where the cops are and how brave do you feel?

Plus, you have almost zero time to make this critical decision; boats are swarming around like bees, even out to .4 and .5 over sometimes—way out in "ticket country." And if you see an open set—room to set in illegal waters, but within your comfort zone, someone will else will take the spot if you don't, like instantly. As the expression goes, "Your turn's over as soon as your buoy hits the water;" It is totally a take-no-prisoners sort of place. And, in the chaos, it's nothing to get whacked so hard by another boat that it knocks you to your knees. Engines roaring, people yelling: your adrenalin is pumping!

When we got to the line that first time there appeared to be good stream of fish ebbing in, but boats were going way over and the fish cops were there in force. It took a few minutes for us to even try to get our net out, a little to the outside of the most intense part of the action. Barely had we got half our net out, setting at three quarters throttle—our first really fast set—and worried about getting a backlash (setting fast always carries the possibility of a net-tearing backlash) when a boat setting at full speed whacked us so hard as he cut us off, that it almost knocked the three of us over, and I had to hit the reel brake and jam the engine in reverse to avoid running over his net. The guy never even looked back. And all that for just 30 fish.

After that we only reluctantly convinced ourselves that it was best to stay with our group at Egegik. So it did my spirits little good to hear the hot reports of five day a week fishing on the Kvichak while we waited for a midnight opening off the bleak South Spit with a 40 knot easterly howling through the rigging. When the opening finally came, it was disappointing and my growing feeling that the Kvichak was the place to be was only fueled by reports from the Shumigans (a group of remote islands on the inbound route of Bristol Bay salmon) of the heaviest fishing on record. The arithmatic was compelling; say the harvest went to 10 million fish in the Kvichak, and there were 1,000 boats. The average would be 60,000 pounds (10,000 six pound fish) and we always beat the average. And if it was a really big run, as all the signs seemed to point to, and those fish were mostly bound for the Kvichak, say 15 million fish in that river alone, that would push the average to 90,000 pounds. Of course, some of those fish had already been caught. These were torturous decisions.

Meanwhile, "Plenty of Gas," had become a constant scramble for a barrel here, a barrel there, as our small tender fleet scrambled with the demands of constant openings on multiple rivers with little time to make it up to the fuel dock on the Naknek. And what if we transferred to the Kvichak, and the fishing was hot but we couldn't get gas?

Finally a tender with what looked like a fresh set of drums on the back showed up, and we slid alongside in the three-foot swell and cross chop to pump what we could. But when the guy plugged the barrel pump into the extension cord, the cord smoked, spat out sparks and finally shorted out completely. They frigged around and finally got hooked up again, but when the when the guy grabbed the pump to turn it on, it was obviously hot as the shock almost knocked him over the side into the water.

By then I'd come to realize that gassing up with these guys looked like a dangerous deal, and was ready to cut the lines and get the hell out of there if a fire started.

Fortunately we'd just finishing up actually filling up, and had just passed the hose back to the tender when our tie up lines parted when another gillnetter blasted by at full throttle. Unfortunately, I was still aboard the tender.

"Well," I shouted to my tense looking crew as they jogged a boat length away, rising and falling three or four feet in the swell and chop, "you always complain that I never let you make a landing; now's your chance." Finally they slammed into the tender's fenders long enough for me to jump aboard without breaking anything.

Plus with what I called the Brand X tenders, the crews were so tired from basically going around the clock, that we'd be lucky to just get unloaded and get out of there with enough of a squirt of water and gas to just keep us going. Food? Forget it. If we didn't have a bunch of mushy canned goods left over from the last season, four big boxes of minute rice, and a cook that made a mean mayonnaise-baked sockeye, we would have been hurting.

On one of those get-unloaded-and-try-and-get-gas-deliveries to yet another king crabber turned tender for the salmon season, I was sitting in the galley, signing my fish ticket and just getting up to go when something struck me as familiar.

"It's a Marco, right? I asked the skipper.

"Yeah, a 104. The only one they ever made. For some reason they stretched them to 108 after this one."

It was the old *Flood Tide*, the name changed to *Sea Venture*, the crabber that I'd spend most of 1971 on. The bookshelves of paperbacks were gone, replaced by a TV, VCR, and shelves of video tapes.

"Yeah," I said, "I crewed on her, Bering Sea, 1971. No knuckle cranes then. We were basically human fork lifts pushing those heavy pots around the deck." Like most modern king crabbers the *Sea Venture* sported a versatile hydraulic crane amidships, sort of like a backhoe on steroids, that made moving the 700 pound crab pots around the deck a lot easier.

Meanwhile our little floater/processor was having a great season. Ever since things started popping in the other rivers, they had been operating a full capacity, day after day. One of the guys in the group that owned it, my friend who didn't seem to have been bothered by processing fish with tundra water was aboard another processor during a closure. The owner had turned to him, "Hey, aren't you Patrick Murphy, one of the guys that bought the old *Nicole N*?"

"Why yes," my friend Patrick had said, puffing up a bit, glad to be getting some recognition, "and we're pretty proud of our little . . ."

"Why that rig's the scummiest floater in the whole Bay," the other man interrupted. "Those guys have fish guts up to their ankles. If the State ever came aboard, they'd shut her down in a minute."

Later, I took Patrick aside, asked him about conditions aboard the floater. She was pretty small and I'd heard there were 70 guys all crammed in there somehow.

"Oh," he admitted offhandedly, "It's a hell ship."

Finally on the 28th, a good charge of fish came to Egegik and we got our net in front of a few. Our 8 bags put our little Shore pretty well down, and I felt pretty smug until we saw a big Rozema with her rail almost under, and deck brailers rigged to the back of the house. We watched her unload 14 bags.

Meanwhile, while we battled it out at Egegik, the guys who had followed the 'least effort theory,' transfering to the districts with the fewest boats were killing them. We heard a report from the Nushagak of a Rawson (a smaller older 32 footer) delivering 26,000 pounds. In a RAWSON!

"Man," the story went, "good thing the guy had splashboards . . . he had to reach underwater to put the tieup lines around the cleats, and even then he had two brailers basically almost floating beside the boat . . ."

By this time 'plenty of gas' had become a bitter joke. Finally on the evening of July 11, our market had no gas and I was about dry. I called around trying to find some when a tender from another market called to say he had plenty of gas if I'd sell him our fish.

"Plenty of gas," I thought ruefully,"What would it mean this time?"

But when the *Ocean Harvester* hove into sight through the early morning gloom, and I saw another handful of rusty drums on the stern and an oilskin clad crew member dragging an electric barrel pump across the deck, I felt like banging my head against the bulkhead. 'Plenty of gas,' turned out to be two barrels when I needed at least four.

That next morning I was about out again.

"Yeah, we got twenty barrels." It was the *Pac I* this time, coming up to the north line to bring me some gas and buy my fish.

I looked in awe as his brillant quartz iodine lights parted the fog to reveal a huge mud boat—originally built to carry drilling mud and drill pipes to oil rigs in the Gulf of Mexico—rigged to buy fish. All I wanted to do was pitch off, fill up and get the hell out of there. Maybe, if we actually got a fillup, we could actually stay on the fish for a change istead of worrying about where the next barrel of gas was coming from.

After we'd sold our fish, I called for the gas hose.

"We haven't got a pump. But no worries," he yelled down over the whistle of the wind and the throb of their gen sets, "We'll just hoist one up, hang it over your boat and you can just siphon as much as you want."

Just then our boat dropped sickeningly in the chop, came up tight on the lines, and lurched sideways into the VW-sized fenders, almost knocking me off my feet. As much as we needed gas, I wasn't willing to have a 55 gallon drum hanging over us in those conditions.

I picked my moment, jumped aboard and went up to the penthouse-like pilothouse to get paid. It was getting near the end of the season and everyone liked a little going home cashola.

The skipper was a real big boy. Across from him, sitting thoughtfully in the other corner was an even bigger guy, with his hand inside his coat. The skipper opened the cashbox. It was mostly 100s, banded into neat inch thick $10,000 bundles. They were jammed in there so tightly that he had to hold the cashbox down with one hand while he pulled out some money.

Holy Shit! There must have been two or three hundred grand in there, easy. I pulled my pen our real slow like, thinking it would be a hell of a way to end my Bay season—getting hosed by some security guy's Uzi because I made the wrong move around the cash box.

When I threw off the lines, some buddies called with a good fish report from the south end, but when I stuck my tanks, there was the smell of gas and nothing else.

So we waited two hours until a tender arrived from Nankek with a hand pump and two sealed drums of nice fresh gas for us. The tide was running with the wind so there was no lee, and as we pumped by hand, the boats would slam together violently, the seas hitting the big fenders and erupting all over us. Just another day in paradise!

The end of a Bristol Bay season has its own powerful dynamic. One day the fish are coming good and you're thinking you'll hang until the 20th of July or so. But then maybe the next day will be a real slow one and someone will get to talking about home and all of a sudden the urge to go is impossible to resist. I was tired of risking injury by simply trying to get gas for my boat, I was tired of sitting on a bucket as it was sliding back and forth in the the fish hold (we had no toilet). I was tired of being cold and wet. But most of all I just missed my family; and all of a sudden whatever season we had was good enough. We radioed our market for them to get plane reservations for us and headed east for Naknek and home.

By then, our second year in the bay, we had the drill pretty well down for getting out of town: strip the nets and wash the boat down on the long run up from Egegik, so that once we were hauled and parked in the boatyard, all we had to do was borrow the truck, take the gear—lead and corklines, buoys, etc. up to the locker, and pack.

Of course, like everything else in the Bay, there were a lot of other guys doing the same thing. So as soon as you decided to bug out, you had to radio your market, and have them put your name on the haulout list at Lummi. In later years Lummi would buy another big tractor and hydraulic trailer for pulling the boats out of the water and parking them for the winter. With one tractor they could only haul about 20-25 boats on each high tide, so it was important to get your name on the list early as usually going home fever hit everyone in the Bay about the same time.

So as soon as we knew we were three or four boats away from being hauled, we radioed one of the taxiis with our ritual pizza order, and our timing was perfect: we'd just been set down on the jack stands and the big green tractor was pulling the trailer away when the taxi arrived with hot pizza and a case of cold beer. Just that little thing and the cares of the season faded away!

The next day, the airport at King Salmon was in full end-of-the-season chaos mode as MarkAir, PenAir, and Alaska Airlines tried to deal with a crowd of fishermen that filled the building and spilled out into the parking lot. All had extra flights and Alaska had even done a last minute schedule change to allow a big 737 to fly direct to Seattle without an Anchorage stop.

King Salmon is also the jumping off place for a number of fishing lodges catering to the very well heeled. When I finally got close to the check-in counter at PenAir, there was a middle aged couple ahead of me, all decked out in new bush gear, obviously headed home from one of the fancy lodges.

A big Russian gillnetter blasts by at 20 knots powered by an 800 horsepower MAN diesel. Usually with a family aboard with the mother and children dressed in traditional garb, these boats were a dramatic presence in the Bay.

Ahead of them was a friend of mine from Petersburg days, Grant Thompson, one of the guys who came to Bristol Bay early and made it big. Like me, he had young kids at home, his season was over and he wanted to just get the hell home. Unlike me, he only had to get to back to Southeast Alaska, so he had come right off the boat, figuring he'd clean up when he got back to Petersburg. He'd been fishing hard, and looked a bit like something a raccoon had dragged out of garbage can: greasy coveralls well flecked with salmon scales. The conversation went something like this while the well-to-do couple, probably thinking Grant was a homeless guy wanting a free ride out, looked on in amazement:

"I'm sorry, Mr. Thompson, everything today is booked. The earliest seat we have is tomorrow at."

"How much is a charter?" Grant didn't let her finish. PenAir also operated charter flights.

"Ahhh, just let me look." The agent did some key clicking, consulted some papers, "Ahh, we do have a plane available, one way to Anchorage is $2,200."

Grant pulled out a thick roll of bills and started slapping down 100s. He turned to some friends in the very large standby line: "Got three seats to Anchorage. Who wants out now?"

And for myself, once again that stunning transition, a little more than 48 hours from picking fish with the grim sight of Aniachak Volcano, venting steam far downwind looming over us to stepping off the afternoon ferry in Maine, looking at the lobsterboats coming in from hauling, and walking up the ramp to my waiting family.

You get what you pay for in the fish biz. We didn't have a chopper or a spotter or a big tender fleet, a great cannery on the beach, or groceries on the tenders—all those things you take for granted when you have a market with one of the majors. But we settled at a buck twenty plus before the first of September, with the promise of another price adjustment in the fall. This, when the majors were only paying a buck and there were rumors flying that the Japanese had rejected 12 million pounds of salmon from some big player, in hopes of buying them back later at a lower price.

Our little floater had had a checkered past before my friends bought her. Her previous owner had a cavalier attitude about paying his help and had been rewarded with mishaps aboard that basically amounted to sabotage.

But new management, lots of fish, and fair treatment of the crew, hell ship or not, had made her into a profitable high producing operation.

In the spring she'd arrived at Togiak—a native village further north— just in time to start off on herring. Then, at False Pass, south of the Alaska Peninsula, the Peter Pan Seafoods fleet had been mighty glad to see a new cash buyer, so she did well there too. In the Bay she had processed around the clock for almost four weeks at full capacity.

I remembered the first time I'd seen her up there. She had some nets that I needed, so I tracked her down out in the maze of trampers and floaters in the 'Y,' the confluence of the Naknek and Kvichak Rivers, about two miles from shore.

Our floater looked pretty small tied up and transfering frozen salmon to the 800' Japanese freighter.

"We're alongside the *Washington*." her skipper had radioed me, but when I found the *Washington*, a big 800' freezer tramp freighter, with the binoculars, there wasn't any sign of anyone tied to her.

Finally, when I'd gotten a little closer, the blue splotch on the side of the *Washington* revealed itself as our little *Ocean Pacific*, the top of her rigging barely clearing the deck of the big tramper.

Next stop for our floater after the Bay was Southeast Alaska for pink salmon. Being narrow, she had to be loaded carefully to maintain her stabilty. But when she was anchored off Ketchikan processing pinks, literally right in front of the Coast Guard base, she took on a load of pinks from a tender, while the engineer, who normally manages such transfers, pumping water around the ship to balance the load, was ashore.

In slow but eventually inevitable motion, in full view of the Coast Guard and hundreds of stunned people on shore, she developed a sudden list that submerged some of her lower deck openings, laid over on her side and sank. All aboard had plenty of time to get off, but in just 30 minutes, our floater was gone.

It was a heavy blow for our group, which just a few weeks earlier, had breathed a collective sigh of relief after having gone way out on a limb and having done so well her first season.

All that effort and work and now it was back to square one.

THE BUST

"Criminals, all I'm getting are criminals. Of my first ten deliveries, seven were from fishermen forfeiting their fish to the state."
              —*tenderman, F/V Oregon, Egegik, June 29, 1987*

THE FIVE PRIMARY BRISTOL BAY DISTRICTS (the mouths of the Kvichak, Nushagak, Naknek, Egegik, and Ugashik Rivers) are large areas. Typically a fishing period (usually 12 hours) starts at the beginning of the flooding tide. Before the start boats cruise around, looking for signs of fish, usually jumpers (female salmon leap out of the water to loosen their eggs before they spawn). Often groups like ours will also share the costs of a spotter plane, who can scout a whole district and report on jumpers or visible schools of fish riling the waters.

At times there were a lot of spotters in the air, especially above the district lines around the peak of the season. I remember our spotter occasionally saying, "Shit, that was a close one. I think I'm gonna set down on a tundra pond and chill for a bit." Our spotter used a floatplane, so he had plenty of choices of where to land. The "close one" was a near mid-air collision. It was a potential problem and the State of Alaska tried to get the pilots to adopt protocols to reduce this possibility. Finally after two deadly mid air collisions in 1990, aircraft were banned over district waters when the fishing was actually in progress.

There are roughly 1,800 32' gillnetters registered in the Bay, spread among the 5 rivers. If they were all spread out evenly—360 to each river—the Bay would be a great mellow fishery. But what happens is that as the short season progresses and skippers listen each night to the catch totals of the day and get information from the tenders as they deliver their fish, and from their buddies on the radio, this huge fleet migrates to the most productive two or less often, three rivers.

This means when for example Egegik is having a strong run, there might be 900 gillnetters plus maybe 40 or 50 support vessels—tenders, net barges, processors, etc. Think about it: 900 boats and each one with a 900' net: almost 153 miles of net!

So as the start of the opening or fishing period approaches, you'll find a promising looking spot, but then as the actual moment nears, other boats will begin to filter in around you, limiting the area you can set in. In the last minute before the start, you might have to move quickly to find a spot that was still open, just to get your 900' net out. Often that first set will be a significant part of your catch for that period, so getting a good first set is very important.

Then within an hour or so, the fish within the district will be mopped up, and a good part of the fleet will migrate to the outer lines, the boundaries of the district, to capture fish moving into the district, and what's called the line fishery or the line game develops during the ebb. The line fisheries are most pronounced at Egegik during the ebb and at Naknek during the flood, as hundreds of thousands of fish, or even a million or more at the peak of the season, pushes into the district with the tidal current.

So, your challenge to find a place to put your net begins. A truly legal set would be way out by the outer marker, where there are few fish. So you maneuver, watch your loran, try and find an opening and meanwhile the clock is ticking.

And if you really feel like a pirate . . . there's another strategy, occasionally tried, but sure not to make you any friends among the fleet: go way out into ticket country, far over the line, maybe even a whole microsecond over and set out your net without the big orange end buoys with your vessel identification numbers on it. Then just run back into legal waters, and wait as your net, full of fish, gets swept slowly by the current into legal waters, at which point you could hook onto it and start picking out the big haul. Such a net, without the big end buoys is unlikely to be seen by the fish cops. But, its also likely that another fisherman seeing such an unaccompanied net, would feel pissed and call the cops, who would buzz over and attach themselves to it to see who comes to claim it. (Probably no one.)

Tight quarters fishing: with boats close all around you, not only is it important to get your net out quickly before someone else "corks" you (sets their nets right in front of yours) but to pick the fish out as fast as you can so that you can move back to where the fish are (remember the current is running swiftly) and get your net out again. Shortly after this photo was taken the Cheap Thrills *got sideswiped by an aluminum boat with a particularly sharp corner to its stern, opening up her bow so much that you could see the crew's sleeping bags through the slice!*

Also the 60' fish cop enforcement vessel *Trooper* typically anchors exactly on the line more or less in the middle. Which at least keeps fishermen legal in that small area. Here's an example of how many fish are pouring over the line at the peak of the ebb at Egegik. One day I was cruising the line near the *Trooper,* moved out into illegal waters—but not far enough out to get a ticket I hoped—and started setting full speed, the net just flying off the stern of our boat. Because of where I set: just over the line and next to the fish cops, no one dared cork me (set in between my net and the stream of incoming fish) so it was that rare event—an open set, or a front row seat. As I approached the *Trooper* I realized that the bow of my friend Jim Smith's boat, towing his net, was literally nudging the *Trooper's* stern, giving me no place to go. But, in an unexpected move, Jim, up on his flying bridge, saw us coming full speed, eased off his throttle just enough for the current to open up a 12' slot between his bow and the stern of the *Trooper.* We shot through the gap, our net spilling out off our stern and continued until it was completely out. It was a full 90 seconds before anyone dared set in front of us. A minute and a half during which our net was boiling with fish hitting it! Finally someone set in front of us, and after waiting for maybe 5 minutes we started picking what turned out to be our best set of the whole season: around 2,000 fish: 12,000 pounds, more than half of a boatload!

This gives you a sense of the pressure and the competition on the lines during big tides.

For some reason the competition in early July 1987 on the Egegik north line was particularly intense. The pre season forecast had predicted a smaller run than usual. There were a lot of new boats around and new boats usually mean big boat payments. The result was that a lot of folks came resolved to fish harder to make up for the poor prediction and their big debt. Except that almost everyone fishing the north line on the ebb was already fishing hard or they wouldn't be in such a rough and lawless place in the first place.

Anticipating a long struggle with hungry fishermen, Fish and Wildlife Protection (the fish cops) decided to make a strong statement to fishermen at the very first opening, citing many boats, often making their very first set on the North Line, ticketing at least one was a brand new boat: welcome to the Bay!

When you get a ticket, the cops take your fish and your nets, plus the fine is usually $10,000. Then you have to make a court appearance and usually lose a day of fishing.

But even with the aggressive enforcement presence, for many the North Line rule of thumb was simple: "How brave do you feel?"

Despite the two enforcement skiffs, the sheer numbers of boats setting over the line those July weeks made it easier to step out into "ticket country." Many boats, with or without the aid of a plane, simply took their chances, routinely going three and four microseconds over, hoping for a shot of fish, and that they'd either get carried by the tide into legal waters, or get corked by another illegal boat before the fish cops came by.

> *"I hate it when no one sets in front of us . . ."*
> —An Egegik crewman

Almost every opening you'd see boats with fresh new gouges on their sides or windows busted out from being rammed or sideswiped by other boats. I remember remarking on how nice this shiny brand new fiberglass gillnetter named the *Cheap Thrills*, looked, then a few minutes heard a particularly loud crunch as two boats collided just outside of where we had set, and looked over to see the *Cheap Thrill*'s whole bow sliced open so badly that you could see sleeping bags through the rip in the fiberglass.

The next day I saw a friend with someone's aluminum window frame with half the glass still intact, hanging off the anchor on the bow of his boat.

"Hey, Dave," I called on the radio, "What's up with the window?"

"Oh, some shit-fer-brains laced me cork to cork this afternoon, twice."

Getting laced means that another boat had set its net literally right next to yours, considered provocative even in the tight quarters fishing of the Bay.

"At the end of the opening he was jogging waiting to unload, and I drove my anchor right into his window. Another six inches to the left and I would have gotten his spice rack too. I think he got the point that he had pissed me off."

It was at this intense part of the season when the Loran signal failed on the morning of the 4th of July 1987, the traditional peak of the run. Aboard the enforcement vessel *Trooper*, steaming for Egegik, watch officers immediately noticed the failure of the Loran signal, and anticipating the kind of chaos it would cause, they got on the sideband radio to ADF&G headquarters to delay the upcoming 12 hour opening until the signal could be restored. The delay was denied and the fishery opened as advertised, at 5 a.m.

We were fishing at Egegik and first noticed an issue when we got up around 3:30 a.m and our Loran wouldn't acquire a signal. At the time we were anchored off the South Spit with a couple of hundred other boats. Assuming that the problem was with our set, we fiddled with the antenna connections before hauling out the manuals to trouble shoot.

After about 15 minutes a voice on the radio: "Hey, I guess the Loran's out . . ." alerted us to the fact that the problem was fleet wide and not just in our set.

Given the fierce 'feeding frenzy' style of fishing on the Egegik boundaries when the Loran was working, we elected to begin our opening deep inside the district, well back from the Loran defined lines.

Fortunately there was a good body of fish around, and by the end of the flood, we had 10,000 pounds aboard, our best day of the season so far with the ebb still to fish. But we knew that by then most of the fish inside the district had been scooped up and that if we wanted to make the best of it, we should move closer to the North Line for the ebb, Loran or not.

As we approached, even from three miles away, we could see the haze in the air from all the exhausts of the crowd on the line. The action seemed even more chaotic than usual, so we made a few sets along the way, hoping to find a few fish and not have to mix it up with the crowd on the line.

Typical crowded and chaotic conditions at the district boundary or line. The pressure to find a place to legally (or as close to legal as you are comfortable with) is intense. And often somewhere in this churning crowd are the fish cops in an outboard boat, ticketing boats that are over the line and fishing illegally.

Meanwhile, on the North Line, the fish cops, in just a Zodiac inflatable were trying to keep the 200-300 boats inside where they thought the district was—remember, no Loran. Usually the 60' *Trooper* anchored itself halfway along the line from the beach to the outer buoy, to aid in enforcement, but that afternoon the *Trooper* was busy keeping the south line under control.

However, by giving written warnings, pulling 16 permit cards and requiring those boats to anchor up, they managed to bring the line back under control.

At about 11:20, the Loran signal re-established and the fleet quickly moved back into legal waters and began the usual dogfights along the 32570 Loran line.

However, within a few minutes, the signal failed again and the fleet immediately started pushing over the line.

About this time the fish cop inflatable was low on gas and motored over to the tender *Bull Harbor* to try and gas up.

While they were refueling, a number of gillnetters came alongside to express their anger and frustration that so many boats were fishing so far over the line.

Finally, around 12:15, the Loran receiver in the skiff started displaying a signal again, and the head fish cop, Trooper Brent, checked his Loran against the Loran on the big fish tender *Bull Harbor*, and satisfied that he now had a valid signal again, and glad to finally have the tool to ticket fishermen in closed waters, started up and headed out into the swirling crowd of boats far over the line.

This was the situation that we were about to unwittingly insert ourselves. Of course, the prudent thing to do would have been to fish conservatively, trying to see the marker on shore and the outer buoy to make sure that Loran or not, we were within the district. At the same time to be candid, the situation reminded me of the cartoon showing two guys fishing out of a boat in some lake. They are staring at a mushroom cloud rising over the horizon.

"I tell you what it means." goes the word balloon, "It means screw the limit."

In any case, as we approached the North Line, our Lorans were reading all zeros on both displays so we assumed that the transmitter was still inoperative. Maybe if we had read the manual a little more thoroughly, we would have understood that after a signal failure, the receivers had to be turned off and then back on again to reset themselves.

The area near the North Line was very crowded, and only by running over many nets, taking our engine out of gear each time were we able to get near the front of the fleet.

Because of the many boats, we were unable to see either the marker on shore or the outer buoy. But we came to a place where the majority of the boats were concentrating, and having heard earlier that the cops were patrolling, assumed that it was the line. In addition beyond where we thought the line was were a number of anchored boats that we assumed had had their permit cards pulled and had anchored to clear the fish out of their nets.

At that time there were probably 50 or 60 boats fishing way out beyond where we thought the line was. So we figured no worries, and laid out our net, and began to tow a hook in the outside end.

A minute or so later we noticed the fish cop inflatable approaching us from the shore end of the line. Figuring we were legal with so many boats outside of us I didn't even stop towing the hook.

So we were stunned when they came alongside and told us we were in closed waters. The conversation went like this:

"Skipper, you're fishing in closed waters. Please give us your permit card."

"But . . . but . . . but . . . our loran's all zeros . . . and there's guys way outside of us.

"The Loran's been back on for half an hour and we warned all you guys . . ."

"But . . . but . . . but you didn't warn us. Hey, c'mon on board; look at our Loran."

"That's too bad. You can take all that up with the judge. Just give us your card, pick up your net and go over to the *Bull Harbor* and unload your fish."

That was it. They took our card and sped off.

But what happened next really pissed us off.

Next to us was another boat, towing his net, just like we had. If we were over, he obviously was too.

The cop boat went alongside and just told them to pick up their net. No ticket, no warning, just "Pick it up, boys, and move back." Plus this was hot, hot fishing; we started getting hits as soon as the first meshes hit the water. We watched, flabbergasted as they picked up, ran back a little ways and reset, getting the hits the whole length of their cork line.

When I went back into the pilothouse and turned the Loran off and back on again—something we'd been doing at intervals all morning, it started to acquire a signal–the transmitter was back on the air. It must have come on just after the last time we tried; it didn't seem fair.

Sick in our hearts, we slowly picked the fish out of our net, stunned at the sudden reversal of fortune—one moment we were watching the thrill of hundreds of fish hitting our net, the next we were shocked and depressed beyond words.

But when we got over to the big Bull Harbor to unload, there were at least a dozen other ticketed boats there waiting to unload.; I hoped that when it came time to go to court and fight what had happened, there would be strength in numbers.

When we'd finally unloaded and got up to the pilothouse to get our fish ticket, I tried to bring a little humor: "Ah, we'll just take cash for these fish today." but no one seemed to be smiling too much.

And double bummer—not only were we up there signing a $15,000 check over to the state, but because all the fish cops were up there in the pilothouse with us, we looked out to see the rest of the fleet having the best fishing of the whole season, going way over the line without a care.

Looking for that elusive not too illegal set can be extremely challenging. In situations like this there is essentially no place that you can legally set your net unless you move away from where the fish are.

They also took our nets, so by the time we'd gone back to the net barge, and found three of our extras, the opening, the biggest of the season was over.

We still made a season out of it, but we'd missed a big day, and it hurt, emotionally as well as financially. I was determined to fight it in court.

As our early October trial date approached, and I resumed mussel dragging on the Maine coast, I hoped and assumed that the State would make a deal: lower the charge from a misdemeanor, which requires that the State prove the fishermen was negligent, to a violation, which only requires that it be proved that the fisherman was fishing in closed waters. And if there were ever a situation where it would be hard to prove negligence, I figured it was when the Loran signal was down.

But it was not to be—the State played hardball, so I traveled 5,000 miles to King Salmon to plead my case.

The reader board on the one motel in town said it all: "Welcome Defendants."

Early on Oct. 7, I headed out for Naknek with two Yugoslavian Bay fishermen in a borrowed '59 Apache Chevy truck that steered like a bow heavy boat bucking a five knot tide. The sky was black, the stars bright, the air crisp and cold, all this at 8 in the morning.

The jury pool was all native, as were most of the inhabitants of Naknek after the frenzy of the fishing season was over. Each was asked if they could judge driftnetters without prejudice. I hoped their true feelings weren't all like the one native who candidly said, "I don't really like drift-ers," and was quickly dismissed. Drifter is the local term for gillnetters like us.

The white D.A. started his case: that while the Loran had been out that morning, it had been a clear day, and that both the marker on shore and the outside marker had been clearly visible when they came alongside each of the 10 defendants.

By the time the prosecution rested its case, the trial recessed until the next day. We headed back to King Salmon, but stopped at Lummi to check in on our boats.

I found our leased, battered '73 Shore, an anonymous workhorse, and the Slavs their brand new Curry, a graceful state-of-the-art fishing ma-chine. I walked along the shore of the river, the swollen ball of the sun making all of Kvichak Bay magenta. In the mud was the hull of what looked like a very old steam tug. And I wondered if it hadn't been the one who had been standing by at Unimak Pass to help the big square riggers through, the *Star of India*, the *Star of Russia* and their sisters as they arrived from the long passage up from San Francisco.

We hung out at Eddie's Fireside Bar in King Salmon that night. It was moose season and outside, giant moose racks—antlers—filed the whole beds of pickup trucks, their tips taped with foam rubber for the long ride back to the states and someone's trophy wall.

"Dey say dey could see de markers," said the Slav skipper in his heavily accented English. "You see de markers? I no see de markers. I see fish cops in skiff giving away tickets way outside of me, figure we be okay, way inside de other boats like dat."

"I couldn't see the markers," said I, "How the hell could you see the markers with so many boats around you.?"

The prosecution had shown the court this map showing where the line was and where the boats that they had ticketed were. We drew up our own map showing that actually in addition to the ten boats they had drawn in, there were easily 250 others churning around, setting and picking in the same area.

I'd brought some photos too, to show the jury what conditions were like on the North Line. The photos of the chaos that is almost every day there really got their attention; they made the prosecution's claim that it would have easy to determine our position visually seem very dubious.

Then the Yugoslavian skipper of the new Curry boat took the stand. While they had been unloading to the *Bull Harbor*, he had been knocked to the deck by a wildly swinging full bag of fish, and had lain there for several hours, unable to move. Aside from ascertaining that he was not paralyzed, the troopers and crew of the *Bull Harbor* made no effort to help him.

When the Curry boat finally got unloaded and went alongside the recently arrived *Trooper* to unload its nets, the injured man asked for medical attention.

The Yugoslavian then testified that the public safety officials aboard the *Trooper* said that they couldn't help him.

The courtroom was unusually still during this testimony and the prosecutor seemed eager to get him off the witness stand as soon as possible.

Our lawyer wrapped up our defense with the suggestion that we and the other defendants were guilty of nothing more than "not being able to afford a 1987 Loran," a reference to the fact that the newer units reset themselves automatically when the signal reestablished itself. And then it was in the hands of the jury.

The troopers came over after that to inquire about the Yugoslavian's injuries.

He shrugged and said, "I'm OK now."

Then the fish cop who had given me the ticket said, "If I'd known you were coming, I would have brought my copy of Alaska Blues (a book I had written) for you to sign."

That kind of broke the ice and we stood and chatted for a bit. They mentioned their futile efforts to get the opening delayed and their frustration at trying to control the fleet with the Loran out.

I had to leave and get my plane before the jury got back. Not until a big steak at the Anchorage airport and three big drinks aboard a 727 with the pink mountains of the Queen Charlottes lifting through the haze below us did I get the verdict.

The jury found all of us not guilty on the misdemeanor charge of negligence, but guilty of a violation and fined $300, and we got our fish money and our nets returned.

"They got off," you might say. Yes, we got off without a misdemeanor conviction on my record. But between lost fish on the rest of the ebb on July 4th, the peak of a big run, lost fish on July 10th when we had to fly to Nankek for our arraignment, lost fish from fishing way conservatively the rest of the season, legal fees, airplane tickets, and all those drinks at Eddie's Fireside, it only cost me maybe $25,000.

1989: SKIM MILK

Never transfer out of good fishing.
—Bristol Bay Rule Number One

Never transfer out of good fishing.
—Bristol Bay Rule Number Two

ONE OF THE BIGGEST CHALLENGES FOR Bay fishermen is choosing the best river to fish in. Each winter ADF&G (Alaska Department of Fish and Game) releases its estimates of what the upcoming runs will be, giving us fishermen plenty of time to talk about where we should fish.

Plus remember, and this is a huge one: when you change rivers (districts) in Bristol Bay—making a transfer—you have to wait out 48 hours without fishing, before you can start fishing again in the new district. With a season so short that a single 12 hour fishing period might be 10% or more of your entire season, it's a step only to be made in extremis.

My fishing philosophy was to avoid if possible the stressful crowded conditions that occur when one river gets 800 or 900 boats. Also there was the issue of timing: the peak of each of the runs headed for the four rivers or districts in Bristol Bay area slightly different. So ideally, you might be able to fish one river until it got too crowded as it approached its peak, then transfer to another river, losing 48 hours, but then, hopefully, becoming legal just in time to get in on that run's peak.

And then there was the wild card: the Kvichak River. In Bristol Bay glory days, when the Alaska Packing Association sent up a fleet of square riggers from San Francisco loaded with boats, fishermen, canning and construction supplies, to return after building a cannery, loaded with canned salmon, it was the Kvichak that was the big river. Where the really big canneries—Koggiung, Lockanok, Hallerville, Diamond X, Nakeen, Graveyard and others—were built to process the huge runs. Until the Japanese fishing fleets moved to within sight of land after World War II, when the Federal Government (they pretty much ran Alaska then) figured it was easier to let the war shattered country feed itself off Alaska fish than send them food aid.

And so the runs from the mighty Kvichak slowly shrank. The great Kvichak canneries were abandoned, canning moved primarily to the other rivers: Nushagak, Naknek, Egegik, and to a much lesser degree, the far to the west Ugashik.

And yet. And yet. In recent years there had been a growing outmigration of smolts (young salmon) from the Kvichak, that for some reason, had not yet translated into significant actual returns into the river.

In a Kvichak year, the old Bristol Bay hands all said, that big river was the place to be. That was where the big scores always came from, loading your boat day after day. When a big Kvichak run came in, it was in awesome numbers: a million, two million fish in a single tide, surging up the west side, along Deadman Sands, past the gravel bars, or maybe up the middle through where the floaters and trampers hang out in the deep water. Plus, it's a giant area; it can soak up at lot of boats. At Egegik, 800 boats means that a 12 hour opening can be almost a one set show, unless you want to push your luck at the line. The same number of boats in the Kvichak is hardly a crowd.

"It can be like a spark in a dry forest," one of the old timers said once, "nothing, nothing, but then something changes and that spark explodes the whole forest. It can be like that in a Kvichak year. Places where there haven't been fish in years will suddenly explode with fish for reasons no one can understand."

But for us, in 1989, after only three seasons of experience in The Bay, we still viewed the Kvichak with skepticism.

Living in Maine and fishing The Bay, I'd always leave for Alaska on June

10th, the day after our daughter's birthday, to hang gear—tie the brand new gill-net netting into the cork and lead lines. Not a lot of guys were up there that early, and to walk down the silent rows of 32' aluminum and fiberglass gillnetters was an eerie feeling. Between our yard—Lummi and Leader Creek next door, there were probably 300 plus silent boats, almost like an invasion fleet waiting for the word.

The early part of the season, when the rivers are open around the clock is called Free Week, as you don't have to register for any particular river. Then as the first fish start to show up, you enter the Emergency Order Period, when fishing is only allowed during specific fishing periods—usually 8-12 hours a day—rivers and times announced on the radio.

So "free week"—when you could fish anywhere around the clock (though usually not for many fish) was usually a time for mellow fishing. But not in 1989.

We started on the southern boundary of the Egegik district, looking around to see if any fish were coming in before we set. The first thing we saw was the high bow of the *Silver Warrior* flying past, net flying off his stern. Then coming at him from the other way was another big aluminum boat both going for the same set from opposite directions. They both poured on the coal and turned out, each trying to get their net in front of the other, running inches apart, engines screaming. But then the cork line of the other boat broke, the *Silver Warrior* got the set and the little game was over.

Curious, we ran his net on the way by and didn't see a single fish. "Wow, "I thought, "guys are really hungry; what will the action be like when the fish really start to show?"

After Free Week, we went back into the Naknek River to tie up at Lummi and wait for the first announcements of fishing time and to figure out what would be the best river for us to fish in. There were about twenty boats rafted out from the small float, with a brand new fiberglass Modutech the inside boat—the only one actually tied to the very small dock. Bad move: when the tide started to run hard, the strain of the twenty boats tied outside of him started to pull his big bow cleats up through the deck, and the line of boats broke up in a frenzy of men and boats swirling upriver with the tide, trying to avoid the many anchored boats in the swift current.

Which river, which river? That year, Egegik, with a projected catch of 4 million fish, looked like a good bet. But each day that we waited for an announcement, more boats would register, until there were almost 800;

a huge fleet. So I'd talk to my friends as we waited, look at the pre season predictions, listen to the radio updates on where the fleet was, trying to figure out the right move. One day we'd be sure we should register for the Nushagak, the next we'd be sure Naknek would be the sleeper.

In the end fate decided it; Egegik got the first opening, so we headed down for the nastiest kind of buck against a Sou'west gale, with all the windows leaking, a rotten trip and a rotten night's sleep after we got there, rolling and pitching at anchor.

Finally on the 27th of June we set somewhere off the mouth of the Egegik in the windy chop.

"Hits," I yelled, pointing at the net.

"No pointing!" my crew yelled together. Quickly I dropped the offending arm. Pointing at fish in your net was a good way to get corked by any of the boats cruising by, looking for action.

And so the pattern of the '89 season was quickly set: maybe a good set or two at the start of the fishing period, but then after four or five hours, the fish inside the district had been caught up and the giant fleet migrated to the outside line, 750 or 800 boats battling it out. Lots of brand new boats got that Bristol Bay battered look pretty quickly. The scramble at the end of the 12-hour period was almost as bad as 800 plus tired crews headed into unload. When we finally sold our fish and headed up to the upper river and dropped the hook, I looked back in amazement at the city of noise and light that was the tender and support fleet.

But did we get any sleep? Not much—just more violent pitching and rolling in the short wind driven chop. Finally we picked the anchor and moved in close to the beach where there was a bit of a lee.

Then around 5 a.m., a eerie and ominous sound woke me with a start— the shriek of the wind. Not since king crabbing in the Bering Sea had I heard the wind tearing so violently at a boat. Luckily we were anchored close to the beach so there was no sea.

But the wind—the power of it was stunning, the gusts slamming into our little boat with all the power of a sea hitting a breakwater. It was literally picking up the surface of the river and filling the first five or six feet of the air with it. In the higher gusts, we could barely see the shore or the boats around us. Now and again in the thin light, we'd see a boat dragging past, with someone up on the bow in rain gear, on hands and knees, just trying to hang on as he winched in the anchor.

Nasty or not, we figured we better get out there and get our net in the water and hope the wind eased off before we had to pull the net in.

On the radio from the tender anchorage, further down the river in less sheltered waters: the big floater *Bristol Monarch* reported a gust over a hundred knots, just before her anchor chain parted. About the same time eight other tenders and net barges, broke free from their anchors, in one case actually breaking their anchor in half! The tenders started up and jogged into it, and the barges blew out to sea, to be chased down later.

By 10 it had eased up a bit, to say, 60 to 80 southerly. ADF&G came on the radio to say they were extending the 2 p.m. opening for another 12 hours "so that fishermen wouldn't feel pressured to fish in the extreme weather." That was a shock—we were hoping that the opening would be postponed. I mean who would feel pressured, owing three or four hundred grand for a new boat and license, and facing the skinniest prediction in a decade?

So we bumped our way over the shallows and anchored in a 5' chop downriver from Coffee Point to wait and see. As 2:00 approached, a few of the larger 32 footers headed out, but Laland Daniels, on his tender *Ballaena*, further out the river, reported gusts of 85, so we decided to wait a bit longer.

But when a guy set his net out below us and started getting a few hits, we decided we'd better go for it.

As I was up on the bow in rain gear, guiding the anchor chain in, the bow dropped into an especially steep sea, the chain jumped the bow roller and flayed my finger against the side of the drum. Nothing severed, but pretty ugly, with blood running down my rain gear and splattered against the windshield so much that my crew inside thought that I'd at least torn off a finger.

A guy was jogging a few yards away up on his flying bridge, and as I switched hands and kept the chain coming in he yelled out: "That's the spirit, guy, don't let a little scratch get you down!"

"Maybe Fish and Game will delay the opening until the weather is better," was our thought as the first grim light of day revealed particularly nasty sea conditions.

I bandaged the finger as we looked for a place to set, and I remembered what one of the guys in our group had said about Ugashik: "Nah, we don't like Ugashik too much. It's too damn windy down there." So far Egegik hadn't show us much for weather either.

Fortunately the wind didn't shift to the West, which would have put the fleet at risk in the evening when the tide started ebbing out over the bars. And of course, we missed out on the best fishing by not being out there at the start, wind and all.

But then in the windy dark of 2 a.m. a radio voice: "Hey, this is Dave. Where are you guys?" I gave him our position and he gave us his: "It's happening here, maybe you should head down."

So for two hours in the meanest and blackest night I'd seen yet in the Bay, we picked our way between the sand bars and the nets, laid out our net, and just hung on as the seas exploded into our stern.

But now and again, I'd pick the right moment, slide the door back and peer out into the black. There was a slice of moon up there somewhere and when it broke through the racing clouds for a moment, I could see fish in the net where it was exposed beween wave crests, and further back the splash of steady hits.

It was 800 plus fish—a great set. The next day we got lucky with a nice 600 fish plus set. We'd picked half of it, but the tide started to carry us across the line, and we had to pull the rest of the net aboard, fish and all, into the stern.

"What a nightmare," one of my crew, a fellow east coaster, still new to the Bay, said. To him it was a hopelessly confused tangle of fish and net.

"Nightmare?" I replied, as we dug into it, picking and throwing fish forward as we sorted our way through the pile. "You kidding me? This is only the easiest money you'll make all year; this is what guys up here dream about."

The next opening at Egegik came with fog and strong westerlies. A little flurry of fish at the end of the opening saved our bacon and we decided to unload on the outside to a big tender in rotten conditions, pitching up and down three or four feet in the swell, and lucky to get unloaded and out of there without an injury or ripping one of our big cleats right off the deck.

By then, it was so cloudy that it was actually dark, the rest of the fleet had gone on into the river to unload and we were alone. It was the bottom of a big minus tide and I knew that the seas would be breaking heavily on the bars on either side of the narrow river channel.

My compass light was out, the guys were already in the bunk and it was very hard to stay oriented as I fought the boat swinging in the big quartering seas as I tried to get to the 32593 line that would carry us into the river. Once we got too close to the edge of the channel, and got sideswiped by a sea that I thought was going to take out our windows before I got back into the deeper water, badly shaken up.

Whenever I tried to use the flashlight to see the compass it would ruin my night vision that I needed to see the big seas trying to broach us side-ways. A couple of other boats had already lost windows that night trying to get into the river, so I opened my side window and tried to steer by the angle of the seas. But every time I thought I was on a good heading, and my eyes had gotten used to the darkness outside, I'd sneak a quick glance at the Loran and we'd be way down to 91, or maybe up to the 95 line and almost in the breakers.

Earlier that evening a boat with engine trouble had gotten too close to one of the sand bars. A sea had come aboard, flooded the cabin and engine through the open back door, and if a friend hadn't darted in between seas and gotten a line on them, they would have been in a tough spot with the night coming on.

I was on the verge of waking the guys up so that they could at least be awake and able to find their survival suits if we got into the breakers, but then finally I saw the glow of running lights behind me in the fog. I figured it was either Mark Perovitch on the *Pattie Marie* or Joel Ludwig in the *Blue Sky*. They'd been behind me unloading and both had radar, so I just throttled back and let them lead me in.

A day or so later I saw Mark and asked him how it was getting into the river that night.

"Ah," said he, "it wasn't bad with radar and all, but geez, you should have seen this guy we passed on the way in. He was all over the place."

I didn't tell him it had been me.

A little before 2 a.m. the faint glow in the foggy black ahead became the support fleet, twenty or thirty big tenders lit up like a city. By then the tide had turned and was boiling into the river at a strong 5 knots, making for an ugly cross chop and even the largest tenders were pitching and rolling heavily, and only taking fish on their leeward sides. But even so I could see that the boats unloading were getting slammed violently into the tenders.

A sand bar, extends all the way across the Egegik River at Coffee Point. An hour or so earlier a hundred or so gillnetters, either already unloaded, or seeking to unload to tenders anchored further up, headed for the bar, thinking there was enough water to get through.

There wasn't and the first 20 or 30 boats hit the shallows and were quickly slewed sideways and shoved over on their chines by the current. Behind them, the fleet followed. By the time the boats following realized that the lights ahead of him weren't anchored but stuck on the bar, it was too late and they were quickly aground as well. And behind them came more and more boats, seeking the shelter of the upper river. Within a few minutes perhaps 200 boats were aground in a big tangle, grinding on the sand bottom and into each other before the tide rose a little more and little gaggles of boats would scrape along the bottom in the current before finally floating free. And all on the meanest kind of windy, black night.

The next opening we had another good first set and were steaming to the front line, over dozens of nets, taking our engine out of gear each time we passed over a cork line. There was a line of boats ahead and behind, all doing the same thing. The guy right behind us, some cowboy in an ugly looking thing called the *JB* was in such a big hurry to get back to the front line and get another set that he didn't see that we were slowing briefly when we passed over a net. He had gotten so close that when we slowed for a net, he hit our stern with a glancing blow, knocking one of the horns, the vertical side pieces, completely off our stern net roller. He shouted something like: "What did you slow down for, asshole?" Like it was our fault, and disappeared off into the melee of boats and nets and choppy seas and exhaust smoke.

A little shaken, the guys covered the broken and jagged part of the roller with duct tape, and we finally got to the front and went for a set. But barely was the net even half way out when two other boats were already passing us with their nets out, shutting off the incoming fish, followed quickly by other boats setting in front of them.

We quickly picked our 50 or 60 and headed to try and get in another couple of sets while the fish were still coming. But it was kind of a double bind—if you went out where you could get your whole net out, you were over the line and the cops were patrolling with a plane and two outboards.

The majority of the fish were sliding down the beach, so the action was most intense in the shallows, in 6 or 8 feet of water. We moved further out from the beach, where at least we thought we might be able to get our whole net out.

With our one-horned roller, we were handicapped—we had to set in a slight turn to port to keep the net on the roller. But then with the net half out, another boat appeared out of the crowd, apparently looking the other way and the only way to avoid him was to turn to starboard. As we did, the net climbed out of the power roller, and the fine webbing climbed over

my new crew member from Maine and ripped the gold earring right out
his ear.

"Welcome to Bristol Bay," I told him as he stared at the blood in
amazement.

We limped through the rest of the 12 hour opening, unloaded early and
headed for Naknek, a five hour run. My guys hit the sack, and as I steered,
I pulled on some dry clothes and poured a tumbler of red box wine and
tried to unwind; getting whacked like that had really gotten the adrenalin
coursing through me. The stove had gone out, but the guys had snacked
on hot dogs. One was left in the pan. I pulled it out of the congealed fat
and ate it: dinner.

"Alaska Airlines Gold Streak's your only shot," Big Tom at Lummi in-
formed me. "No one's got a roller here. Maybe one of the canneries, but
they wouldn't sell it to someone who wasn't fishing for them."

Shit. That would mean at the earliest, I'd get the new roller the next
day, and still had to install it. That might mean missing two openings. Shit,
shit, shit. Not to mention that a new MARCO roller air freighted to King
Salmon would probably be at least 5 grand.

"But," Tom went on, quick to realize my dilemma, "there's an old wood-
en boat on the bank, up the river a ways, seems like I remember seeing an
old Clackskanie roller on it. The boat's just been setting there for years; better take my chain saw. You might have to saw the whole stern off to get it."

We took the saw and headed off through the bushes and along the river
bank to a slough that was more of a boat graveyard: early plywood gillnetters slowly composting away; even a couple of old double ender sailboat
hulls with bushes growing up between the rotted planks. But just like he
had said, there was a plywood Bryant, one of the first built-just-for-the-
Bay power boats to arrive in 1952, with a set of hydraulic powered net
rollers. I grabbed the rubber ribbed roller, sure that the sand and the salt
had frozen it solid over the years. But, it rotated! There was hope!

Six hours later we were headed back to the fray with our 1958 rollers
attached to our 1978 boat with 1988 hydraulic hoses; thank you, Tom!

But then Egegik boats started to transfer to Ugashik. We would hear
them on the radio, calling their markets to make the transfers. Almost half
of the projected fish had already been caught at Egegik, and the fleet there
was still huge. On paper, Ugashik had 3 million fish headed its way and the
fleet was barely 200 boats.

Once again we agonized: stay or go? Every few hours we'd talk about it, but then Egegik would get another opening, we'd catch a few more fish and decide to stay. Finally, on the 9th of July, way after the traditional peak of the season, we had a slow opening with very few fish even on the North Line of the ebb so we figured it was time to make a move.

Only by cutting much of the stern off a beached and abandoned boat were we able to scavenge a set of old rollers and get back to work without missing a fishing period.

We were pretty sure Ugashik was the best bet—the poor guys who had transferred down there five days earlier hadn't had an opening while Egegik had had three. But now it seemed like it might be Ugashik's turn. If we were lucky, we'd transfer out of Egegik after the opening on the 9th, wait our 48 hours and then get in on an opening at Ugashik.

But then we started hearing rumors about the Kvichak—a large body of fish had been sighted and the fish count past the towers was rising, though there was a long ways to go before the Kvichak reached its escapement goal. There was even wild speculation about a possible opening there.

The Kvichak? I mean, this was the district that hadn't had an opening in three years, and for which the pre-season forecast was for getting 3 million fish less than their escapement goals.

But in the past, before I had even come to the Bay, the Kvichak had been a legendary place, the place with the biggest fishing.

I finally convinced Marvin and Chris that Ugashik was our best shot.

You can Monday morning quarterback all you want, but still on the 8th or 9th of July, it would have taken a brave soul to pick the Kvichak over Ugashik for the next action, at least with the information that we were able to glean over the radio.

At the net barge: make sure you have your nets in distinctive and well marked bags!

So on the evening of the 9th we steamed for Ugashik, but as usual, our guess was a little off—both Ugashik and Egegik got openings for 10th and we were confident that there would be another one on the 11th and we'd be legal and ready to get in on the big action.

Then as we were steaming for Ugashik, 5 hours down the coast, more news: Kvichak got a 12 hour opening, the first one in years! My heart sank; even if we wanted to go, it'd be another 48 hours before we could fish, and we'd be legal in Ugashik in 12—like it or not, the die was cast.

The guys hit the sack and I steered down the beach in a dirty sou'west chop, trying to convince myself that we'd made the right move. I knew that the clock was running—in a week or so Bristol Bay '89 would pretty much be history, and we still very much had to make a season.

Then, about halfway along that bleak and lonely shore, I passed a couple of boats headed the other way. What the hell???

It was a stab in the gut—what would make them leave Ugashik in the middle of a opening? Where were they going and what did they know that we didn't? A dozen ominous thoughts rushed through my head. What if we were running away from fish? It was the worst hour of my season.

After a while I could make out the loom of Cape Grieg, and we got in amongst the boats, everyone was picking fish so I felt a lot better about our move.

Our whole late season strategy hinged on getting in a couple of good openings at Ugashik before a bunch of boats transferred in. As we lay on the hook that night, things were looking good—a pretty small fleet and reports of good fishing.

But then the next morning, when we listened for the fishing announcements on the radio, there was nothing for Ugashik!! But . . . Kvichak got a 24 hour extension of fishing time, and the 48 transfer period was waived, but just for the Kvichak—all signs of a lot of fish there! We could take off right then, steam up there and start fishing as soon as we got there. Chris and Marvin were hot to go, but I convinced them to stay.

And the clock is running: the anchored fleet at Dago Creek, Ugashik. All are waiting for a radio announcement of a fishing opening that might salvage a season that seemed to be slipping away.

"I mean, listen," I counseled, me, barely in my third year in The Bay, "there's still supposed to be three million fish coming in." I held up the tattered and much studied pre-season forecast sheet like it was gospel.

"Suppose we transfer out of here right now, and Ugashik gets an opening tomorrow and it's hot, and we get up to the Kvichak and the party's over, or they close it. We'll have run away from making a season. Remember here last year, they opened it with just two hours notice.

Dago Creek, Saturday evening: no announcement for Ugashik, but another extension for the Kvichak. I was wild. I bummed some smokes off another boat. I never smoke, but I went out and sat on the deck bucket in the back cockpit, beating myself up.

Dago Creek, Sunday morning: "Ugashik fishermen should stand by at 9 p.m. for an update."

"Update, UPDATE? What the f--- did that mean?" It sounded ominous, and right after the announcement boats were calling in their transfers on the radio. Once again, we rationalized why we should stay, but it was torture.

The update turned out to be an announcement for a 12 hour fishing period for Monday noon, after all. It had better be good, we said—we had a lot of catch-up ball to play—it had been four days since our net had been in the water and now the clock was running even faster toward the end of the run and our season.

Our first set was terrible, the second even worse. My stomach was in knots, I was chewing Di-Gel, an antacid, like candy. Plus Marvin and I swapped off openings running the boat, and of course, it was my turn.

"You guys can come in for a bit if you want," I said after we'd gotten the last discouraging hundred feet of net aboard, "I'm just going to steam until I see something."

For two hours we ran around the district, looking at nets and guys picking just a little handful here and there, feeling intensely the sands of the '87 season reaching down toward the bottom of the hourglass, sure that we'd blown it with our rational "looks-good-on-paper" strategy.

Then finally on the edge of one of the bars, we saw a pretty good looking net and dumped ours in off his end. Hits, right off the bat, on both sides of the net! We went from depression to exhilaration with no stops in between. In three sets we salvaged our opening, but at the end of the period, it totally died.

By then we were convinced that something was out of whack—it just wasn't the kind of fishing you'd expect with a small fleet and a lot of fish headed in.

Plus, by then the Kvichak had been open steady for the last three days and the rumor mill was full of stories of big scores.

So as soon as we had unloaded and gassed up at the *Farwest Leader* at Cape Grieg, we threw off the lines and beat feet for the Kvichak, hoping just to keep our net wet for three or four days and salvage our season.

The current from the incoming 26' flood pushed us quickly up the shore: we'd unloaded at midnight and by 7:15 the next morning we had our net in the water off the Pedersen Point cannery in the mighty Kvichak.

And bang: hits right off the bat. Instantly we felt good about our decision. But then, in radio range of friends for the first time, we got the details out on what we'd missed out on: 1200 fish sets, 20,000 pound deliveries.

In the vastness of the mighty Kvichak. In still waters like this it is easy to tell when fish are hitting the net!

"You guys ought to think about coming over here for the flood," said a friend way over on the West Side, "it was pretty good here yesterday afternoon."

So like the gambler, going for the longest shots when his money gets low, we went for it, ran three hours. The Kvichak is so huge—from the west side the tender fleet down was hull down on the horizon.

All that for just four hundred fish.

The real killer was when we cruised into the *Alaska Eagle* that night to unload. A guy we knew was there, we'd seen his boat that morning off Pedersen Point next to us before we took off on our little wild goose chase. His boat looked pretty well sagged down; he must have 25,000 pounds on, a big, big load.

"Where'd you boys go, anyway?" Said he in an overly chummy but smug way, "we had a little handful on the flood."

That was pretty much the story of our '89 season—skim milk coming and going. The only thing that gave us any hope was the price. With the run coming in smaller than forecast, the price was climbing.

We kept fishing, figuring we'd go until Saturday and then haul the boat. But then Friday afternoon came with a 30-knot easterly, so we called it quits for the season and hauled out.

Then Saturday morning, when I was walking back from a really nice long shower at Lummi, feeling that even if it wasn't a big season, at least it was over, and that I would be getting back to my family, a guy called over from up on another hauled-out boat.

"Hey, get this," he said. "I just talked to some of the guys in my group. I guess they really loaded up last night; guess we should have stayed out."

It's agony up there, don't let anyone tell you different.

I mean, the Kvichak, who'd have figured it?

The next spring someone noticed a curious phenomena: beulga whales (pale white, 12-15 feet in length) hanging out around the mouth of the Kvichak River just about the time 20 or 30 million two to three inch salmon smolts were heading out into the ocean. This happened again the following spring, but that time with more belugas, and this was a cause for alarm. In that the Kvichak empties into Bristol Bay via several channels, it wasn't a stretch to imagine a half dozen hungry belugas eating enough of the outbound smolts to have a big impact on the run, just when the Kvichak seemed to be getting back on its feet and yielding significant salmon returning to the river again.

And if that occurred, there's wasn't a lot of legal options for the fishermen as belugas, like all marine mammals, are a protected species under the Marine Mammal Protection Act.

There was a lot of dark humor among fishermen about someone having to hire a chopper and shoot the belugas and the rest of the fleet having to chip in for his legal defense.

A similar though less consequential problem used to happen every summer at the outflow of Seattle's Lake Union/Lake Washington on the south side of the lockst. Steelhead returning to the lake milled around the entrance to the fish ladder up which they can swim into the lake system.

So did several California sea lions: a perfect arrangment for them: usually three or four big males—1500 pounds plus—just hanging out and chowing down. Again the issue was that the sea lions were protected, but fishery managers thought that they had a solution: capture the sea lions and take them far away, like the coast of Oregon. Less than two weeks later, the biggest one was back. How did they know it was the same sea lion? Because of the number they had spray painted on him!

Eventually the worst predators were captured and transferred to Sea World in Florida.

Fortunately, for whatever reason, back on the Kvichak, the belugas did not return in large enough numbers to threaten the run.

THE SECRET

By January of 1989 back in Maine, it was starting to look like the Casco Bay mussel bonanza might be coming to an end. Our original aquaculture program—moving small mussels dragged from inter-tidal beds to the deeper sub-tidal flats of our leased bottom didn't work out. Instead of the "three or four bushels for every one that we plant" as was advertised by a biologist, Carter Newell, who worked for the company that advised us and bought our mussels, we were lucky to get one back. Did the eider ducks eat the other three? We never knew. What we did know was that there were no more economically draggable mussels on or around our base and cabin on Vinalhaven Island and it appeared that ourselves and the other four boats that had the shallow bays and mussel flats of Casco Bay to fish for the last four years had basically cleaned them out. We'd been spoiled by four winters of load-your-boat dragging. Could the party really be over? There were hundreds of miles of shallow bays and winding shallow channels that looked like they might be good mussel bottom. The best way to cover all that territory was by outboard.

So off we went, my fishing partner, Mike Mesko, and I, exploring down these miles of winding channels lined with shuttered summer cottages, floats and boats pulled up on the shore and covered for the winter. It was cold traveling in an open 12' outboard; sometimes we'd be breaking glass-like skim ice in the morning and at the end of a day of exploring our hands would be so cold that we had difficulty putting the tie up lines around a dock cleat.

We'd find a few days of fishing here and there, but nothing like the big loads day after day for four winters in a row that had spoiled us. We squeaked through the winter but at the end it was obvious that for us to continue in the mussel fishery, we'd have to change our game substantially and go "Down East," or to the remote, eastern part of the Maine coast. Where there were few easy places to unload mussels directly to our truck as we had in South Freeport. Where we would have to put the mussels into 90 pound onion bags—the net bags that wholesale quantities of onions are shipped in—aboard the boat, run into some beach at high tide and throw them into the water. Where we'd have to come back in our four wheel drive truck when the tide dropped enough and pick up the 90 pound bags and load them into our truck to take them to our market. Stay in motels near where we were fishing, come home just on the weekends.

That was not appealing to either of us. For my partner, who already fished a hundred or so lobster traps out of a skiff, it was an easy decision to start buying more traps, with the goal of building up to a full string of 800 traps and using our mussel boat to fish with.

For myself, lobstering wasn't a option. I didn't live full time on the island as Michael did, and while there were no laws about who could or could not fish for lobsters, there was a effective practice which we called 'The Law of The Knife,' which basically meant that if you weren't from the island, don't try fishing there or your pots would be cut off by the locals.

Alaska had the legally more correct Limited Entry system to control the number of people fishing, Maine had the equally effective Law of The Knife.

After struggling to get gas from tenders year after year, I decided I needed to ramp up my search for a new boat with a diesel engine. Getting a new commercial fishing boat is more like building a house than going to a dealer and buying a new truck off the lot: most fishermen have pretty specific ideas what they want in a new boat and work closely with the boat builder to get those features. Plus the Bay was booming and most boat builders were booked at least a year in advance. There was one boat build-er, Bob Pleier, who had a small shop back in the woods near Mt, Rainier, who produced two or three hulls a year. My friend Patrick Murphy had a Pleier hull that we really liked. But we thought if we could convince Bob Pleier to make the hull a foot higher all around, and raised the floor of the cabin a foot we would get a bigger cabin and an all around better boat.

I'd been in the fishing business some 14 years by then. I'd started with a piece of shit wooden boat, made enough money king crabbing to buy a nice used fiberglass gillnetter/troller, moved on to Maine and 70' seventy-year-old woodie that needed a new engine room. Next was a 37 foot glass mussel dragger, again used. Then in The Bay I'd started off with a once-state-of--the-art-but-now-tired aluminum boat.

So the idea of a brand new boat was more than exciting, it was totally thrilling!

When we'd finally committed to it, we rented out our house in Maine, and moved to a small waterfront rental in Poulsbo, WA, so that I could participate in the construction of our new boat.

It also looked like the State of Alaska was going to lift or modify the 32 foot limit in Bristol Bay to accommodate fishermen who needed slightly bigger boats so as to also be able to more effectively seine for herring in the spring at nearby Togiak Bay. It wasn't clear if the new limit would be 33' or 34', but in any case it seemed that larger boats were on the horizon.

So instead of building a 32 footer, I'd decided to build a 33. I mean, what the hell, it's only 3 percent longer than a 32. Did those extra few inches really give me a competitive advantage? No way, Jose. It wasn't a big deal, there were plenty of long boats in the Bay. In fact most of the really big new aluminum boats built in the last few years had those "bolt on" bows that taken off, made the boats legal at 32' but most guys just left on. Besides, my buddies in the know had assured me that the state had okayed those bows as long as they didn't provide additional flotation.

Of course, at the same time, I knew that there were a lot of guys who didn't like to see those big boats coming and that if they ever had their way with the Board of Fish that sets the rules for such things, all those bows would be in the locker for salmon season and bolted back on for herring. And I knew that I didn't want to be running around with a big flat spot instead of a nice pointy bow. So we built it long with a nice bow instead of bolt-on job. I figured if they cracked down, they'd just go after the guys with the bolt ons, and not worry about small potatoes like me. Right?

So the 33' hull got built and the builder, Bob Pleier, trucked it from his shop up in the woods near Mt. Rainier up to the Petrzelka brothers' shop in Mt. Vernon, WA, where the interior, engine, etc would be installed. Bob just used his old '57 Chevy Apache half ton pickup to tow that big boat and trailer, but he'd rigged an extra radiator, bolted to the frame behind the cab for a little extra cooling capacity for going over the passes between his shop and Mt. Vernon.

Ugly enough? Fishermen wanting to fish spring herring in nearby Togiak would build 34 footers with removeable bows so as to be legal for Bristol Bay salmon season. The last thing I wanted on my brand new boat was an ugly flat spot where the nice pointy bow was supposed to be.

Another Pleier hull, a conventional 32 footer with the lower sides was already at the brothers' shop. Having the two hulls side by side at the shop gave me a chance to feel good about my decision. The whole cabin was bigger, the foc's'le was bigger, and there was noticeably more fish picking room on the back deck.

One night that winter when I was reading to our 11 year old, Matthew, the phone rang.

"Hey, did'ya hear the news?"

It was a friend, another Bay fisherman.

"No, what news?"

"The Board of Fish. They decided to enforce the 32 foot limit."

"What d'ya mean?"

"Well, it was kind of a surprise they way they sneaked it in. A lot of guys figured there was half a chance they were going to throw out the size lim-it altogether. Then they changed their minds and put in this thing about strictly enforcing 32 feet."

I got that sharp pain in my stomach when I know that I've screwed up bad. "So what's the bottom line you think?"

"Ahhh, I wouldn't worry about it. Grant and Menish and those guys that are building 35 footers say you shouldn't sweat it. They're hiring a law-yer; they might get the whole thing thrown out. But I think you made the right decision about not having a removable bow. If this reg sticks those'll be the first to go. "

After I hung up, Mary Lou turned to me, "What was that all about?"

"Ah," I tried to soft pedal it, "the Board of Fish decided to enforce the 32 foot limit. But it's no big deal; it'll probably get throw out in court."

"See," said she, "I knew you'd get in trouble if you built a long boat." This was a sore point between us; I'd already had a brush with the fish cops and she thought I shouldn't take a chance with an over length boat.

"I'm not in trouble. Anyway, the boat doesn't look long. It's just that boats that look long that they're after. I mean there must be a hundred ACMs (American Commercial Marine fiberglass gillnetters) that have been up there for years, and they're all 10 inches too long. They're sure as hell not going to make all those guys cut their bows off, right?"

Pretty soon, each time I came back from the boat shop Mary Lou would ask me the same question:

"Did you tell anyone?"

"Hey," I'd always tell her, "it's no big deal; the state's not after guys like me that are just a little bit long, they're after the jumbos, you know, the guys that really push it. Hey, there's some thirty five footers out there! I mean, that's really pushing it.

Right?

I became evasive with my friends. I started to stretch the truth.

"Hey Joe," I'd run into an acquaintance around town, "Too bad about the Board of Fish decision: what a pain to have to whack your bow off."

"Naw," I'd say guilelessly, "I got cold feet about building a long boat, good thing, too."

Then the rumors started: the state was hiring a bunch of college kids to measure every boat; the state was calling builders to see who had built over-length boats.

I began to have trouble sleeping.

Still, I rationalized, no one knew that the boat was long, and it didn't look long, so I was probably OK.

And it was all tempered by the simple joy of seeing the boat come together. Petrzelka Brothers let me work on the boat along with them. One of the challenges was the design of the back deck right behind the deck house, specifically the placement of the 6' diameter 20" wide gill-net reel. The use of the reel to store, set and retrieve nets from was a big change from sailboat days. Of course in those days there were no reels as there was no engines to power them. And when engines were allowed in 1956, the so called power rollers were developed to take advantage of it: a mechanically operated roller on the stern of the boat. The roller had cleats on it so that when the power was engaged, it pulled the net, fish and all, out of the water and into the stern of the boat. There the fishermen would pick the fish out, casting the net forward, ready to be set out again.

However, almost all the other salmon gill-net fisheries in Alaska and Washington State used reels, usually wide ones with cores maybe 8" in diameter. So when gillnetters from other areas came to The Bay, it was natural for them to put reels on their boats as that was what they were used to. But it quickly became apparent that in the take no prisoners style of Bristol Bay gill-netting, reels had to be adapted to set the net sometimes at full speed, as well as being able to retrieve it quickly. So big cored narrow reels quickly gained popularity. A narrow reel didn't take up much deck space, allowing for more fish holds. (A big day for a gillnetter in Southeast Alaska might be 5 or 6,000 pounds. A big day for a Bristol Bay boat would be filling the boat, often over 25,000 pounds.) The big core meant that when you started reeling the net back in, it came in much faster than the traditional small core reels. Additionally we wanted to put in an engine room access hatch with a ladder down to the engine so you could check the oil and the fuel filters without having to pull up the floorboards in the cabin. Plus there had to be a well underneath the reel to allow it to sit lower in the boat, but the well couldn't be so deep that it impeded access to the top of the engine. And the whole thing had to be designed to be able to be removed in one piece in case it was necessary to remove the engine. Luckily I was working with Bob Anderson, a cracker jack mechanic as well as a good friend, and he came up with excellent design ideas.

Then one day, a total stranger, a Bay fishermen I'd never even seen before, tire kicking Bay boats at the shop, came over to where I was working.

"Say," sez this guy, "what'ya going to do about that extra foot?"

YAAA, it was like a stab in the chest. After that I looked at the bow again and again. Then I remembered—when I'd started the boat project, I told most people who had asked that she was a 33; back then it had seemed that it wouldn't be a problem.

All ready to head north on the big barge: son Matt and our new boat just before she was hoisted up to the top of the shipping containers. With Bristol Bay some 2,000 miles by water from Seattle, most fishermen send their boats north by barge.

"Hey, they went through this whole thing 10 years ago when MARCO figured the 32 foot limit was going to be thrown out and shipped up those 34 footers. Now all of a sudden everyone's trying to push the rule again and the State's clamping down. It's just the same thing all over again." This from John VanAmerogan who'd worked at MARCO (Marine Construction and Design—a major Seattle builder of large and small fish boats) during the early '80s when Pete Schmidt made such an impact in the fishery with the 34 foot prototypes and then the barge load of 32 footers he sent up to the Bay.

I'd had another friend who'd ordered one of the first 34 footers. Keeping his bow on hadn't been easy—he knew the fish cops were looking for him, so he kept changing the name of the boat. He threw the carpet over the bow each time he came into the cannery, and even then had to be sure to always tie up next to big 32 footers, so his length wouldn't be obvious.

It began to seem that having a long boat was going to be a big hassle. Maybe my wife was right. Why did I build an over limit boat? Why didn't I have the builder flatten the nose when it was in his shop? The questions tortured me. I'd been hugely excited to build a new boat, but now all I could think about was why didn't I make it shorter.

I couldn't believe I had this big beautiful boat built then whacked off the bow!

Then I started getting this recurring nightmare: I had a big load aboard and was headed to the tender, over the hump of a big season at last with my new boat. Then from out of nowhere the fish cops show up. "Skipper," they'd call out again and again in my nightmare, "Skipper, you're fishing an illegal vessel!" They'd take my fish, and make me shorten the boat before I could fish again. But that wasn't all. I'd get to town and there would be no welders who could help me on short notice; I'd miss three openings before I could get shortened and out again.

It was a terrible dream and I had it every night.

The rumors got worse: the fish cops were meeting each barge (Bristol Bay was almost 2,500 miles by water from Seattle, so most new boats were shipped up on the top of three layers of full shipping containers on big barges) and measuring all the boats, whether they looked long or not.

Finally Bob Anderson and I went up to the boat shop to talk to John Petrzelka about possibly cutting off the bow. On the way up we stopped at All Points Marine in Marysville where three giant Bay boats 17 feet plus wide by 35 feet long, were being built. The bows were detachable and on the ground when we got there. The flat spot was 8 feet wide at the deck and extended all the way down to the waterline, it was unbelievably ugly. It made me feel a lot better about possibly cutting a foot off of mine.

Still, when we went to the boat and started laying out how big a flat spot it would mean, it was just too depressing. Cutting up my beautiful new boat, the first brand new boat I'd had in 20 years of fishing was too much to take. Bob and I went over to a nearby truck stop to have a bite and hash it all over again. I was bummed.

"How about cutting off six inches and calling it good?" Bob suggested.

"What d'ya mean?"

"Well," he reasoned, "if the cops see a boat with the bow already flattened, they'd naturally figure that no one'd be dumb to cut it off and not get it right."

Right?

I grasped at the idea, at anything to avoid the big flat spot that cutting off the full foot would mean. But then, like a toothache, the gnawing fear kept coming back.

We went back and measured some more.

Then we looked carefully at the stern. Our transom, like many Bay boats, was not only raked aft, but partially rounded as well. We hung a plumb bob, began drawing curves to see how much we could gain by cutting out a piece, flattening it, and welding it back in again. Our cockpit deck also formed the top of the water tank, so we decided to limit our possible work to the area above the waterline.

Our measurements showed us that by flattening a wide U-shaped area, we could gain another three or four inches. It wouldn't be easy—the transom was made of two different plates at different angles. It would also mean moving the power roller.

It would be a tricky job, but if it came to it, it could probably be done on the beach between openings with a saber saw and enough blades and a drill. In theory at least.

I figured what the hell, they don't give you a speeding ticket for going 68 in a 65, do they?

So we cut nine inches off the bow and called it good. I mean we were just three inches over; we'd made a good faith attempt to be legal, plus the cops would see that we'd cut it off. No one would know.

This time I didn't tell anyone. Only the welder and a few of the guys at the shop who had walked us through the various options knew we were still a little long. I even got enough stainless flathead screws and aluminum flat stock so that if we got caught at the peak of the season, we could beach out, cut it out with a saber saw, and cob it back together with the pieces I had brought. It wouldn't be pretty, but it was something we could do between openings. If we had to.

And hell, it was only three inches. Who'd make a big deal over that?

We launched the boat at the end of March, in time to go for a family cruise up to the San Juans for the kids' school spring vacation.

For a single shining week, the new boat had the bare feet of children and the sound of happy voices across her cold metal decks. She got filled with happy family memories before she ever got put on the barge north, like as not, never to return. It was great—the kids loved the double deck bunks in the fo'c's'le, it was hot and dusty every day, and I got plenty of practice explaining the nose job to yachters.

"Ah," I'd say, ever so casually, "the State of Alaska changed the rules to 32' after we built a 33, so I had to whack off a foot. But I'd probably do it again like this even if I had known. That extra foot makes a big difference, and the hell, the bow doesn't look that bad.

The nightmares slowly went away.

The Togiak boys went up for herring and came back after their short season, bringing stories of fish cops using plumb bobs to measure new boats, but they didn't bother me much any more.

Until I heard a story from a friend at one of the canneries. One of the fishermen there worked winters at the Petrzelka shop. When the talk around the table got to long boats, he told them how he'd cut the bow off one, but that it was still three inches long. Thing was he'd left the shop to get north before the name went on, so he didn't know which boat it was.

I tried to be calm, but felt like my blood pressure went up and down with the ebb and flow of the various rumors floating down from Dillingham and Naknek.

In the middle of May, our son, Matthew, and I took our boat from the mooring off our rented cabin in Poulsbo up the Duwamish River to the Northland Barge. I felt a bit better about our bow when I saw a couple of brand new Kvichak 34s looking pretty nasty with two feet whacked off.

But the first thing I noticed when I got up to Naknek to finish up the last items on the new boat and get ready to start the season was staging and tarps up over the bows of a whole bunch of boats, including all of the ACMs. The ones that had been around for years, the ones I was sure that the fish cops would never require to be shortened.

In the end, crackerjack welder Ed Thompson did a careful "stern job."

In fact guys were cutting and grinding even if they were an inch over; paranoia was running high. And the rumors were flying again: "If they catch you with a long boat, they'll fine you the value of all the fish you caught that season." "Even if it's just an inch, you're still long."

The fish cops, naturally, were milking it for all that they could, sowing paranoia wherever they went—getting back at the boats that made it so hard for them to enforce the district boundaries.

The question that the fish cops were asking folks was how much would it cost to be out of the water at the fourth of July, the peak of the season, trying frantically to shorten your boat. It was a great strategy—people were asking to be measured, just so they wouldn't have to face any hassle during the season. Fiberglass workers and aluminum welders were getting flown in from Seattle!

I talked the delicate situation over with friends, and finally figured that once we got launched and away from the raging rumor mill, everything would be OK

Then a few days before we were to go into the water, we had a visitor, a guy who owned another Bob Pleier boat, a 32 footer. What was weird was that I didn't really know the guy, certainly not enough for him to get a ride all the way from his cannery to talk to me.

He asked me what I was going to do about the 32' limit.

I told him we were legal.

On their way out, he and the guys he was with spent what seemed like a lot of time studying the way my bow looked.

After they left, I turned to my crew, "You guys get any weird vibes from those guys?"

They looked at each other, finally Jake Magel said, "Hey Joe, you're getting pretty paranoid about this. Let's just get the boat in the water and get the hell out of town."

The next day when I was looking for some net light batteries at the Leader Creek boatyard, a short walk down the hill, two fish cops showed up at Lummi, our boatyard. There were couple of hundred boats jammed into the dusty yard but they went right into the office to ask where we were, went to the boat and started doing their thing with the plumb bobs and measuring tapes.

While they were working, a friend stopped by to ask them how they picked out boats to measure.

"Ah," one of the fish cops answered, "usually Dick (Richard Dykema, the boss fish cop) drives around the yards and makes a list of boats that look long, but this one's different." He waved an arm up at our bow, "We got an anonymous phone call about this one."

I came back just as they were packing up their stuff.

"You're three inches too long," the taller of the fish cops said, looking down at his list. He paused, looking at me again, "You're that writer guy, aren't you?"

I nodded and he went on.

"It was weird, there was this pencil line, drawn right on the bow at 32 feet. But then you cut it off three inches too long. What happened?"

But in the end it all turned out fine: by flattening the stern 3" we became legal without having a really ugly "nosejob!" This is a typical unloading scene: a bag of salmon—about 1,000 pounds—being hoisted out—Note that our bowline goes to a boom rigged off the tender with a tire as a shock absorber. Also note: the brailer is made of fabric, much less bruising to the fish than the earlier net brailers.

I sighed, "Any more than nine inches off would have made it look really rotten."

"Yeah, but now you'll have to cut it all off anyway."

"Naw," I said, "I think I'll whack off the stern this time. I'm done sawing on that bow."

He looked at me as if I were nuts.

But in the end, it didn't come out too bad. Of course it was more work than I figured. I spent a whole day measuring and marking, wanting it to look good, if such a thing were possible. Ed Thompson of Frontier welding, who'd done work on the *Joe H* made time in his busy schedule for us and spent a lot of time making sure that the transom wouldn't get wrinkled in the flattening and welding process.

I slept better, relieved that we were legal, but pissed that someone had stooped so low to put the cops on us.

When it was all done, some guys from around the boatyard came to look at the job. We were the only boat in the whole fleet of some 1800 boats in the Bay that had both the bow and the stern cut off. But of all the cutoff boats, we had the best looking bow.

"Still think you could have done it on the beach between openings?" One of the guys asked.

I shrugged, "Anything's possible if you're hungry enough."

Once the fishing started myself and everyone else forgot about the whole 32-foot issue.

And when the season was over and I was back in Washington State again, I showed some photos to a friend who raced sailboats, another activity with a lot of rules about length etc.

"This is terrific," he said excitedly, "you whacked off the bow and the stern, but without affecting performance a bit. God, it's the ultimate rule beater. All Bristol Bay boats would be like this if guys had any brains."

MR. BIG HELPS US OUT

A big moment for Bay fishermen is actually getting into the water. For the week or so of getting boats and nets ready before you actually launch, the crews in the big boatyards are living and cooking aboard their boats, climbing up a ladder to get aboard, climbing back down to use the bathrooms in the boatyard, tracking sand and dirt back into the boat's cabin. Of course the cannery guys were all enjoying their nice rooms at night and meals and mug ups in the mess hall.

Launching is a relief, as finally you can sweep out all that sand and dirt and have the boat really clean for the first time. And for a lot of us independent fishermen, once we are aboard our boats, we don't step a foot on shore until the season is over four or five weeks later and we haul out.

This is my bell, ringing: the exquisite pleasure of getting up while the guys were asleep, scribbling in my journal and having a quiet moment before the day started. This pix was before the season really started: once the fish came, such moments would be rare.

For me with a new boat launching was especially sweet. We had a couple of days of just laying at anchor with probably 600 other boats in the Naknek River, waiting for fishing to open. There was a couple of hours of net work to be done each day but I let my guys sleep as late as they wanted.

So for those couple of days I had the exquisite pleasure of getting up early, making a pot of coffee, and just sitting at our teak trimmed galley table, and just enjoying all that Petrzelka Brothers, Bob Plier, Bob Anderson and I had created, before the rush of the season that I knew was coming very soon. The *Katie Anne*, named for our daughter, was probably the only brand new boat I would ever own and I wanted to savor it.

1 a.m., June 21, a Naknek River beach, black, windy, with spits of rain:

"Crews, man your vessels." The scene could have been at a forward tor-
pedo base in WW II. The tide was coming up and 30 beached gillnetters,
caught by a surprise 7 a.m. Egegik opening, waited to float. A blow was
making up outside the river mouth and rain gear clad crews, silhouetted
by deck lights, tied things down for a rough passage. The rising tide in
the river started to slap on aluminum transoms, the shallowest draft boats
started to lift. Engines started up and down the line.

One by one, boats backed off the gravel beach and were quickly swirled
away by the current, lost in the cloud-thick black and the rain of the short,
high latitude night.

As we picked our way out of the river, our radar screen (radar . . . the
new boat had radar!) was an air traffic controller's nightmare: totally full of
targets. Running lights would appear out of the fog, change course quickly
as they saw us, and as quickly disappear.

The Egegik bound boats not only had each other to contend with running down the Naknek River in the black, but also with 350 or 400 anchored Naknek-Kvichak boats, 20 or 30 big anchored tenders, net barges,
plus the usual high tide cross river traffic between canneries. And all this
in a narrow river channel with the tide boiling in at five or six knots to a
26-foot-high flood.

But if there were ever a night to have a brand new boat under you, it
was that one. The wind gathered strength. The current, running against
it in the shallow waters, pushed up a steep short sea. Two boats, bucking
across the Bay from Dillingham, had already lost pilothouse windows. In
our old Shore boat, we would have been throttling back for the big ones
and bailing water inside the cabin from all the window leaks.

Instead that night, my crew, David Murphy and Jake Magel, slept, the
autopilot steered, and I got to sit back and just watch the radar and all the
little gauges and digital displays that these new rigs seem to come with.

Then, in the first mean light of day, we arrived off the mouth of the
Egegik River. The channel in is a winding trough between breaking sand
bars, neither charted or buoyed, different each year. For a long time we
jogged back and forth around the 32595 line, looking for a place where the
seas seemed to be breaking a little less. Of the fleet we'd departed Naknek
with the night before, there was only a couple of running lights, like us
searching for the channel.

It was one of those times you sort of wished you were in another profession. Where you could wake up in your own bed, slip downstairs without waking your family, have a coffee with the birds singing and the light just starting to steal over the land.

Instead of heaving up and down in a confused sea off some lonely river mouth. Trying to pick your way between breaking sand bars in a howling wind blowing all the way down from the Siberian steppes.

And if you only see the awesome power and drama once that is the Bay, it should be on such a morning. Riding those big gray hills into the Egegik River in the wind and the fog. Watching boats ahead and behind surfing downhill and out of sight in a welter of foam and spray. And finally staring ahead in awe as a city of light appears out of the swirling gray, bobbing and swinging ponderously in the swell: the support fleet of tenders, floaters, barges, and assorted small craft.

If getting into the river was difficult, getting out two hours later after we'd unloaded our extra nets to the barge and wolfed down some breakfast, was even worse. You'd think you were in the channel when all of a sudden your depth-finder would go from 12 feet to 5, and your bow drop so quickly you'd be sure you'd hit bottom, and all you could see ahead was a big wall of water. The kind of morning you could get in a real jam, just on your way out of the river.

Like Larry Reed, at Ugashik, a year earlier. Following the channel into the river in with a big westerly behind him in an ebbing tide, his bow hit the sand, his Shore boat swung around and broached, and the next sea filled it, just like that. A passing boat came by and Larry and his crew scrambled off the bow just as their boat tumbled away in the surf, a good season turned into disaster in less than a minute.

So our season started. Down on the south line at Egegik, in a 10-foot swell with maybe a 2-foot chop on top. A year earlier, in almost similar conditions, we'd had almost 800 fish there.

1990 was different. Jake started throwing up, we had four fish on the first set, our fancy scrambler equipped radio didn't work, and I was soaked inside my rain gear in the first ten minutes on the flying bridge. Only after we'd quit early and run into the river with barely a thousand pounds—before the minus-four tide made the channel into solid breakers—did I figure out that our radio wasn't busted. The other guys in our group were so sick and disgusted they didn't answer.

All of a sudden Bay '90 wasn't looking so hot. A thousand pounds at

South Egegik with a sou'west gale pushing whatever was out there up the beach was an ominous sign. There was more—during the winter the Board of Fish had redrawn the Egegik district boundaries, pulling in the outside and south lines, reducing the side of the already crowded district by 17 percent.

I hadn't thought it would be that bad, until I realized that 17 percent was all deep, fishable water, and at low tide the outside line was now right along the edge of the sand bars.

Sure, I'd headed out before with the last of my money spent on the fuel in the tank and the grub in the galley. But when you build a new boat with no old boat to sell, you get into a whole new dimension of debt. We unloaded our sad two half-bags of fish and motored over the bars to the anchorage in the upper river, my spirits about as low as the clouds that pressed down low over the water.

But I could always rely on my crew to keep my spirits up. As we ran, David called over to Jake: "Hey, Jake, I keep having this really bad nightmare."

"You mean like you were flunking statistics; that bad?"

"No," David replied, "it was terrible—I dreamt you took all season just to pick one fish."

The next morning the guys in our group were talking strategy on our 'secret' radio channel while we waited for the next opening. "I'm beginning to get a bad feeling about this river." was the general gist of the conversation.

Secure communications were always a challenge to fishermen. In the days when fishermen were limited to just a few radio channels on the old a.m. radios we used to pay technicians to create special crystals that we could plug into the radios to give us our own channels. Then everyone was required to switch to VHF radios, where it was almost impossible to create your own "secret" frequency. So then we started using something called a 2 meter radio, giving us many hundreds of frequencies to choose from. However many boats also had frequency scanner receivers, so even using a two meter radio, you couldn't be sure that no one was listening in, so we would use code sheets, a little awkward up on the flying bridge with the wind and the flying spray: "This is Yank over in green 12, got a pineapple on that last one."

The full communications package for a totally dialed Bristol Bay boat would include a single sideband (for talking between rivers and further), CB radio (nicknamed the Mickey Mouse), two meter, VHF, and scanner. That might mean four different microphones hanging down from the pilothouse ceiling. As they say: "He with the most radios wins."

Fishing was so slow that some of us (David and Jake here) would actually take a nap while the net was in the water, pretty much impossible once the fish struck.

The anchored fleet around us was at 730 boats, the kind of numbers you used to see only around the first week of July, the peak of the run, but it was still only June 22. A lot of them I didn't recognize, strangers come to cash in on Egegik's track record of steady big catches.

The new moon coincided with the summer solstice, making for some huge tides, including a minus seven (!!!) at Ugashik. Each evening as the sand laden current scratched audibly at our hull, and the prop turned with the engine off, we'd listen to disconnected, odd-sounding voices on the sideband: the False Pass boys, 600 miles to the west. Their gloomy reports did little for our spirits as usually what they caught was a reliable indication of what was headed our way.

Each morning, when the guys were still asleep, I'd get up early and start going over my finances again: how much we owed and how much we had to catch. Again and again I'd go over the pre-season forecast sheet. We'd been so used to runs that routinely came in 25% over that 1990's slim forecast hadn't been a concern. But now I began to think about what kind of winter work I might be able to line up if the forecast was right.

Then on June 25 came an odd bit of news: the Port Moller test boat suddenly was reporting very high catches: "Based on the Port Moller test indices, a run of 32 million fish is headed to The Bay." That, after our fourth day of waiting for an opening, really made us sit up and listen: 32 was a third more than the 25 million forecast.

And it got better: the next day they bumped it up to 42 million, and I wondered if I shouldn't get on the radio and order more nets; the waiting was obviously the calm before the storm.

Most of the bigger processors had a big barge anchored in the Egegik River to store fishermen's nets. Also on the barge were two steel 40' containers of supplies—non perishable groceries, etc for the tenders to sell to fishermen. One of the containers also had some very basic housing for the barge crew. The net barge had to be crewed around the clock as fishermen might stop by in the middle of the night for a new bag of net. The 900' gill net that we used actually consisted of three 50 fathom (300': a fathom is 6 feet) "shackles' connected together by quick release clips on the cork line and lead line. Although we tried to patch the bigger rips and tears regularly, by the time you'd picked 50 or 60 thousand pounds out it was usually time to replace the three shackles. Plus one shackle might become especially beat up if another boat got tangled in it, etc, so if necessary, you could just replace that one shackle. Usually we like to have at least nine shackles or three complete nets to get through the season.

A barge could have as many 800 or 900 (some boats would just leave their extra nets at the cannery) heavy bags of netting (typically a shackle of gear with net and 300' of cork line and lead line would weigh about 100 pounds.) The trick was to have your **gear well marked** so you could just call on the radio and tell the guys on the barge that you wanted the yellow and green striped bag marked, "Katie Anne 2." Then before you got to the barge you would have rolled off the bad shackle into a bag you had on board, so as to be ready to have the new shackle lowered to you, and the old shackle hoisted off.

But if you hadn't marked your bags well enough for the barge crew to easily find, then you would have to climb up onto the barge yourself, and try to pick through almost a thousand heavy bags to find yours! Most guys put all their extra nets into the stern of their boat before they get launched, and delivered them personally to the net barge, so if they couldn't find them when they needed them, it can be an ugly scene as it possibly means that somehow through carelessness, someone . . . else . . . got . . . your . . . nets . . .!!

My Maine neighbor and ex-mussel fishing partner, Mike Mesko, was crewing on another Bristol Bay boat, the *Chris R* operated by Jim Smith. They fished for Icicle, and one day they went over to the Icicle barge to get a couple of extra shackles of gear. After an exhaustive search by themselves and the guys who ran the barge, they still couldn't find the nets and things were beginning to get heated.

Then their other crew member tapped Jim on the shoulder and pointed to the big sign on one of the 40 foot steel storage containers: Peter Pan Seafoods—they were looking on the wrong barge! They excused themselves without revealing their error and quickly left.

I soon found out that the more experienced fishermen didn't put too much faith in the test boat numbers:

"Look out at that river fer chrissake. If there were 40 million fish headed this way, it'd be full of jumpers . . . I fished this place for 25 years and we never had a big year that this river wasn't full of fish on the 25th. Something has to be whacko."

We hadn't seen a jumper since we arrived.

The test boat had another huge catch and the biologists upped the numbers again: 59 million fish, the biggest run in history was headed our way—if you believed it—but there still wasn't a fish to be seen in the river.

On the 29th, we and 739 other boats had a 12 hour opening. We had four hundred plus on our mop-up first set, and then almost every single boat migrated to the outside lines. In a normal year the chaotic line fishery would develop on the north line on the ebb and on the south line on the flood. But now the entire outside line was one continuous line battle just three hours after the start of the opening.

And we're not talking your usual relaxed, early part of the season line fishery, we're talking intense four and five clicks over boat battles just to stay open a minute or two.

An integral part of the fishing process in The Bay is running your net. Here's how it works: you set your net with a hook in either end, so that fish, running along the net to get around it will gill themselves in the unexpected curve of the hook. Then after you set, perhaps towed on the end to get the hook just right you wait a few minutes and then run at full speed parallel to your net, maybe 15 feet off. Usually by this time a number of salmon, headed to their spawning grounds up the river have come to your net, can faintly see it (ideally your net color matches the color of the water) and are just basically trying to figure out what to do. Running the net scares them and they quickly gill themselves, and splash and struggle to get free. It can be very dramatic, as in a big set your cork line will suddenly come alive with hundreds of fish! After running the net, you might wait, off to one end, watching your net for hits—individual salmon hitting the net—and then run it again.

But on this particular day, with the wind and high seas, four hours into the opening, as I was running the net, a cresting sea pushed us over the cork line, and just like that: "Clunk, clunk, clunk," our propeller scooped it up, stopping us dead. Usually net in the wheel (propeller) would be a total bummer leaving you with the choice of either trying to grind it out, with the possibility of frying your transmission, or missing the rest of the opening.

But, on the new boat we'd installed a six inch removable access hatch right over the propeller with a long vinyl tube-like boot attached to it to allow you to work on the prop and keep the water out. We just unscrewed the hatch, rolled up the boot and could look right down to see the prop and whatever was wrapped around it. A couple of swipes with the knife, splice the net back together and we were good to go!

Of course having a six inch hole through the bottom of your boat carries its own risks. On one of the earlier openings a big new aluminum gillnetter had net in the wheel, and the skipper opened the hatch up to clear it out. When he got done, he yelled to his crew to close and secure the hatch, and climbed up the flying bridge to find another set. A little later she started to settle by the stern, and after they opened the engine room hatch to see water already flooding over the reverse gear, they headed for the beach. Luckily they made the sand before it sank. At first the skipper thought that his stuffing box had come loose, but then when the tide went out, the problem was obvious—the six inch hatch had vibrated loose while they were running.

When we got up past the bar and into calmer water at last, I looked around glumly at a couple of the biggest Russians, still waiting to unload, sagged way down with fish. When you see a rig like the monster 16-wide

Transformer way down in the water with her load, you know she has to be pushing 25, maybe even 30,000 pounds: we'd missed 'em.

We slid past the handsome power scow *Muskrat*, with a boat on either side and a dozen trailing off the stern and dropped the hook in by the beach. It was just 3 a.m.

The Egegik River was home to a native village and a cannery, sleepy in the winter with about 50 residents. But in the summer, it was transformed with the arrival of several hundred cannery workers and fishermen.

It seemed to me like there were two separate fleets at Egegik. Fishing the outer river, participating in the chaotic but often lucrative line fishery were the bigger newer aluminum boats, operated mostly by the independents like myself.

Then there was the upriver fishery, mostly Egegik cannery boats: older, more glass, even a few old "woodies" as the fishery was much less confrontational.

Usually we unloaded our catch either onto a tender on the outside, or among the tenders and processors anchored in a big fleet, sort of in the middle of the river mouth, but downriver from the bars that kept deep draft vessels like most tenders from the upper river. One particularly nasty opening I decided to try the upper river to see if I might find a tender where it might be calm enough to unload without having to worry about one of the guys getting injured or a cleat ripped right off the deck of our brand new boat.

We crossed the bar, only bumping once and found a tender with a cash sign, with a side open (Bristol Bay tenders are usually rigged to buy fish on both sides at once) and slid in, amazed at how calm it was out of the ocean swell and without cowboys blasting by full bore a boat length away. We had maybe 16,000 pounds aboard—not a big day but a good one. But as we were unloading our 16 bags, two of the local boats, with 4 or 5 bags each, unloaded and left. Then another boat tied up on the other side to sell, and its skipper came right over where I was writing down the weights as they were called out.

"What did'ja do, fish all night?" This in a bit of an angry voice. At first I didn't get it; it had been a 12 hour opening starting at 4 a.m. And then another guy spoke up from the boat that had been waiting behind us as we unloaded also annoyed.

"Jesus, that's 14 bags and they're still coming. You had to have been fishing all night."

Then I looked around at the other local Egegik boats waiting to un-load—none looked to have more than 5-6,000 pounds aboard. Then I got it: these guys mostly fished inside the river. In that opening the high boat would have had maybe 8,000 pounds. They didn't fish on the outside where the heavy fishing was, nor did they have a good view of the tenders on the other side of the bar and how many bags they were buying from most boats. So they naturally assumed that we were lawbreakers. We got our money and left; I had the sense that it could have gotten ugly if we needed groceries or fuel.

Much of the fleet that fished the upper Egegik River were old plywood Bryants, not suited for the rough and tumble fishing tactics in the lower River.

The next day after dark another big new Russian roared by, the *Kazbek*, a humbling sight. In our shiny new 13-wide Baycraft, I'd put in a Lugger 440 HP diesel, the modest attempt at speed that our budget could afford. I was satisfied with a honest 12 knots at fishing weight, and I had friends who'd spent twice what I had for maybe four more knots.

But to see that big Russian roar by in the black, all lit up, the guys work-ing on the back deck, and clipping along at 25 knots, the whole hull on top of the water and planing easily through the two-foot chop was to be awed at the dimension of their achievement.

While we were waiting to unload a friend jogged by. "Guess we blew it," he yelled, "the Naknek boys are killing 'em." I reached for the Tums.

I hate to transfer. My timing is always rotten. When I transferred in the past, the river I left got hot and the river I went to died. Plus Naknek-Kvichak was a huge district, hard to fish without a code group or a spotter plane, and my group was staying in Egegik.

But the Egegik fleet had jumped up to over 800 boats, there was hardly any water at low tide, and the fish hadn't shown up. What haunted me was this: what if the Port Moller test boat was right, what if, against all odds, it was going to be one of those legendary Kvichak years: the two and three thousand fish sets, the 30,000 pound days.

And so, with the deepest doubts, I called in our transfer to the Kvichak.

Naturally they got an opening while I was waiting out the 48 hours. We anchored way up the river, so we wouldn't have to watch as boat after boat, their names on the transom almost underwater they had so many fish, came in to unload.

But finally we got an opening. And it was big; the old timers were right about fish pouring in when the Kvichak run came in. And they kept coming, day after big day. ADF&G left it open straight through from July 1st, when were legal, to the 19th, except for 12 or 24 hours here and there: finally we had made the right move! And when they did close it, we needed the rest, as we'd been going straight for three or four days.

When you start unloading twice a day, those fish tickets start to add up.

But easy it wasn't. Often it was the smaller Nankek district that was open, and the Johnson Hill line, where the fish crossed into the district on the flood, was just a frantic churning mass of boats. A good set was just getting your net back in one piece without getting into a mess with someone else's boat or net. Along the beach, early in the tide, the nets would just be 30 or 40 feet apart, and then someone would hang up on the bottom and all the others would collapse around it in the sweeping current.

Or, you'd just get it out, a few fish would hit, and someone else would lace you, cork for cork, and the fish coming through would gill in both nets. Or other boats would drift over your net in the chop and the wind. And each screw up meant lost fishing time.

Now and then the Kvichak would open for a single 12 hour period and the fleet would spread out, way out. The Kvichak District is huge, and as opposed to the Naknek, which has sand bars only along the beaches, has bars like Deadman Sands, way out in the middle, far from shore, changing position every year.

Once in the short black part of the night when we were picking a set, we suddenly fetched up on a sand bar and quickly lay over on our side. The current quickly created a wave that reached almost to the top of our bulwarks. Fortunately our net trailed away down tide, without wrapping us, and there were no other boats above us to smack into us in the current.

But, to have stopped so suddenly and to see the power of the tide, pushing that wave against the boat, was sobering. Luckily the tide was flooding and after a bit, it carried us bumping and scraping over the bar and into deeper water.

In the middle of a particularly bruising flood on July 4th, a friend radioed me: "Hey Joe, get over here." When he called me, he used the latest and greatest in secure communications technology: pushing a button on his radio that displayed his position on the screen on my flying bridge radio, without having to give away his position verbally. I chased his numbers down and found him way off to one side, far from the action. In the failing light I couldn't see if there were any fish in his net or not.

Then my friend picked up a plastic battery powered loud hailer, bagged in plastic against the weather—and screeched at me: "Just set off my bow; there's a ton of fish here."

I did and barely had the meshes hit the water before they were filled with splashing struggling red salmon, the whole net alive from end to end. What a rush!

It was almost 2,000 fish, over 12,000 pounds, our biggest set of the season. By the time we got the fish out, it was 2 a.m. and we ran into the beach across the line and dropped the anchor to get a little rest, figuring we'd have plenty to time to unload in the morning: things were looking way up.

"Hey Joe," this voice kept saying in my nightmare that night, "Hey Joe, pick me up? If you've got fish on still, you better get over to the tender Lafayette (our market) is plugged."

I woke in a sweat, glad it was just a bad dream. I stumbled, blinking from the darkened fo'c's'le up into the bright day lit cabin and looked outside. Something was weird. We'd anchored just a quarter mile outside the south line; the tide was flooding, there should be hundreds of boats there battling it out.

But no one was fishing, every single boat was anchored up.

Then the voice came again, but on the radio, not my head: "Hey Joe, you guys better get up and get over to the tender if you don't want to get stuck with those fish, almost all the markets are plugged. If you can't get rid of those fish you'll have to dump em!"

Yaaaaa! The nightmare was true: our market was plugged.

I picked up the anchor, started steaming and yelled to the guys to get suited up to unload. On the way over to the tender, I didn't see a single boat fishing; it looked like all the markets were plugged.

A big day; good weather and plenty of fish: Joel Ludwig's Blue Sky *and Mark Perovitch's* Entrepreneur *at Egegik. Two or three big days with full loads can go a long ways towards making your season.*

But at least our tender could take our fish. But they were real vague about when they'd be buying again: "No one is telling us much. Listen to the company frequency tonight; maybe there'll be some news then." And they looked a little gun shy, like you might look after having to tell every single one of your fishermen to try and find another market for a day or two.

By then it was pretty clear that the Port Moller test boat got it right: we were in the middle of a giant run. Processors were struggling to keep up: air freighting in cardboard for freezer boxes and pallet after pallet of cans.

But as you can't build a church to seat a crowd that only comes on Christmas or Easter, processors can't afford to have capacity that is only used in a rare huge run.

It was a bitter experience to have spent so much on the new boat, always thinking about how to avoid breakdowns and losing fishing time, only to have our market fail us.

A day later our market started buying again, but put us "on limit," of 15,000 pounds a day. Half the other markets were still struggling to work through the ten or fifteen million pounds of fish still in all the tenders, so a lot the fleet was still anchored up.

I could tell it was going to be another big day; we got our 15,000 pounds by 11 in the morning and the flood was still to come. We unloaded, but were still pumped by the easy picking; we knew we could load the boat if we had a market. I called around to a couple of floaters—small independent processors that I had met over the years. Two guys said they "might be able to take a few fish."

"I think we've got market," I told my crew, "I'm not sure how much they'll take. There's always a chance we'll get stuck with the fish. what do you think?"

"Go for it!"

So we did. With a brand new boat, I needed a big season.

The fishing was great, the best we ever had: uncrowded. UNCROWDED! Lots of fish, set after set. By four, we'd proudly loaded our fine new boat, filled every brailer bag, probably 27,000 pounds. Our little *Katie Anne* had that great feeling fishing boats have when they get a big load: moving ponderously through the water, responding much slower to the controls. Finally, the fishermen's dream: putting the name in the water! It was like musseling days over again, but instead of loading your boat at 10 cents a pound, it was a buck ten. Big difference!

I called the markets that said they could buy our fish. Someone else had gotten there first, at every single one. "Maybe in a couple of days," was the best that they could offer. But we without refrigeration we had to get unloaded today.

Then, over the radio we began to hear bad stories, really bad stories. Like the setnetters who had to dump 20,000 pounds plus of reds because their market was plugged. As we lay there off the mouth of the river, while I talked on the radio trying to find a buyer, a few dead fish drifted by in the current: not a good sign.

I knew this guy, Chuck Bundrant who owned Trident Seafoods, one of the bigger processors operating in the Bay. We'd become friends over the years so I thought maybe he could take my fish. I stopped by one of his tenders in the river, just anchored with a full load aboard, explained that Chuck was my friend.

In trouble: us, on our way to a full load, hoping that we could find a place to sell them. Did we? Stay tuned . . .

"Hey, Joe, I'd really like to take your fish, but we got the word yesterday to not take anyone but our regular boats."

"Is Chuck around? Maybe I could talk to him on the radio. What channel does he stand by on?"

"He won't talk about that on the radio. There's too many other boats wanting to do the same thing. If he's going to help you, he'll have to do it on the sly." He nodded over at the old Farwest Seafoods, now Trident cannery on the North Side of the river. "I think he's there today; that's his cannery now."

So we went over and tied up alongside a tender unloading a full load and I climbed the long slimy ladder up to the dock. As soon as I reached the top, I could tell that things were cooking: beeping forklifts shuttling back and forth, steam pouring out of the long building with all the canning machines. The cannery, like all the other canneries around the Bay was running around the clock trying to keep up with the giant and unexpected run. Chuck's wife, Diane, was manning the phone outside his office and looked a bit frazzled; big runs tend to do that. We chatted for a moment, and then she said, "He's off the phone." and I went in to Chuck's office with its big windows overlooking all the activity in the river.

Just when we thought we were totally screwed, an old friend, Chuck Bundrant, took pity on us and bought our fish. And just like that we became Trident fishermen for the rest of my career.

Chuck was one of those guys like me who'd started his career by walking up and down the docks looking for a crew job. But then he hit it big king crabbing, built the first king crab catcher-processor, and rode the Alaska fisheries boom. But in his heart, he was still a fisherman.

"Chuck," I said after we'd small talked, "I need a favor, a big one." I suspected he'd seen us talking to his tender out in the river, and coming over to the cannery dock, obviously deep in the water with our load. And he also knew I had just built a brand new boat.

"I know." He interrupted me, "I saw you come over here. You got greedy, didn't you?" But before I could answer, he picked up one of his business cards off his desk, scribbled something on the back and hand-ed it to me. He nodded out toward the river. "Take this over to the *Sea Lion* and give it to the skipper, Matt Chester. But here's the deal: you're a Trident fisherman from here on. Are we clear? And this is between us. I've had calls from 50 guys today looking for market and I've turned them down. "Then the phone rang and the radio called for him so we shook on it and I left.

On the back of the card he had written: "Matt: please take Joe's fish. Don't call me on the radio about this. I'll explain later."

Back on the dock I felt exhilarated. Hugely relieved that we wouldn't have to dump $35,000 worth of fish. But more: salmon canneries had al-ways had a special place in my life. My first Alaska job had been engineer on a tender for the Annette Island Packing Company cannery when I was 19; ten years later I'd run a tender for Whitney Fidalgo Seafoods, my wife and I had run a big tender for Icicle Seafoods, our son had been aboard a cannery tender before he was even born.

To me there was something special and powerful being part of a salmon cannery operation. It was like the cannery was the beating heart of Alaska, whole little towns unto themselves out in the wilderness. Way back in gill-netting days back in Southeast Alaska in the '70s, I knew a couple of young brothers whose dad owned a cannery, Petersburg Processors. They lived there, they had cannery mechanics who could work on their boats; I used to have dreams about having a dad who owned a cannery. I'd bumped into Chuck at some Seattle fish function after I'd heard about him buying the Naknek cannery "Hey, Chuck, I heard you bought a cannery. I'm jealous." he'd looked at me as if I'd had too much to drink.

But when we pulled up to the *Sea Lion*, I could see the skipper looking down at us and flipping though some stapled together sheets of paper.

"Outta here, guy" he called out, "we're only taking our regular boats and you're not on the list." He waved to his crew to throw our tie up lines off.

"Hey, wait a minute," I yelled up to him, "I want to talk to you."

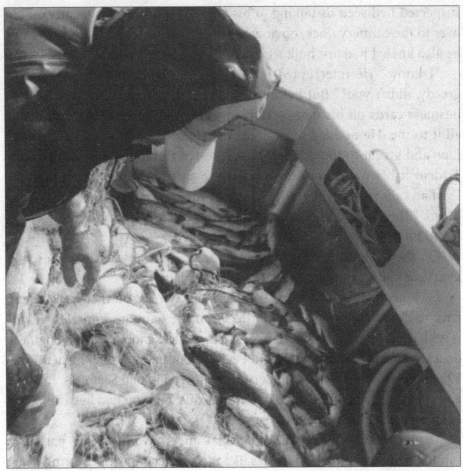

Drifting toward the line with the fish cops headed our way, we frantically pulled the last 300' of net and fish into the stern.

"I'm the wrong guy to talk to," he called back, "look at those guys." He waved at a heavily laden boat pulling away from the other side of the tender. "He had 15,000 pounds on and he had tears in his eyes when I told him we couldn't take his fish."

Other boats were starting to come up behind us. His crew was starting to take our lines off their cleats. And Chuck had told me to keep our little arrangement quiet.

I jumped aboard before they could untie us, pulled out Chuck's business card and gave it to the skipper.

"Huh," he said, turning it over in his hands, "where'd you get this?"

"Up at the cannery," I nodded over across the river, "just now."

"OK, boys," he yelled down to his crew, "we're taking him."

And just like that, our butt was saved and we became Trident fishermen.

For ourselves, the peak moment of our season came on the 14th of July, when traditionally many boats would be calling it quits and hauling their boats out of the water. Instead a huge push of fish came into the Kvichak and the Johnson Hill line got smoking hot.

The fish were literally POURING in. It was crowded and all the nets in front looked like they were smoking from all the fish hitting them.

But the amazing part was this: usually when the flooding current stops the fish stop coming until the current turns to flood again at the end of the ebb. But on the 14th, the fish kept coming even after the current had turned to ebb. But of course the problem was that unlike at the Egegik north line where the current from the ebbing tide carried you into legal waters, the Naknek ebb pushed you into closed waters. The big cop boat *Vigilant* was anchored outside the line and the fish cops were somewhere close in their skiff, so you had to be careful.

Finally we wiggled just half a shackle out (150') and almost immediately we started ebbing over the line into ticket country, so we power rolled it back aboard with about 200 fish, still flipping and fighting in the thin netting. As we picked, I looked over and saw the fish cop skiff ticketing guys who had drifted over. And still the fish pushed into the district against the current.

After a bit we found another spot, and got two (600') of our three shackles out in a long curving hook. The fish started hitting heavy immediately, but of course the current was taking us toward the line, so I started towing the net to keep it legal. It took me a few minutes of towing and looking at my Loran to realize that with all the fish in the net, I couldn't tow hard enough to keep us legal without ripping the net in half. By then we were starting to go over.

"Roll it, ROLL IT!!" I climbed down into the cockpit yelling to the guys, jammed the roller into gear and we started pulling net and fish over the roller. "PULL, GODDAMMIT, PULL!"

Sixty yards away, the fish cops were just climbing back aboard their skiff after writing some poor guy up. One of the cops looked over at us and nudged his partner. Then they started the motor and started coming our way. I throttled way up to get all the speed we could out of the hydraulic system, and kept yelling, "WE GOTTA GET THE F------ THING IN!"

With the three of us back there pulling with all we had, the fish started flying over the roller. Astern of us the net was all smoking white water—the fish were still hitting hard, and we still had a half shackle to go. The cops got closer; they were definitely coming for us. Some of the fish were flipping free of the net as they came over the roller, flying forward and hitting the back of the cabin.

Headed in to the tenders after midnight in clear weather. (Remember: at that time of year the sky never gets really black unless it's clouded over.)

Then the cops stopped their skiff and just lay there for a long moment, 20 or 30 yards off our stern, just watching the drama of it all: the corks smoking with the heavy hits, the panic on our faces, the net, a solid rope of fish a foot and a half in diameter coming aboard with meshes ripping and fish flying. And then, they motored off the other way, toward some boats that were a little further over the line and hadn't even started to pick yet.

The last of the net came aboard and we collapsed back onto the pile of fish and net that almost filled up the entire stern of the boat.

From then until we left five days later, it was about the only action there was—the evening flood at the Johnson Hill line. It was the modern Bay in every respect—a no holds barred, no quarter asked, take no prisoners business. Your turn was over when your end buoy hit the water, and if you couldn't take the heat you'd better get out of the kitchen.

After a stormy start to the season, the weather had turned cloudless, even hot; we'd be picking fish with sunglasses at 11 at night.

The tides were building and the current ran hard. When the cops weren't there, the fleet quickly leapfrogged out, almost to the anchored tenders, starting their sets a good half mile over the line. But even then, the current was running so fast that unless they set at almost full speed, angling sharply into the current, they'd be back in district waters before they even got the whole net out .

This wasn't your usual Bay fare of 12 on and 12 off or 12 on and 24 off. This was wide-open, round-the-clock, seven-days-a-week fishing. A rare event. So each day we'd fish until dark, close to midnight. Run over to the tenders to unload, and drop the anchor just as the baked salmon hit the table. Savor a big hot meal, and the sight of that huge fleet, coming back from the tenders to anchor all around us, like birds to roost.

Then at first light just a few hours later, with engines starting up and anchors rattling aboard all around us, I'd make a coffee and instant oatmeal, get my sweats and rain pants on, and climb up to the flying bridge. My crew would get up and we'd head out. Put Rain-X on our sunglasses. And get ready to do it all over again.

STRIKE!

A HUGE SIDE BENEFIT TO FISHING FOR Trident was being able to use the facilities of their Diamond NN cannery in South Naknek, across the river from Naknek, When I tied up there in 1992, it had been in continuous operation—though first as a saltery—for over a hundred years since 1890, when a big square rigger dropped the anchor in the river and sent a crew ashore to start driving pilings for the first three buildings. By the time I arrived, it had grown to a mini industrial complex with over 30 buildings, a three line cannery, a freezer plant, bunkhouses, warehouses, staff houses, helicopter landing platform, air strip, warehouses, and most importantly, the mess hall. With big meals at 7, 12, and 5, and almost equally large mug ups at 10, 3, and 9 in the evening, it was basically the center of cannery life, and the cook's was usually considered the most important job in the cannery.

In decades past, places like the NN often had separate mess halls for Chinese or perhaps Filipino workers, who had their own cooks preparing ethnic foods. Now at the NN it was one happy family, except for a smaller dining room for the superintendent, engineers, accountants, etc.

Graves, South Naknek, with Russian Orthodox style crosses. The Spanish Flu took a terrible toll in Alaska's remote native villages.

Before we had access to the cannery and its great mess hall through Trident, our Bristol Bay friends were largely guys who came up from the Petersburg area of Southeast Alaska, guys I had fished around in the 1970s, usually with 200 or 300 thousand dollars in debt for their boat and license, hungry aggressive fishermen. But at the mess hall I'd find myself and my crew sitting next to a wide range of folks who for the most part had been part of the salmon world up there for most of their lives. There were Slavs and Croats from Puget Sound, Italians from San Diego, and Scandinavians from Astoria, Oregon, on the Columbia River, another place where there had been a huge sail and oar powered fleet before small internal combustion engines became available. And a lot of natives; both from the nearby villages of North and South Naknek and up and down the rivers that fed into The Bay. But also from more distant villages and settlements: along the Bering Sea coast and on the main stem and many tributaries of the big Yukon and Kuskokwim Rivers further north.

The natives were generally a quiet bunch, but when on occasion I'd be next to one at mealtime or mug-up, I'd try to draw them out a bit, and I was always taken by the different worlds that we inhabited. After fishing I joined my family at our island cabin on the Maine coast and then when the kids' school started, to the wealthy bedroom community of Bainbridge Island, a crowded ferry ride across Puget Sound from Seattle.

For the natives often after the Bristol Bay season was over, they'd go to fish camp: a couple of tents set up on the shore of a good salmon stream, where they would catch and dry salmon into leather-like planks, to help get them through the winter. They were only a generation or two removed from a time when a family's survival in the bitter winters was a function of how good a hunter the man was. And when a winter was particularly hard and the caribou or seals or whales scarce, it wasn't unknown for grandma to walk off alone into the darkness of a winter night to die so not be a burden on her family.

More recently the cash economy had come to the villages, especially with the Alaska Native Claims Settlement Act in 1971, Limited Entry, and better salmon prices. But still, almost all the native settlements and villages dotted across the vast landscape of Western Alaska were isolated, not connected by road to anywhere. In the summer they could receive supplies by tug and barge, brought over twenty five hundred miles up from Seattle. But after the rivers froze in the fall, supplies had to come in by bush plane:

very expensive. And so the old ways of hunting and gathering were very much a part of their lives: salmon they'd smoked or caribou they'd shot was cheaper, healthier, and more dependable than food flown by expensive bush plane.

Summer Camp: painting by Ken Lisburn. After the Bristol Bay season, many of the native fishermen returned to their remote villages and a very traditional life style.

And it was these villages, especially the ones along the lakes and rivers that fed into Bristol Bay that were very instrumental in keeping the runs from being decimated in the first half of the 20th century. By the early 1920s it became clear that Bristol Bay salmon were being over harvested. One of the consequences of that was that the river and lake native communities that depended on the salmon that had to make it past all the nets suffered genuine hardship. These fish were a good part of their winter food as well as food for their dog teams which were also a critical part of their lives—allowing them to hunt and trap over a wide enough area to sustain themselves. These hardships were one of the reasons that the sophisticated river management schemes—measuring the upriver escapement to dictate fishing times—came into being.

These same native villages and settlements had also just been devastated by the Spanish Flu Epidemic of 1918-19. Whole villages disappeared, canneries had to set up orphanages for the children left behind, and one older native told me every single adult in his father's village had been killed by the flu, and that dogs had eaten their bodies after he and the rest of the orphaned children were taken away.

In more modern times, the money made available by rising salmon prices and bigger runs had a darker side. A friend was a cannery superintendent whose cannery had housing for the natives that brought their families with them to the cannery each season.

"It broke my heart," he told me. "I'd see these beautiful children playing around the cannery when they were young. Then they'd be teenagers, huffing aerosols, gasoline, anything they could get their hands on."

It didn't help that until 1987, fish buyers and processors—including myself on two different vessels—gave away free booze to their fishermen as an incentive to sell to them. This became a real problem when herring fishing spread to some very remote native villages where alcohol was banned. Finally the Alaska Alcohol Control Board sent letters to all processors and canneries, reminding them that giving away booze, even to adults was actually illegal, and would be prosecuted. After that the practice died out pretty quickly.

Being around the Diamond NN taught me something else, something unexpected: humility.

Running around up on the flying bridge in these big diesel boats, it's easy to think you're tough, that you're really something. On the occasional days at Naknek when we weren't fishing, we'd tie up at the Diamond NN and I'd walk out to the west, past the native settlement of South Naknek and its 45 residents and the Russian Orthodox crosses in the little graveyard, then the busy Bumble Bee cannery, and finally two more, the abandoned Diamond M and Diamond O, now just rusty sheet metal covered buildings and lines of pilings.

And boats: a history of the earlier Bay. Dozens of the old double-ended sailboats, side by side, put to pasture together in '53 or '54, when big freighters like the Alaska Steamship Company's *Tanana* and others would arrive with 20 or 30 of the newest powered 32 footers stacked on deck.

The monkey boats—essentially little tugs—that towed the sailboats out in the morning and back in the evenings if there was no wind. Now skeletons with grass growing up between their planks.

Laland Daniels chopping applewood chips for his smoker aboard his tender Balaena. Rarely would we come in to deliver our fish without leaving with a bit of fresh smoked salmon.

Humbling to see what the old guys fished in.

And the conversions: old wood double-ended sailboat hulls upgraded with now rusted engines, some with the steel cabins bolted to the bow to provide at least a bit of shelter and a place to steer from.

Finally the first "modern boats"—early planked wood hull and plywood cabin Bryants and Commercial Marines, now 40 years old and abandoned as yet better, aluminum and fiberglass boats showed up to replace them.

But the one that humbled me the most was right there on the dock at the old Diamond NN—in those years the largest cannery in the whole state. Trident's carpentry gang had taken the best of the old sailboat hulls, stored inside all these years and restored it, complete with the heavy canvas sails, the Diamond NN logo on both sides of the boat and two sets of those heavy 14' oars.

Hard not to look at that and be humbled. We knew what the weather was like out there; lots of time even our beefy diesel boats seemed small. But the thought of working the 14' oars against the wind and the seas, of trying to reef the stiff stiff canvas when a squall came up made us realize that we were hardly the tough ones up there.

Another great benefit to fishing for Trident was Laland Daniels and the *Balaena*. A friend from earlier days when we were each running different tenders in Southeast Alaska, he had upgraded from the 80' classy but single deck *Christian* to one of the biggest power scows, the 110' *Balaena*. It was the perfect Bristol Bay tender. Wide and flat bottomed she could settle at low tide onto the mud bottom in front of the cannery. With her big fish tanks on deck, she could open the chutes and the fish would slide easily into the the fish elevators between the pilings. On her stern there were two rooms specifically for fishermen: a bathroom complete with shower and washer and dryer (!!!) and a one room mini-store with shelves for groceries and a big chest freezer. And let me repeat that first part—dedicated shower, washer and dryer. Plus, delivering to the cannery every few days, she could also fill up with water while she unloaded (some tenders delivered to the floating processors, where fresh water was a bit scarcer) and be able to offer it to fishermen, whose fresh water tanks were generally small.

Laland's arrangement with Trident was a daily charter fee plus poundage—so many cents for each pound that he bought. So although in any river there were usually several tenders buying fish for Trident, and at the end of a fishing period, most guys just wanted to get unloaded, washed down, and get dinner on the table, Laland had a loyal following of boats that didn't mind waiting. Sometimes you'd see another Trident tender with both sides open, ready to buy fish, and there would be the *Balaena* with four or five boats waiting on each side!

Laland was a big friendly guy, eager to help and full of stories. He would always have a smoker going, and when you delivered to him there would be a little bag of home baked cookies, maybe a chunk of great smoked fish, or even, a couple of times a season a fresh baked apple pie! Have a mechanical problem? He'd send over his engineer. Medical issue? Talk to one of the gals.

Life is good: David, Jake and I make a big delivery to the Balaena *and get rewarded with an apple pie hot from the oven!*

He was close with our old friend Ethel Hamar, a Haida native whom loved apples but who had never seen them on a tree. So one year when he was running his fish all the way down to Bellingham, Washington, from Tree Point, Alaska, 50 hours steaming each way, he invited Ethel along, said he knew where there were some apple trees.

In Bellingham, there was only enough time to unload, fuel up and head north again. But he showed Ethel where to go: across the Burlington

Northern RR tracks, through a hole in a fence, and down the road a piece. So off she went and made it back just in time with a canvas sack full of nice Granny Smiths.

Plus he had installed a soft serve ice cream machine on his stern, so when you got close enough, you could send a crewman forward to bring back soft serve for the rest of the gang. It took the sting out of a long wait to unload.

But he saved the best for his good friends, his special boats, and due to our long friendship, we made the cut. After a particularly challenging opening in very wet, chilly, and windy conditions, we were greeted with, "I just changed the water in the hot tub. You boys are welcome to give it a try."

"Hot tub?" Did I miss the memo?

So, towels in hand, the three of us climbed down into the engine room, past the big twin Caterpillar diesels, the noisy GM generators, and then down the long alley between the hull and the row of big timbers and posts that supported the deck mounted fish holds. Way up to the bow, almost under the anchor winch where Laland and his sons had installed a space with a big shower and a changing area with a bench and hooks for clothes! And a door that led to a totally magic experience: a salt water hot tub with room for four, almost like this little fiberglass cocoon. The magic part was this: because it was salt water—filtered, so it was clear, not muddy—you were buoyant. And since the *Balaena* was rolling in the long swell, when we entered the water we slowly sloshed back and forth! We just soaked and laughed, floated back and forth and let the cares and worries of a harsh season slowly evaporate.

1990 was one of those amazing years in the red salmon business. Even with the huge run, the market was very strong and buyers were continually raising the price during the season. There was one cash buyer with a big illuminated reader board sign on his stern showing the price he was paying. Each day he'd be up a nickel over the day before, and we'd say to ourselves, "That's another six or seven grand," as we knew that our market would most likely match what the cash buyers were paying.

But it was even better than that: it was the winter of multiple price adjustments. Typically the big processors will pay a "grounds price" with the understanding that depending on the market in Japan (the majority of Bristol Bay salmon were frozen and shipped to Japan) there would be an additional payment usually after New Years. I'd only been fishing the Bay five years, and each year there had been a price adjustment, usually in the 15 or 20 cents per delivered pound range. For A 150,000 pound season, that was a very nice check. And in the winter after the 1990 season, there were several such welcome checks!

The principal owner of Trident Seafoods, Chuck Bundrant, worked hard to get the best price for Trident and its fishermen. Most years he would fly over to Japan after the season was over, park himself in some hotel and just start negotiating and selling salmon. He must have had some good juju that year for we got three separate big price adjustments: very exciting, especially since I had headed up to Alaska that June in a new boat with a ton of debt and a lot of anxiety.

"Was I doing better than I should?" For me, with boat and license payments, and a new house to build, I was just keeping my head above water, and mighty glad that my wife had a good teaching job with health benefits. On the other hand, my crew, who worked for me five weeks in the summer, and basically skiied all winter, the answer might be yes . . .

Chuck also worked hard to cultivate good relationships with his fishermen. Usually at some point during the winter several Bristol Bay friends and myself would meet Chuck for lunch and talk over the market and the Bay forecast for the upcoming season.

When we got together that winter, something came up that prevented him from coming, but he sent Bart Eaton in his place. Bart had been a successful king crab fishermen with his big house aft crabber *Amatuli*, eventually becoming one of the partners, along with Kari Ness and Mike Jacobsen, that came together to create Trident Seafoods. Bart was vice-president, spending a lot of time shuttling between Trident's various plants putting out fires. His message to us wasn't what we were expecting.

"Did you ever feel you were doing maybe a little better than you should?" He said, alluding to the particularly high prices we'd been paid the past season. Our own production had been good, but nothing like the big numbers some of the more experienced fishermen in our group put up. Several had caught 250,000 plus pounds, which with price adjustments and all was edging up toward a half a million dollar season, not bad for three guys in a 32 footer fishing for a month.

"There's a feeling among the Japanese fish buyers that they overpaid for salmon last year. It's just rumor now, but you put it all together and it looks like the price next season (1991) could be a lot lower than last year."

He wouldn't commit to a price other than it might be low and we went away from the meeting sobered. But most of my Bristol Bay friends, like myself were pretty busy with our families and our young children, and just figured that if the price was down, the volume would probably be up so that it would all work out.

I had just purchased a nice property by this sweet little harbor, Port Madison, on Bainbridge Island, Washington, and was in the process of clearing the land and designing a house to build starting after the 1991 season, so I was extra busy that winter.

Then in the spring, the phone rang with the rumor: we'd be lucky to get fifty cents. And the only way around it would be to strike. Fifty cents?? I was stunned. Bart had suggested we better get ready to tighten our belts, but not in my darkest nightmare had I even imagined such a low price.

And the strike word. I knew that a lot of the old time Bristol Bay fishermen were union guys—longshoremen from the docks of San Diego with the union attitude of "You gotta show them who's boss."

But Bristol Bay was a short intense fishery once it got going; at the four or five day peak of the run around July 4th, it was easy to have a single day mean 10 or 15 percent of your whole season. The salmon business was like farming: you had a window to harvest your crop, and once the window closed, you were done for the season.

Most of my Bristol Bay friends had been through a strike year and the collective conclusion from that experience was that the price bump you **might** get from striking never made up for the fish that you didn't catch while you were on strike.

Usually when I head up to The Bay on the 10th of June (our daughter's birthday was on the 9th) between what I owed to Seattle Ship Supply for nets, etc, Trident for boat insurance and airplane tickets for my crew and I, and my master card, the first 20 or 25,000 bucks that I made went right to paying all those bills. Having the low price and the looming possibility of a strike, made me even more anxious.

It didn't help that strike was on everyone's lips and minds around Naknek when we got there. I just wanted to get the boat ready, loaded with nets, launched so that we could stay away from the controversy. But when a big rally was announced for the big open space between Naknek Marine Center ("Lummi") and Leader Creek Marina, I felt we should go.

Spartan when compared to the canneries' comfortable facilities, Leader Creek and Lummi had no heated mess halls, no bunk houses with cable TV, or phones in the rooms. Little more than dirt boat parking lots with a gear store, showers, and laundry, they were a recent innovation in the remote bay where the canneries had traditionally taken care of fishermen's needs.

Yet in a sense, the key to any Bristol Bay strike lies in the actions of the 400 or 500 independent fishermen who keep their boats there and at a similar yard, PAF in Dillingham.

It is there that many new fishermen put their boats when they came to the Bay along with the change from canned to frozen processing in the late 1970s and early 1980s. Less dependent on processors for their logistical and financial needs, most of these fishermen are truly independent, less bound to any one market than other Bay fishermen.

Cannery fishermen who have fished, eaten, and worked together for decades are more apt to be united in their political action than the independents, men who often barely know the names of the men in the other boats around them.

During the Bristol Bay strike of 1991, it was natural then, that these two facilities became the place for the biggest meetings and rallies.

We stuck around for the rally, which seemed more designed to get fishermen wound up about what a raw deal they were getting from the processors than serious discussions of possible ways forward. As soon as it was over we headed 5 hours west to the relative peace of the Egegik River, where the strike had a grassroots beginning on the 18th or 19th of June when setnet fishermen, disgusted by the 45 cents offered by one processor, joined with village driftnetters to sit out the next fishing period.

Egegik was the site of a cannery and a small native village built on one side of the river mouth and a tiny settlement, Coffee Point, on the other.

For fishermen like myself and others seeking the quiet of an anchorage off the cannery at Egegik, the news of a strike was a bolt from the blue, an unwelcome addition to a season that already promised the lowest salmon price in a decade.

Pat Murphy, right, and crew, in 1995. In his earlier years as a setnetter, flying his own fish off the beach in a twin-engined DC-3 fish freighter, he had been right in the thick of it in the last strike year.

"I tied up at the cannery to go up and make a phone call," the skipper of another gillnetter told me. "They were all having some sort of meeting on the dock and one of the guys came over to me. 'We're not fishing for no god damned 45 cents! Are ya with us or not?' A couple of his big buddies came over to hear what I had to say.'

"'I don't know a thing about it,' I told 'em, 'I just work on one of the tenders.' I made my call and got the hell out of there. Strikes can get ugly.'"

Patrick Murphy, the skipper on the boat rafted up next to us put a yoga tape in his Walkman to try and mellow out as soon as he heard the strike news.

"I hate strikes," he said as he adjusted the volume. We watched as a setnetter put a shotgun in his skiff and headed across the river. "Lookit that. Now you tell me what a setnetter's going to do with a shotgun if not make trouble.

STRIKE! Basically the entire Egegik upriver fleet, all loyal cannery fishermen, beached or tied up their boats, striking against the low prices offered by the canneries.

"I was setnetting and buying fish in the last strike year, 1979, and I was paying more than the strikers were asking for, and they came over to my beach and hassled me for fishing. My setnet neighbor was an ex state cop. 'You go talk to them, Patrick,' he said, and then he ran up into the bushes with his rifle.

"I hate guns. I went down to the beach and told those guys I was going to load up my DC-3 with rocks and when I dumped it on them there wouldn't be anything left. They probably thought I was joking until another pissed off setnetter buzzed their shack with his 185 so close he clipped off a couple of antennas with his wheels."

June 21, the first opening of the emergency order period came cloudless and fair. Of the several hundred drift-net and setnet fishermen from Egegik village, perhaps fewer than 30 boats fished; it was a remarkable show of solidarity.

If it were only the Egegik fleet fishing on the Egegik River their boycott would have been a stunning success. But the lower anchorages at Coffee Point and the South Spit were a forest of masts before the opening, as Dillingham and Naknek fishermen, mostly independents like ourselves, were prepared to fish. Some hadn't even heard about the strike. Others had already resolved to not miss a single fish in 1991—no matter who struck; they had bitter memories of strike years when you never make up for the fishing you miss.

The fleet was reported as fewer than 200 boats, much less than the five or 600 that would have been there, had there been no strike. But it was a poor omen for the success of a Bay wide strike—if that many boats would fish on the 21st of June—so early in the season that no one really expected to catch much, how many would decide to fish when the reds really started to run.

Back in Naknek a day later, I spoke with Chuck Bundrant, president of Trident Seafoods. Bundrant's operation had come to symbolize the "new" Bay. Starting as an independent cash buyer in 1979 with a small floating processor, Trident had become the largest fish buyer in Bristol Bay, with over 300 boats delivering in 1991.

Frequently the price of frozen sockeye rises over the course of the winter and cash strapped processors who have to sell their pack early miss the higher prices of late winter and early spring. In 1990, however, the reverse occurred and Trident and other holders of frozen sockeye took a bath in the spring when they had to unload heavy inventories right before the beginning of the new season.

That evening Bundrant was sympathetic with the fleet's frustration, but uneasy about committing to a price. The Port Moller test fishery which had been the only indicator of the monster run the year before, was again showing a very large run headed in.

The problem, Bundrant said, was that their Japanese customers simply weren't committing themselves to any price. Furthermore, the wholesale price for frozen reds at the big Tokyo fish market had suddenly taken a dive, apparently because a joint Soviet-Japanese high seas fishery on Siberian sockeyes had unexpectedly produced almost 30,000 tons, more than four times what the market had been anticipating.

While we talked, Bart Eaton, Trident's number two man, also an ex-crabfisherman, left to attend a meeting between fishermen and processors. He returned a few minutes later, shaking his head.

"There were about 40 people there, including this state senator. He walked right in and said, 'OK, we've got about 700 boats in favor of a strike, so we're going to blockade the river and the docks.' When he started saying that, I got up; that was no place for me."

Earlier in the day, fishermen at many of the Naknek canneries had polled themselves as to the price they would agree to fish for. Bundrant and Eaton choppered over to their South Naknek cannery to try and find a way out of the impasse. They found a full rec hall waiting for them.

Bundrant cautioned fishermen about Japan-bashing, noting that they'd still be looking at 30-40 cents a pound from the domestic can market if the Japanese hadn't started buying frozen reds in big volumes. He then shared a fax from a Trident representative in Tokyo:

"Survey of a dozen contacts indicates that as there is no need for the fish, their anxiety is more for the poor quality that will result if there is a strike and production is accelerated and quality suffers."

The hottest issue at the meeting was whether to trust Bundrant and fish on an open ticket. (An open ticket just shows the pounds and species delivered without a price) Many assumed that although Trident hadn't set a price, it would only be 50 cents.

"I can't make my boat payment on fifty cents; I can just squeeze by on seventy five," one fishermen said, "What else can I do but strike?"

Some were more philosophical. "We fish herring on an open ticket, why not salmon?" Said one fishermen involved in several other fisheries.

Bundrant's response was that as soon as he put a price on a ticket, it would quickly become the final price the Japanese would pay, negating the over-the-winter price adjustments that prior to '89 and '90 had become the pattern for Bristol Bay settlements.

With no movement on the open ticket issue, fishermen sought some way out of the impasse. One older fishermen stood up. "I've fished in the Bay for 51 years, and like it or not, Chuck, you're God up here. We expect you to help us."

"I believe in God," Bundrant said, " but we have to help ourselves."

Next Bundrant singled a fishermen out of the crowd: "When did you start fishing for Trident?"

"In False Pass, in 1983."

"And did you ever feel, in all those years since, that you could have done better somewhere else?"

"No," the answer came, "I've always felt that Trident treated me a cut above what other companies did."

Another fishermen stood up, "Do you think we can exist on 50 cents a pound?"

"We're in for some tough sledding, all of us," Bundrant said. "I've tried to hold an umbrella over the whole market and we couldn't do it."

One man asked about possible profit sharing as a way out of the impasse. Bundrant's reply was that in year's past there had been profit sharing with the fishermen when there really wasn't profit to share.

Several times Bundrant urged fishermen who were unhappy with Trident to seek a market that would give them what they wanted: "I'd rather you fish for someone else and still be friends than have you thinking I didn't give you the best deal I possibly could."

Next Bart Eaton took Chuck's place to discuss some of the unintended consequences of a strike.

"Probably when this thing gets settled, three rivers are all going to open at the same time. Fish and Game has so far managed to avoid this in the past by juggling openings to even up the load on processors. But when everything pops at once, it means that quality suffers; we end up with more number twos and threes. It's possible that we may have to go on limit, just to be able to handle things."

"It used to be in Alaska fishing," Eaton continued, "that you tried to overcome all your problems with more volume. But we're only going to dig our way out of this with quality."

Finally Bundrant got up again at the end to try and convince fishermen that the open ticket was the best way out of a difficult situation: "Trident has always done as good to its fishermen as it possibly could, and this is no different . . ."

It was obvious that it was a difficult meeting for Bundrant

Sign of a big run: a small power scow with a big, big load!

The 26th through the 28th were hard days for fishermen. The State of Alaska decided to not open the rivers for fishing until the fishermen and processors had come to an agreement. Those who supported the strike sensed the unwillingness of the processors to move very far at all. Those who wanted to fish were unable to because of the Governor's decision. Furthermore, the fragile dialog between fishermen and processors seemed to have broken down entirely.

And the fish weren't waiting for anyone; on the 28th 300,000 fish pushed up the Naknek River past the canneries and the 1,000 or so waiting boats.

One fishermen who supported the strike told me he felt that the fishermen had become trapped by their own rhetoric. After staking out a position that was clearly impossible (many asked for a higher price than '90), organizing a successful boycott and getting a great deal of media attention (TV watchers in NYC for example, were treated to footage of the waiting fleet churning around in the Naknek River. What must they have thought?), it was pretty hard for the strikers to eat humble pie and settle for 60 or 70 cents.

But the real test of the striker's resolve was yet to come. On the afternoon of the 28th, an Alaska judge said that it "was not appropriate for the State to use closures for other than regular management purposes."

Sometime, probably in the early hours of the 29th, near the top of a 19 foot tide, the Naknek River reached its escapement goal of one million fish. Before the tide was over, another 100,000 or so followed them up. A few hours later, a 12-hour fishing period for the Naknek was announced starting at 2 p.m. on the 30th. It was to be open almost continuously for the next 20 days and the stage was set for the next phase of the strike: confrontation.

While hundreds of Bristol Bay fishermen rallied on the beaches at Naknek and Dillingham, testing the resolve of "Japanese Masters" and railing against the "company store," a fleet of independents with tenders and markets of their own was already on the grounds, determined to harvest the sockeye crop come hell or high water. It was a recipe for trouble, seasoned liberally with threats, anxiety and bitterness. Humor was in short supply when 28 million reds showed up and the kettle was set to boil.

With fishing about to open on June 30, two thousand setnetters and gillnetters including myself, had to make a very personal decision: to fish or not to fish.

"I was at Kenai Packers during the last strike," one Everett-based fisherman told me."I told all those guys exactly what I thought: that we were shooting ourselves in the foot by not fishing. But I stuck with them. We sat on the beach for two weeks, let the run go by, and got an additional two cents. I'm not doing it again."

"If we fish for fifty cents this year," one fisherman said, echoing the feeling of many of the strikers, "what'll it be next year? We have to make a stand now."

Mindful of the damage violence could do to their cause, strike leaders urged fishermen to stay tied to the dock, except for a few that would go out and take the names of the boats that were fishing.

Trident's South Naknek cannery also had a baño, essentially a big sauna that harked back to the days when many native Alaskans including some Eskimos worked at the cannery. One particularly nasty afternoon with rain sweeping across the cannery in sheets, I took my crew up there, discovering to our surprise that it was empty but that the wood stove still had a good fire in it. Stoking up the fire even more, we stripped and just sat on the benches, savoring the dry heat. But then a little later a couple of big natives came in, and threw even more wood on the fire, and I remembered someone telling me something about being careful to share a sauna with the natives as they really liked it hot, hot, hot!

And then the biggest of them started ladling water onto the top of the stove, and instantly the sauna was transformed into a steam bath; and I figured that what was really happening was that the natives were trying to use the steam heat to drive us out.

"Mmmmm," I said, winking at my crew, who followed my example: pretending that we liked it hot, and I even ladled another cup of water onto the hot stove, bathing us all in searing steam once again. We kept it up, until the steam was really excruciating and just before we jumped up to get the hell of there, the natives grunted and left first: we'd defended the honor of the white man!

But it was quickly obvious that I'd picked the wrong place to hang out during a strike year. I'd already decided to sit out a day or two to see if the strike would get us anything, but what with boat payments and a new house to build that fall, I had to fish sooner than later.

All these cannery guys had fished together for years, often decades; one guy I talked to started back in sailboat days, before engines were first allowed in 1951. Plus most of the guys had gotten their permits free, having fished in The Bay before Limited Entry was imposed, or had bought in the 70s, when permits were few grand. I didn't meet a single fishermen who had both boat payments and permit payments (my permit had cost 90,000$) like I had. Additionally many of these guys had longshoring or other jobs to go back to.

And I learned why my friends who had fished The Bay for a while called many of the cannery guys, "Ham and eggers." With a great mess hall, comfortable rooms in the bunk house, and generally a lower debt load, it was much more convenient for these guys to just fish the Naknek River, sleep in their own rooms at night and eat in the mess hall than move aboard their boats like my crew and the rest of the "independents" did to chase the fish to whatever river seemed the most promising. Some of them even referred to The Bay as their "summer vacation." I could see how they could look at it like that: up in Alaska, away from their families, just with their buddies, maybe even come home with a few bucks after their expenses.

I learned that I had to be careful what I let on.

"You new around here?" A conversation might start at mug up.

"Yeah, I'm a Trident guy, just came over to see what cannery life was like."

"Where do you keep your boat?"

"Lummi."

Wrong answer, I sensed, as it immediately identified me as an independent, someone from The New Bay, upending the old ways the cannery guys were used to.

"You're striking, right?"

"You bet, can't make it at half a buck."

"What's your boat name?"

"*Katie Anne*, new Plier boat."

Wrong answer again; now not only had I identified myself as an independent, but with a new boat too, i.e. hungry to put in a big season. Plus, I'd given him our boat name.

I was a marked man.

And our boat was boxed in at the cannery dock, tied with cannery boats on either side; as soon as fishing started there would be many guys watching on the dock to see who was going out to fish. And even if I wanted to leave, it was possible that might turn into a confrontation unless I was careful about it.

"Hey, Joe, you catching the vibes? We gotta get outta here?" This was Jake Magel, who fished with me ever since *Joe H* days.

"I'm getting them too. We just got to pick our moment."

On the morning of the 30th the river in front of the cannery was a steady stream of independent boats like myself, headed out with the ebbing current to scout out a good place to start fishing. They were all coming upstream from the anchorages in front of Lummi and Leader Creek. As the fleet passing thinned I looked upstream and it looked like every boat up there was on their way out to fish.

But at the same time at the Trident cannery on the other side of the river, and at all the other canneries on either side of it and the two canneries downriver from us, the big fleets were all tied to the docks in long rows; the divide was stark: the cannery guys were striking and the independents were fishing.

We ate as much as we could at morning mug up and headed down to the boat to keep our heads low; we knew lunch would be ugly once the word got around about all the boats breaking the strike and headed out to fish.

Strikers, waiting, Diamond NN Cannery. Very hard to sneak out with everyone on the dock keeping an eye to make sure no boats left to go out to fish.

Overheard as we walked along the wharf to the dock ladders:

"That asshole told me he was with us." This from a guy pointing out a passing boat to a buddy. Next to him was a guy with binoculars, calling out boat names to the guy next to him who was writing them down.

"Fucking scabs. I know what we did with guys like that in the old days."

We crossed the dock and climbed the ladder down to our boat. We couldn't go anywhere anyway as not only did we have boats tied on either side of us, but there was a row of 8 or 10 boats ahead and behind. And it was low tide: we were all sitting on the bottom.

At all the canneries in all the Bristol Bay rivers, life revolves around the tides, as at low tide most docks are dry, with mud for several hundred feet, and gillnetters and the big flat bottomed tenders all sit on the bottom together. High tide is when the tenders can come in to unload, guys can head out to go fishing, etc.

"We should be out there." This from David Coble, who'd also been with me, fishing through thick and thin for five years. I knew his winter life depended on how much he made on board with me in the short Bay season.

"I'm gonna' give it one tide." I said, "We're stuck here anyway until half-way through the flood. Maybe there'll be a chance to slip away undetected." It always seemed like there was a boat shuffle when the tide got up; someone might need to go over to the other side of the river to the store, someone else might need to get to the fuel dock, under the hoist to load nets, etc.

We had to turn our radio off. The rest of our group was out there, and there was a lot of fish.

Finally at the top of the tide a big tender needed to come into the dock to unload some freight and the big raft up broke up to jog around in the current until there was room to tie up again. When they retied, we were long gone, out the river to join our buddies.

They were all deep in the water with almost full loads from the flood, and the opening wasn't even half over.

We got right to work. Catching fish was what we had come for, and with a house to build and a new boat and permit to pay for, we put the strike and all the bullshit of the spring and the last week behind us.

It was once again, full on fishing, around the clock, 7 days a week. Now and again, some guys in a cannery boat would come over and harass us about fishing, but there were no guns, at least that we could see, so we just kept our heads down and picked fish.

With more than half the boats still tied up, it was big, big, fishing, with plenty of room, a rare, rare scenario in the Bay. Every now and then there would be a Kvichak opening and the fleet would spread out even further. One day in the Kvichak we were so far over to the west side that the processors anchored up in the "Y," the area where the Kvichak and Naknek come together were all hull down over the horizon, with just their rigging visible.

Today you'd fish the Kvichak with a nice GPS plotter which would show you where you were in real time on a little digital map, with you as a little boat icon, and the sand bars clearly marked. But the Kvichak is a huge area, and it was foggy and cool one afternoon, GPS plotters hadn't been invented, and charts never survived long on the windy and often wet fly bridge.

So without warning we fetched up on Deadman Sands, and within two hours we were so high and dry that we climbed down off the stern to walk around. I'd fished in Alaska for fifteen or sixteen years by then, in all kinds of boats, in all kinds of places and situations.

Once we ended up high and dry on Deadman Sands, and we walked around in the windy dusk. With no other boats in sight it was a spooky and otherworldly feeling.

But that walk around that sand bar, with the wisps of thin fog slowly floating past us, with no other sign of man's existence anywhere around us was a strange and otherworldly experience. The weirdest part was to walk to the sand's edge, where it dropped off quickly into deeper water, that rushed past at the speed of a jogger. And then to look out at the vast expanse of water, and then at the acres of sand around us, it wasn't too hard to imagine that it was the water that was fixed and that it was the sand bars that were moving through it.

It was near here where one of The Bay's most dramatic rescues occurred.

On a particularly stormy day in the early 90s a body washed up near a setnet site on the west side of the Kvichak river. Initially due to some poor communication it was thought to be a setnetter from a nearby site. By the time the mistake was cleared up, it was obvious that the body was of a crewman off a gillnetter, and that there might be others out there. It was coming on dark, and the nearest Coast Guard chopper was 500 miles away in Kodiak. However, at least three of the bigger processors, Trident, Icicle, and Lafayette had choppers, and when it was clear that there might be fishermen in the water, all were launched.

Without a signal from an EPIRB (Emergency Position Indicating Radio Beacon) or a mayday from a stricken vessel, all the potential rescuers had to go on was where the body washed up—down wind and current from Deadman Sands. Bundrant and his pilot headed over in the little Bell Ranger, finding a wasteland of breakers, and dark water rapidly covering the sands as the tide came up. At very last light they spotted what looked like two guys standing marooned on a tiny sand bar that was quickly being eroded away by the swift current around it.

As they approached they realized that there was no time to pick up one man and run him in to the beach and come back for other in order not to exceed the chopper's maximum load. It also looked like one of the men was already in the sand partway up his calves.

"Just set 'er down, and I can pull that guy out." said Bundrant to the pilot.

But when the pilot set the skids onto the sands and throttled back, he noticed the skids disappearing—it was essentially quicksand. "Can't do it, Chuck," he called.

"Just hover . . . I think I can grab 'em" Bundrant replied.

The chopper pulled out of the muck and edged sideways toward the guys. One of the fishermen was able to climb up on the chopper's skids and into the cabin, but the other was stuck in the mud that was quickly starting to wash away from the current.

Bundrant, strong and wiry at 6'5", stepped out onto the skids, put one hand around the edge of the cabin door, reached out and muckled onto the stuck-in-the-mud fisherman, yelled to the pilot to get them the hell of there. The chopper lifted into the air, as Bundrant wrenched the man out of the mud and tumbled back into the cabin with him. At the time Trident was close to being the largest seafood company in the US, and that Bundrant, the CEO, would go out personally to rescue a fisherman who did not even deliver to Trident, spoke a lot for the loyalty its fishermen felt toward Trident and Bundrant.

Each tide a few more of the boats tied up at the canneries would join us out in the river, and when the strike finally settled around the 10th of July, we and the other fishermen joined in a week of round the clock chaos, as we mopped up the last of the run.

Over the course of the last couple of seasons I'd become friends with the Bundrants. For us independent fishermen that delivered our fish to Trident, Chuck's wife Diane was the one to whom we went to get our settlements. Though we were independent in that we owned our boats and permits, it was convenient to be associated with a big outfit like Trident.

For example, Trident owned a travel agency, through which I arranged air travel to and from Alaska for myself and my crew. They had a fleet insurance program through which I insured our boat. During the course of the season, we purchased fuel and food off the tenders. In addition, Trident owned an interest in Lummi Fisheries Supply, which operated the boatyard where we kept our boat, and the marine store where we purchased much of our supplies.

So when it came to settle up, it wasn't uncommon to have ten or fifteen thousand dollars on the debit side of the ledger. In addition, some fishermen were in the habit taking cash "draws" from Trident—essentially interest free loans—to help them get through the winter. (You can see why we occasionally referred to the company as "Mother Trident.") And it all came together on your settlement sheet.

We were lucky that season—we'd started fishing early, hadn't taken any cash draws over the winter, hadn't gotten Trident POs for any big ticket items, so there were checks in the settlement envelope. (Trident divided the final figure into checks for myself and each of my crew.)

"You guys did well." said Diane. "The run had pretty much passed by the time a lot of the regular cannery guys decided to fish, so many ended up with negative balances at the end of the season. Some of the guys had to get their wives to buy them a ticket to get home."

I don't remember exactly what the strikers settled at. But the guys who said at the beginning of the strike that you never make back the value of the fish that you missed got it right.

And for us, there was another negative side to it. I didn't think we'd be hitting the baño at South Naknek anytime soon. We were on the list.

A BOY GOES NORTH

FINALLY IN 1994, OUR SON WAS 12 and my wife agreed, though with some reluctance, to let him come up to the Bay at last. He certainly knew what it was all about, listening eagerly to my stories, and meeting my crew when they needed a place to stay on occasion. Plus each year he'd helped me pack "The box"—the big 4'x4'x4' crate that we loaded up with nets, groceries, boat parts etc. in the back of my pickup truck each April and delivered to a Trident Seattle facility to be put on the barge to Naknek.

Logistics—sending our 12-year-old on the not so easy journey to the remote areas we usually fished—were a bit of a problem. Until our friend Diane Bundrant came up with a great solution: arranging for one of their Naknek cannery staff, a big, big Samoan, to meet Matt at the Seattle airport, accompany him to the cannery via Anchorage and King Salmon. Once at the cannery, they would sign him up for a crew license, put a life jacket on him and put him on a chopper headed out to the net barge on the Egegik River.

Picking lesson: getting fish out of the net quickly without ripping more of the net than you have to is an art.

The two big 40' steel storage containers side by side on Trident's Egegik net barge also served as a the helicopter landing pad. It was a bit rough and ready with just a rough ladder up to it and no rails, and probably not FAA approved either as there was a radio antenna mast closer to the landing pad than I was comfortable with.

Many of the bigger fish processing companies had their own planes and choppers. Trident's chief chopper pilot was a tall lanky guy nicknamed "Whisper," as he had his voice box or larynx shot away in Vietnam, and talked in this hoarse whisper that could be a bit hard to understand.

Matt and Whisper came out an hour or so before a fishing period was to start so the air over the river and near the barge had a lot of other aircraft, primarily single engined spotter planes, but also at least one other processor's chopper, inbound with freight. Matt and Whisper were both wearing earphone/microphone rigs that allowed them to talk to each other over the noise of the chopper's gas turbine engine. Matt told me later that as they approached the barge, Whisper came over his earphones in his raspy voice:

"Hey kid, there's a lot of traffic here and I got to focus on my landing. So you keep an eye out for other planes or choppers and if you see something that looks like it might get too close, sing out."

When the chopper appeared above the anchored fleet I made sure we were tied to the net barge, and I clambered aboard and got halfway up the stairs to the top of the containers as they came in. The scene: a young man exiting a chopper, ducking low with a sea bag on his shoulder, reminded me of some Vietnam War movies.

So began some wonderful Bristol Bay seasons.

Not your usual summer job: the Trident Seafoods chopper delivers our 12-year-old son to the landing pad at Egegik: on top of a 40' container on the net barge.

My crew those years were Jake Magel, Bruce McGowan, and David Coble. Bruce and Jake fished with me summers in the Bay, and spent the winter skiing out of their home town in Park City, Utah. For an impressionable young man of 12, they were all wonderful mentors: full of advice and stories. Sometimes I'd be up on the flying bridge looking for a set and I'd hear snatches of their conversations wafting up to me: "College . . . naw. Matt, there's so many things you have to do before college, you've got to spend at least a year surfing, and then at least a year hanging out in Amsterdam." Sometimes I'd have to yell back down to them to knock off polluting our son's brain with their fantasies.

The first year Matt came up, I arranged for him to arrive after the peak, when basically we'd made the bulk of our season, a lot of boats had left, and the Bay might even be described as if not mellow, at least, not the 10 day frenzied madhouse that was the peak of the season.

At the peak, in the thick of it, we would be occasionally smacked by another boat as we maneuvered in tight quarters to get our net out. Mostly they were just fender squeaking encounters, (In Bristol Bay, your fenders were attached permanently to the sides of your boat, not like yachts where they are only deployed for docking, rafting up with other boats etc.) but at least once a season someone would hit us hard enough to dent the boat, and once, hard enough to knock my crew to the deck. And to be candid, one of the reasons I waited until after the peak was to make it extremely unlikely that Matt or my crew would be injured by some cowboy smacking into us.

A particularly vulnerable area to get rammed in was the stern control station—the steering wheel and engine controls in an aft corner of the cockpit that allowed the skipper to operate the boat while he and his crew were pulling the net in and picking the fish out. Fortunately ours, like most newer Bay boats, was well protected. We did however, get into the habit of what I'd observed in a lot of Bay boats, but nowhere else in Alaska: protecting your anchor. We used our anchor almost every day and only carried one anchor. Plus anchors are expensive: our 33 pound Bruce claw anchor cost almost 300 bucks, so each day after picking it up, we'd pull it off the anchor roller on the bow of the boat and tie it to one of the big cleats on either side of the anchor winch. That way if we smacked someone with our bow, we might bend the anchor roller, but we'd still be able to anchor.

After Matt had his little chopper adventure getting into Egegik, we moved down to the relative peace and quiet of the Ugashik River.

And cell phone coverage had finally come to The Bay! It was still spotty and you had to have what were called bag phones—big, clunky, pocketbook sized units—to have enough power. And this was way before iPhones and the wonderful Facetime technology that Steve Jobs brought to so many of us decades later. But still, every evening when we anchored up at the head of Dago Creek with the vast green rolling tundra outside spreading south to the steaming volcanoes that were the spine of the Alaska Peninsula we would be witness to what then seemed a miracle. The phone would ring and there would be my wife, Mary Lou, listening as her still big-eyed-at-it-all boy described what he had done that day.

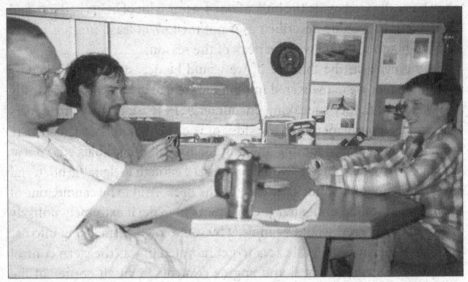

Before we really got into the peak of the season, we had time to teach Matt how to pick fish, and a few evening hands of UNO.

There were only about 60 or 70 boats fishing Ugashik at the end of the '94 season: plenty of room for everyone, and we settled into a easy routine: net in the water by 7, unload by 6, dinner on the table at 7, and even time afterwards for a couple of hands of Uno.

For us as well, it was kind of a magic time: seeing The Bay through a youth's eyes. His excitement at seeing the fish hit the net when we ran it with the boat, the drama of a 25 pound king salmon coming over the roller unexpectedly. And then something that was a first for us as well.

One afternoon we were fishing close to the beach up on the northern boundary of the district, under the high bluff at Cape Grieg. Fishing was slow and the Bering Sea was calm, so we had lots of time to enjoy the austere scenery. Matt called our attention to what looked like moving sticks up on the top of the bluff. We got the binoculars and peered up, There was something up there that looked like oddly shaped sticks that were certainly moving. After a bit the mystery resolved itself when half a dozen caribou peeked their heads over the edge of bluff to see what we were doing down there: what we had been seeing earlier were their antlers!

Sometimes when it was choppy out in the wider waters by the outer district lines, we'd do what we called the "one shackle thing" in the narrow confines of the river itself. The shallow winding channel had just enough room for a single shackle (300') of net. So we would set that out, putting a buoy on both ends and cruising off in the boat to one side watching, and then running it every few minutes to drive the fish in. After 30 minutes or so, we'd pull that shackle into the stern, fish and all (we'd maybe get 70–80 fish) and set out another single shackle. Then as Matt and the rest of the crew worked in the stern to pick the fish out, I would watch and run the shackle that was in the water.

And all this in a little gutter of shallow winding water with the muddy tundra banks moving swiftly by as the tide pushed us up the river. After a couple of sets of doing that, the current would have pushed us far up the river, near the upper boundary for the district, so I'd pick up the net and steam back to where we had started: the buildings of the old Diamond U cannery built by a crew brought up on a square rigger in 1918.

And always in the distance rising above the muddy river banks and the green tundra fields beyond; the snow covered cone of Aniachak Volcano, shining in the light, steam venting from its flank, blowing downwind.

I'd take Matthew with me aboard the tender when we were unloading, give him the pad to write down the bag weights as the tender crew called them out before dumping the fish into the refrigerated water of their fish hold.

Like most Bristol Bay Rivers, Ugashik had few docks (actually just one: far up the river at an abandoned cannery) so if you wanted to go ashore for some reason, like just getting off the boat if you had a day with no fishing, you just drove your boat up onto the beach and let the tide go out. This was standard practice, called beaching. The trick was to do it with another boat so that when the tide went out, you weren't laying over on your side. The protocol was that if you were by yourself and wanted to beach, and you saw some other boats that were already beached, you would just slide up next to them. Sometimes you'd see 40 or 50 boats beached out in groups of 4 or 5 on a no-fishing day.

A proud boy with the first really tangled fish that he picked totally by himself.

Sooo, one day, when there was no fishing at Ugashik to let the escapement (the number of fish going up the river to spawn) catch up, we decided to go ashore and have a walk. The rest of the boats in our code group were either fishing at Egegik or hauling out and going home so we had no one to beach out with. But I noticed a group of four boats had just beached themselves so we headed over to join them.

Except for a brief few minutes at high or low tide, the current in the river was always pretty strong, so it can be tricky in a beach landing to slide alongside another boat already beached with just enough momentum and in the right position. As we slid in, the current was a bit stronger than I had anticipated so we hit the boat on the beach harder than I had planned. Normally that wouldn't be a problem—boats get whacked hard all the time in the Bay; that's why we have fenders permanently fixed along both sides of the boat.

But as soon as we'd come to a sliding stop and shut off our engine, I realized there was a problem. The boats we had slid up alongside were all owned and crewed by Alaska Natives, and it turned out they were all celebrating the arrival of a brand new boat into their little fleet: the boat that we had whacked, hard enough to chip off a piece of fiberglass about the size of a quarter off his port stern corner.

And these folks had been drinking and they were pissed! I quickly realized that I'd stirred up a hornet's nest. The angry natives came over to yell at us with some pretty bad language directed at me, my crew, and the somewhat tender ears of our 12-year-old son. It was an embarrassing and ugly situation.

Fortunately about then it started to rain pretty hard, we and the Natives retreated into our boats, and the situation seemed to have been defused. But then about five minutes later: wham! Another boat slammed into our other side and pretty soon I could hear angry voices outside again: apparently they had called some of their friends, the rain squall had passed, they'd come out of their boats and were getting all worked up again.

Then there was a loud knock at our door.

The window in the door was all fogged up so I couldn't really see, but I was pretty sure it was trouble.

I turned to our son and my crew:

"Hey guys, I'm really sorry I got you into this. It's totally my fault. They're going to break their way in here and beat us up. Just try to protect your teeth and let's hope it's over quickly."

Mending your net: after each fishing period the net had to be overhauled and any rips or tears repaired.

Slowly I opened the door. There was a really big guy standing there and I started to apologize profusely. Then I realized the big guy was holding a plate of steaming caribou meat.

"Are you Joe Upton?" the big guy asked in a heavy native accent. "My dad said you were a really good writer. Do you want some caribou? We just shot it yesterday."

And so an ugly situation passed. My annual story about the Bristol Bay season, published in the Alaska Fishermen's Journal was widely read in Alaska. Our new friend invited us aboard his boat, where the skinned carcass of a caribou lay on the hatch cover. They were whacking off pieces that would fit into the small oven on the boat, cooking and passing them around.

Fishing dropped off after that to a bag (a thousand pounds) a day: for us the traditional sign that it was time to hang it up.

The end of a Bristol Bay season has its own dynamic and that year was no different. We'd have all these great ambitious plans to stay to the end, to catch the last fish, etc. Then one day we'd wake up, and as we were having our coffee and looking out at the grim and austere world all around us, the feeling of just wanting to be home with family became too strong and just like that, we knew the season was over, and we'd head to town stripping gear (cutting the gill-net off the cork lines and lead lines of our net so that the lines would be ready for new nets) all the way.

Timing was critical; as soon as you figured out when you wanted to leave, you got on the radio and called your cannery for them to make your plane reservation. (We all came up with open returns on our plane tickets.) At the end of the season there was always a jam-up at the King Salmon airport, as not only did most of the 2,800 gillnet and setnet crews try to get out at the same time, but there were also probably a couple thousand cannery and freezer plant workers trying to go home as well. Even if they couldn't get a seat a lot of guys would just go out to the airport anyway, so the little King Salmon airport would get pretty chaotic. Sometimes when it got really bad Alaska Airlines would find an empty 737 somewhere and send it to King Salmon for a direct flight to Seattle (most of the time you had to change in Anchorage).

We left Ugashik right after breakfast for the 9 hour run up to Naknek. It's a straight run up a low coast with the volcanoes in the distance, so I'd swap off stripping gear with the guys to give everyone a break from the chilly wind.

On watch—usually when we had to run from one district to another, we'd have Matt steer and we'd all get some rest. Inside the actual districts during fishing periods, there were too many nets in the water for us to feel comfortable with him steering.

When we got to the "Y"—the confluence of the Kvichak and Naknek Rivers that was the traditional anchorage for the big processors and trampers (freighters) waiting to load frozen salmon, there was only one processor, the big *Yardarm Knot* still there. And the barges with the pack. When we'd headed out from Naknek to start our season just four weeks earlier there had been two huge barges stacked high with vans (40' long steel shipping containers), both reefer vans (with refrigeration systems to keep what was inside frozen) and regular vans on moorings. Now the vans were all full of canned and frozen salmon, and the barges were deep in the water with the weight, waiting for the tugs that would tow them west to Unimak Pass and then southeast across the Gulf of Alaska to Seattle, with a stop in Dutch Harbor in the Aleutian Islands where the Asia bound vans would be offloaded to await Asia bound freighters.

Luckily for us the peak of guys wanting to haul their boats had already passed, so Lummi could haul us as soon as we arrived. If we'd arrived a couple of days earlier, we might have had to wait until the middle of the night, or maybe even a whole day at anchor before we could get hauled out. Here's the way it worked: a huge 4 wheel drive tractor with wheels 8 or 9 feet in diameter would push this big trailer into the swiftly moving river current. When the trailer was in water deep enough, the tractor would stop and the driver would wave you on.

Then came the tricky part: fighting the 4 or 5 mph current to get onto the trailer. You had to approach slowly heading straight into the current, at right angles to the trailer then turn and quickly drive your boat onto the pads before the current could sweep you past and against the PVC pipe upright guides with enough force to break them off.

I'd guessed at when we'd get hauled and my timing was perfect, just as the tractor had finished lowering and blocking us up in the boatyard with our stern backed up against the steel shipping container that was our locker, the taxi that I had radioed arrived with three big pizzas and a case of cold Pabst Blue Ribbon!

Some guys just shut off their stove (which also serves as a cabin heater), tie a plastic bucket over their exhaust pipe and get the hell out of town. But I was so proud of our new boat and big 440 hp. Lugger diesel, that I really wanted to treat it right.

So full of pizza and with a bit of a buzz on, we started our final end of the season ritual. A year earlier we had converted an old 40' shipping container into two lockers with big doors. The guys put the nets and fishing gear into the locker, I unscrewed the plug at the bottom of the bilge, changed the oil, washed the engine with soap and a hose, and soon as it was dry, spray painted anything with the least bit of rust with Rustoleum white and we were done.

By the beginning of the '95 season, Matt, now a fast boat smart fish picker was ready for the big time: Egegik.

And it looked like we'd be joining a crowd as the atmosphere around Naknek on the afternoon of June 19 was like the East Coast of England in June of 1944 as upwards of a thousand boats prepared for the invasion of the continent to attack Hitler.

Matt actually got to be a good picker and by the end of the second season, I had to start paying him in real money. He took it and bought his dream boat, a '70s 13' Boston Whaler. The seller wanted $1,400, Matt only had $1,000 but after five phone calls the seller relented: "OK, kid, show up with a grand in cash and it's yours. But DON'T CALL ME AGAIN!"

In the big boatyards at Naknek Marine Center, Leader Creek and Dillingham, and at the eight big canneries on both sides of the Naknek River, fishermen were working feverishly to get their boats launched and ready to fish.

Out in the river, hundreds of boats, anchored singly, or in groups, were testing their equipment, rolling on nets, checking radio frequencies, and waiting for the turn of the tide to set out for the passage down to Egegik.

A relatively small fleet of 650 boats at Egegik had been the hands-down winner of the '94 season. But the first light of dawn on the 20th dashed any hopes for an orderly fishery in '95. A forest of masts filled the Egegik outer anchorage from Coffee Point to Red Bluff light as a fleet of over 900 boats, possibly the largest fishing fleet ever assembled in a single place in Alaska began to stir, and late arrivals were still streaming in.

The huge fleet filled all the anchorages and some boats were forced to anchor in places where they would go dry. The swiftness of the incoming tide would often carry them down to slam into other boats before their anchor rodes came tight.

And if the action on the North Line was intense during the first few openings, it became truly wild on June 26th and 27th, when the openings ran into the few hours of what passes for darkness at that latitude in summer. Most skippers reduced setting speeds in low visibility and crowded conditions, but a few continued to set at full speed, weaving in and out of the churning fleet, risking injury and serious damage.

How bad was it? The best indicator was simply the damaged boats. Rammed or sideswiped by accident or on purpose, literally dozens of boats were sporting Splash Zone (an epoxy patching material) warts, plywood band-aids, or crudely welded aluminum patches over bows and sides ripped open.

A particularly vulnerable area was the stern control station—the steering wheel and engine controls in an aft corner of the cockpit that allowed the skipper to operate the boat while he and his crew were pulling the net in and picking the fish out. Fortunately ours, like most newer Bay boats, was well protected. We did however, get into the habit of what I'd observed in a lot of Bay boats, but nowhere else in Alaska: protecting your anchor. We used our anchor almost every day and only carried one anchor. Plus anchors are expensive: our 33 pound Bruce claw anchor cost almost 300 bucks, so each day after picking it up, we'd pull it off the anchor roller on the bow of the boat and tie it to one of the big cleats on either side of the anchor winch. That way if we smacked someone with our bow, we might bend the anchor roller, but we'd still be able to anchor.

Meanwhile as the crowd on the line at Egegik got even more aggressive, a few entrepreneurial fishermen had worked together with boat builders to give them an edge: shallower. At the beginning of the ebb at the Egegik north line, the water was deep enough for most boats to fish all the way up to the edge of the setnets (anchored gill nets on the beach fished by shore based fishermen). Fishing regulations required a separation between gill nets and setnets, but it was difficult to enforce. Then as the ebb continued the dropping water levels moved the fleet out away from the setnets creating an opportunity for even shallower draft boats, which came in several flavors. Most modern Bay boats were already built with a sort of half tunnel in the hull at the stern allowing the prop and driveshaft to be installed higher and the boat to travel in shallower water. Next shallower were the outboards. These were generally shallower draft to begin with, and tilting up the motors allowed them to go shallower still. However outboards were never popular in gillnetters because of the ease of nets getting tangled in props and lower units. But the ultimate answer were the jet boats, using water jet systems similar to those used in jet ski boats, except way, way more powerful. With jet drives there was nothing hanging down below the hull. At first there were just a couple of jet boats, but after a few years there was a regular little mini-fleet of them duking it out in the the shallows.

There was even one very odd boat, a monster of a thing: 32x16, raised pilothouse with a wide and high walkway underneath it, a movable net reel on rails and power rollers at bow and stern. Its twin jet drives were powered by two 500 hp diesels. But with so much in the engine room and probably fish hold for 30,000 pounds, I couldn't imagine that the galley and crew quarters, stuffed in there somewhere, would be very roomy. And hmm . . . rollers at bow and stern: big crew . . . pick both ends of the net at once?

And sometimes the fish were running in just a foot of water or so. If that was happening, and your timing was right and you were the shallowest, you could go in as shallow as you could, and set out towards deeper water. But there was a fine line: shallow was great but if your net went dry, you might be picking the fish out of the mud and wading through it to bring them back to the boat, as your net couldn't be in the water when the tide came in again (the fishing period would be over).

However, even as crowded as Egegik was in 1995, we were able to get in one of the most exciting sets of my whole Bristol Bay career.

It was on the south line at the bottom of the tide near the peak of the season. When the tide is ebbing a large fleet is engaged in the chaos and frenzy on the north line, but there's always a small fleet working the south line, carefully staying back as during the ebb the current sweeps you across the line into closed waters: ticket country. The protocol is to set back from the line, watch your position on your Loran display and start to pick with enough time to get all your net in before you go across.

Then as the tide slows, the strategy changes: watch how fast the ebb is moving, estimate when it will stop—there is a period of slack water at the bottom of the tide—and try to set your net back from the line just enough that the current will carry you right to the line and then stop, forcing the boats that have set in front of you to pick up and giving you that elusive "front row seat." Plus often right at the change of the tide a wave of fish will move in with the first of the flood.

Setnetters Camp, near Egegik south line, 1996. Need anything? In the plane, Naknek and the Alaska Commercial store is only 20 min. away!

It takes a bit of courage as sometimes the current fools you: stops for a bit and then ebbs again, carrying you quickly over the line, where the fish cops are often waiting.

On this occasion it took me three trys to get it right. On both the first and second try I thought I'd gotten it right, only to watch the Loran numbers ever so slowly keep changing as the current kept ebbing and we had to pick. Then I moved back but the only open place to set our net had seemed at first too far back: that the direction the water was moving would change before we got to the line.

But then one by one the guys in front of us picked up as they got to the line, I towed our net straight and parallel to the line, and anxiously watched the digital Loran display up on the flying bridge. Slowly, slowly we kept moving toward the line, and to the south I could see the fish cop inflatable making his way through the fleet. The Loran on the fly bridge clicked down to the line at 45140, and then blinked 45140.1 showing that we were still moving ever so slowly west. I got ready to pick, but then the receiver blinked back to 45140 and stayed steady: we did it: got that elusive "front row seat!"

And then, almost exactly at the beginning of slack water, our net started to light up with fish hitting it. And still no one set in front of us, as the cops were right there, watching us, thinking we would ebb over and they'd nab us. But at the same time, maybe relieved when they realized that we were probably going to stay legal; that they could just stay there for a few minutes and enjoy watching the action. I was sure that arguing with angry fishermen and maneuvering their outboard amongst the north line chaos wasn't any fun and that maybe this was a pleasant break from it.

Setnetters use a beamy skiff to overhaul their nets—sliding the skiff under it and picking the fish out.

By the time the current changed and started moving us east, it and the fish had pushed the center of our net back creating sort of a deep "U." The center of the U was probably fifty yards from the guy that had just corked us, and in that space, I quickly realized, were still hundreds of fish. I began running the net; traveling parallel to it at full speed, twenty or thirty feet off, and each time we'd scare another 60 or 80 startled fish into the net! Then we'd wait off to one side for four or five minutes and do it again. And again, another big bunch of fish that had come to the net, sensed something, but weren't sure exactly what it was, would drive into the net to escape the boat! And on each run, Matt and my crew would be cheering the action—it wasn't a secret to anyone around us that we had a big set going!

Plus were totally in legal waters, with the current pushing us deeper into the district so that we could pick without the frantic pressure we would have had just 45 minutes earlier when the tide was running the other way.

It was around 2,000 fish: 12 bags (12,000) pounds: a huge set.

Occasionally we'd get a day off from fishing to let the escapement up the river build a bit, and a couple of times we were anchored down near the south spit, near the cabins of some setnetters. So we got a chance to observe their lives, and from the perspective of being more or less cooped up for the season in our little (but very nice) 32 footer, their program looked pretty good.

Setnetters have essentially a land based life. Some have cabins by the site of their net, others just have tents, but even those would usually be big semi-permanent wall tents instead of the smaller camping style tents. They use a husky, aluminum outboard skiff to tend their gill nets, which have one end anchored or staked on shore and the other, anchored at right angles to shore. They observe the same fishing period or opening times as we do. When the period opens, they set their net from the skiff or use a pulley line to drag them out to the anchored buoy. Then when fish are in the net, they pick them out by pulling the skiff along the cork line, taking the fish out as they go. At the end of the opening they use the skiff to take their catch to the tender, or in some places fly them right off the beach in airplanes.

There was one place, a cabin with a deck maybe 20 yards from the water, with a little fabric covered Piper Cub in the tall grass next to it, a clothesline and what looked like chairs around a fire pit. Then as we watched throughout the day, a volleyball game started, and after the game was over, someone jumped into the plane, took off, to return a couple of hours later with boxes of something that looked like food and supplies from a store. Wow, I thought he buzzed into Naknek for supplies, maybe even a pizza and a beer. It all looked pretty good to us.

In a sense setnetting was a lot like the traditional native fish camp, a riverside site where a family might go each summer for the length of the salmon run, to net and smoke or dry fish. Further north in the Arctic, the catch might include seals and even whales, but it was still fish camp.

And to me it seemed like the setnetters were having more of an Alaska bush experience. Sure, once fishing started, there was a noisy fleet of boats a few hundred yards offshore, but when the opening was over and their fish delivered, they could sit on the deck of their little cabin or around the fire and enjoy the wilderness around them.

The flip side of course is that you can't move: your setnet site is a specific place and if the fish are there this year, great, but if not, they're not and you have a skinny year. I knew that there were some sites on the west side of the Kvichak that had very few fish for a number of years in a row, and then the pattern of the sandbars or fish routes changed and the fish roared in, season after season, enough for at least one setnetter to purchase a DC-3 twin engine air freighter to take his fish to the Naknek airport where a cannery truck would be waiting for them. The beaches and sand bars were so firm that the planes would use them as runways.

On my second summer in the Bay, at Egegik, I saw a mirage way down the beach at the end of a fishing period that looked like a big four engine propeller plane, but found that hard to believe. I put the binoculars on it just as the low throb of the engines reached me; it was! A couple of minutes later it thundered overhead: a Northern Air Cargo DC-6 loaded, I learned later, with 30,000 pounds of setnet fish bound for a freezer plant in Anchorage, using the beach as the airstrip.

A few years earlier another DC-6 was loaded and ready to go on that same beach. The setnetters had a great site, and six other planes including a DC-3, had been pressed into service to fly the hundred thousand or so pounds of salmon, in aluminum totes off the beach before the tide came in. By the time the last flight of the day was ready to take off, visibility was marginal, but the tide was coming in and if the plane didn't get off the beach, it would be in the surf by morning.

The pilot went for it, but in the semi darkness, a wingtip hit the bluff at the edge of the beach, and the plane crashed and burst into flames. The setnetters rushed to the plane, sure that the crew had been cremated, but when they got to the cockpit, they could see that enough wet fish had rushed forward to protect the pilots and flight engineer long enough to be rescued, slimy and shook up, but basically healthy.

By 1995 a notable change was taking place in the Bay. For most of the past decade relatively strong runs and good fish prices had allowed skippers with dependable boats and crews with fast hands to do pretty well for themselves. This wasn't lost on the larger Northwest salmon commercial fishing community. Guys with young children, older guys wanting a shorter season and others found the Bay and its five or six week season very appealing.

And so slowly, the native and local fishermen who were grandfathered into the fishery and basically gotten their permits for free got older, and if they didn't pass their permits and boats down to their children, they sold them on the open market—a price of a drift permit in 1995 was around $175,000. Many of the native and local fishermen had smaller boats, and with little debt, were often content with smaller catches—like the Egegik local fishermen with fished inside the bars in the upper river.

Most of the people that bought permits at those prices were from out of state, though they may have participated in other Alaska fisheries. Often, if they could swing it, they would purchase or build a larger and more modern boat rather than purchase the usually smaller and older boats that the previous permit holder had.

And so one by one the smaller boats with less aggressive skippers were replaced by newer, more modern and faster boats skippered by guys that owed a lot of money. The result was the whole fishery across the five rivers became more aggressive and combative.

And something else as well: more woman in the fleet. A lot of the newcomers had come from places like SE Alaska where it was common to have women working aboard both seiners and gillnetters. There were even, I had heard, a couple of all woman boats.

I never considered myself a super aggressive fisherman. Sure, I mixed it up on the Naknek and Egegik lines, but my sets were usually on the edge of the most combative fishing. My attitude was get as close as you are comfortable with, keep your equipment running, your net in the water and you'll have a season at the end

Then we had a little interaction that made me see myself in an unflattering light.

There's not much that's polite in Bristol Bay fishing. If you see an open set, you go for it, even if it means setting your net off your reel at full speed and cutting someone off who was also setting out their net. It's just the way it is; if you want to be a polite fisherman, you probably need to fish elsewhere.

I'd found room to get the net out, waved to the guys, the end buoy (a big inflated buoy at the end of the net that is thrown into the water to begin a set) went over the stern and the net began to peel off the reel as I sped up. There was another boat approaching from my port side setting fast and hoping to get ahead of me, forcing me to either stop or turn east and go possibly over the line to finish getting my net out. Legally I had the right of way (the nautical rules of the road state that vessels approaching from my port side have to give way), but no one really pays much attention to that in the Bay. In any case I just throttled up and cut him off. He had to reverse hard to avoid hitting me and we passed within five feet of each other. For a moment it seemed like the other skipper was going to say something. Then just as we passed, I could hear one of the guys on the back deck call up to the flying bridge, "Don't make him angry, Dad."

By the time I really thought about what I heard, we were a hundred yards away, I thought, "get ME angry?? Do I look like that kind of a guy??"

I hoped that I wasn't.

In a place like Bristol Bay with such a short season, it behooves fishermen to go to great lengths to avoid a breakdown. You try to be totally proactive: aware of the condition of all your systems; at the end of the season inventorying the problems encountered, sometimes shipping a whole engine south to be rebuilt just to be absolutely sure that it won't fail you when you need it. Ordering the parts you need for the next season, getting up to Alaska early so that you can repair or replace before the thick of the season. Perhaps carrying a spare of the most critical components: starter, alternator, maybe a hydraulic pump

With some 1,900 boats in the Bay, diesel engine dealers make a big marketing effort aimed at Bay fishermen, boasting of the reliability of their products, prepositioning spares in Bristol Bay. For our new boat we installed something called a Lugger 440, a six cylinder, 2,900 pound, turbocharged diesel. As part of their effort to court Bristol Bay fishermen, the Lugger dealer in Seattle had positioned a mechanic in Naknek for the season along with a stock of spare parts to help fishermen who had purchased their engines.

Basically these modern diesels are incredibly dependable as along as they have clean fuel and regular oil and filter changes. To that end we had designed our new boat with a deck hatch and a ladder down into the area behind the engine, allowing me to easily climb down, check the oil in the engine and the reverse gear (the transmission) and check the glass bowl at the bottom of my fuel filter for any sign of water contamination. All without having to pull up floorboards in the boat's cabin.

Bay fishing permits are really expensive. Otfen after purchasing a permit, there wasn't a lot of money left over for a really nice boat, and you had to work with what you had, like this Shore boat with a funky flying bridge that looked more like a weird telephone booth! We called it the "mushroom boat" as in, "With no windows, those guys must be like mushrooms!"

As diesel fuel is lighter than water, any water that happens to get into the fuel will settle to the bottom and be visible in the glass bowl in the filter. If upon inspecting the glass bowl, you see water, then you can easily drain it into a container via a valve.

But still, even with all these precautions, sometimes problems still happen. One day on the way out to start fishing our engine started running really rough, as if it had lost power on a couple of cylinders. Quickly dropping into the engine compartment with a flashlight, I checked the glass settling bowl at the bottom of the fuel filter: all clear. But there was something suspicious about the color of it—lighter than it usually was, so I drained a bit and was shocked to discover that the entire settling bowl was filled with water. Apparently when I had checked it before starting up that morning, I just did a quick look, and not seeing the telltale division between diesel fuel and water, which was easy to spot, figured all good. What I hadn't realized was that when we had fueled up the day before, we'd gotten enough water to fill up the whole settling bowl with water so that there was no telltale line.

First step was draining the filter until all the water was out of the filter, and then trying to assess the damage. Sometimes water won't actually pass through a filter, but will block it and your engine will struggle because it is running out of fuel. In a situation like that the remedy is simply to empty (and sometimes keep emptying) the filter to remove the water. But for us that morning, no such luck: the engine still ran badly, so I figured I had probably blown the tips off one or more injectors—water turns to steam instantly in the hot tips of fuel injectors. By running the engine at an idle and loosening the high pressure injector feed lines, one at a time, you can easily tell which injector are working. If you loosen the fuel line and the engine instantly slows, it means that injector is working. Working quickly, I determined that two of the six injectors weren't working. And immediately got on the cell phone to Paul, the Lugger mechanic in Naknek, explaining our situation. As advertised, he had spare injectors in Naknek, and he made arrangements to get two on Trident's next chopper run to Egegik where we were fishing, and gave me a detailed rundown on the process of swapping out the bad injectors.

Meanwhile it was time to fish: the engine was running badly, but I figured that if I took it easy and made long sets, we could limp through the 12 hour opening and hopefully get the new injectors before the next fishing period. Normally throughout the opening we are setting and hauling frequently, often never returning to the cabin for the whole fishing period. But as we had the engine problem, and being a night opening, I opted for a different strategy: start at the south line where the flood would carry us into the district and try to keep the net in the water as long as possible without starting up the engine to haul it in. Plus we could . . . omg . . . just sleep, alternating guys up to watch the Loran to make sure that we stayed within the district boundaries and away from the sand bars. I took the first three hour watch, kind of enjoying watching other boats pick around us and move back to the line, comfortable that we were making a wise choice because of our engine issues. Six delightful hours later, I was awakened with the happy news that the current had carried us across the district, missing the sand bars and turned to ebb, and was now carrying us toward the still distant south line. Then we started and picked up the net and omg, there were almost 1500 fish in it! Then when the other guys in our group started radioing in with their numbers I realized that we'd caught almost as much as they had, setting and picking all night!

After we unloaded, we limped back and tied up to the side of the net barge, site of the Trident Seafoods helicopter Egegik landing pad where Matt had landed the previous summer.

Then, by disconnecting the steel fuel lines, and carefully levering the two bad injectors out of the head and cleaning out the injector tubes, we were all ready for the new ones. When the clock wound down to two hours before the next opening, I began to get a bit nervous. Finally when we heard the chopper's approach, I dropped down into the engine room to be all ready, and as soon as the chopper landed, Jake passed down the new injectors, I installed them, hooked up the fuel lines, had someone hit the starter. As soon as the fresh fuel pushed the air out of the lines, I tightened the connections and was thrilled to hear the engine's steady beat of hitting on all six cylinders! And with hardly a minute to spare for as I worked the fleet around us was hauling their anchors and starting to head out for the next fishing period.

And sometimes when you break down, your friends come to the rescue. The new boat had Hynautic engine controls, essentially a low pressure hydraulic system, that occasionally needs to have the air bled out for proper operation. In the middle of one opening in particularly bad weather, for some reason the controls got very soft to the point where I could barely get the engine in and out of gear. Luckily we were hanging on our net, but I didn't have the right tool to get the air out. Fortunately friend Bob Anderson had the right tool, and shortly after I called him on the radio, appeared out of the choppy seas and crowd of boats, picked a moment between seas, passed the tool over and disapeared off into the churning fleet and in just a few minutes we were back in business: Thank You Bob!

There were other benefits to fishing for a cannery with a chopper. We weren't a hard drinking bunch on our boat. I'd shipped up a bunch of box wines in the crate with the rest of our supplies, and if we had the time, the inclination and the energy at the end of a day of fishing, we'd break out the wine and mellow out while the salmon was baking.

But sometimes, after a particularly hard day, we'd feel the need for something a little stronger: rum. Unfortunately, Ugashik and Egegik, like many native villages, were dry. There was no actual prohibition against alcohol, and folks could bring it in, but there was neither a bar or a place to purchase any alcohol. So when we ran out of rum, I figured we were out of luck until the end of the season and we made it back to Naknek, where alcohol was plentiful. But then I remembered: the chopper! Checked the cell phone: we had service! So I called the old Farwest Seafoods cannery in Naknek, which Trident had bought a few years earlier. Diane Bundrant answered the phone.

"Hey Diane, it's Joe Upton. I'm at Egegik. How about sending me out a jug of rum on the next chopper run headed this way."

"Joe, I don't do alcohol for fishermen."

OK, I figured, at least I tried. I knew booze was a problem with some fishermen; maybe she had some bad experiences—in her position at the front desk of the cannery, a lot of fishermen came through her door, so she'd probably about seen it all. But then she continued, "But I'll switch you over to Ray. He can help you."

And sure enough the next time we went in to deliver at the *Balaena*, there was a nice big jug of rum waiting for us. Thank you, Mother Trident!

On rare days off, after we'd slept half the day to catch up, we'd raft up with a friend's boat on either side, open up the wine and have a regular old party. Son Matt was a bit of an anomaly, being so young, but the other crews, salty and full of life, made him feel welcome, and as Old Mick had with me on the *Sidney* 30 years earlier, filled him up with wonderful Alaska tales.

David Coble, Jake Magel, author and son, Matt, with a tangle of fish and net, Ugashik River, 1995.

David Cobel was very proud of his mayonnaise baked salmon. It was usually served with green beans or carrots, cooked in the can, instant mashed potatoes, Bisquick rolls and fruit cocktail for dessert, all whipped up in the 30 or so minutes between delivering our fish and dropping the hook and cleaning up. On one of those days when there was no fishing, we decided we'd have a bake-off: see whose salmon recipe was the best. I was confident that it would be Dave's. But as was our custom on days off, the wine box was open, and we all had been making free use of it, including David. Plus there were 4 boats in our raft up with a lot of wandering back and forth between boats, sampling what they had to drink, etc. But in the happy chaos of it all, David overcooked the salmon so someone else won the bake off!

And so we settled into a deeply satisfying groove. Now with Matt making five we fit together like a hand in a glove. For the most part, once the season got rolling, it was 12 on and 12 off, a great schedule. After we'd unloaded, Dave would go into the cabin to get dinner started—we would have saved the last fish of the day to eat—Matt and the guys would wash down the back deck and patch any particularly bad rips in the net, and I would be up on the flying bridge steering in to the anchorage. Sometimes if we were fishing late, it would be almost midnight before the anchor was down and dinner was on the table. We actually had a couple of candles we might light—sensitive guys that we were—and as we ate that fine dinner— basically the only real meal of the day as breakfast was instant oatmeal and lunch was candy and granola bars—we could look out into the semi darkness and see boats sliding in to anchor all around us.

The weather was often windy and rough—with a lot of fish and a lot of boats in close quarters. In order to be out there, not get anyone seriously hurt and get our share of the fish required all of our attention.

It was more than just paying attention. It was like when we really got our mojo going, the gain on all of our senses had to be turned up to the max: an almost zen-like concentration and focus.

And this: Bristol Bay was the Grand Prix of Alaska commercial fishing: top crab, salmon, and herring skippers from all over Alaska, airline pilots, lawyers, wealthy adventurers and just regular guys and women were all here.

And now and again in the middle of a busy fishing period, maybe running fish into the net in a big swell and cross chop, holding on tight with

one hand and steering with the other—"Neckers' knobs" were popular
in the Bay—I'd look around at the drama of it all: the fine boat that Bob
Anderson, Bob Pleier, and the Petrzelka Brothers had crafted, the mountains, the tundra, the busy fleet all around us and just think: "Wow, what
a place."

MEMORY: SPEAK

THE AFTERNOON OF JULY 17, 1997 found us working our net in the upper
reaches of the Ugashik River without another boat or house or setnetter's
shack in sight. The season was about done, most of the fleet had left. We
were about to wrap it up too, but we'd found a little handful of fish and
were having a fun day of it. The channel was narrow and winding: just
enough room to fish one shackle, so we would rotate the gear: I'd work the
300' section of net with the boat, running fish into it, occasionally towing it
to keep it oriented across the channel, while Jake, Bruce, and our son Matt
picked fish out of the shackle they'd just pulled in.

In the distance Aniachak Volcano was blowing a fine plume of steam
downwind, and emerald green tundra shores stretched back to austere
snowy peaks. It was even warm: a rare and perfect Bristol Bay day, and
up there on the flying bridge I mused a bit on the twisting path that had
brought me to that spot.

Our tuna boat, 32 years earlier, fifty miles off the Chilean coast: a starry
night, us alone on the sea, drifting, but with our big deck lights on in case
of a passing ship while we slept. I was restless, came out on deck, looked,
startled over the side. The water around the boat was full of odd sea crea-
tures, writhing and twisting.

The old fellow in the bar of the Hotel Pratt, talking about sailboat days
in Alaska. Me nudging closer, fascinated by the tale he spun.

That riveting conversation with George Fulton: "You should go to
Alaska."

Walking the docks at Seattle's Fishermen's Terminal for almost two
weeks, all but begging for a job on a boat headed to Alaska, deeply frus-
trated, seeing guys I was sure with less experience, get a berth on some
great looking boat simply because they were in the right place at the right
time.

And finally the *Sidney* and the unforgettable 1965 season: ALASKA in capital letters, bigger than life. Old Mick, the kindly mate taking me under his wing, teaching me the skills I needed, how to tell salmon apart. But mostly filling me up with his richly embroidered stories of almost 50 years on the Alaska and British Columbia coast.

The fiasco that was the *Denise:* how could my big dreams, all that I learned in Fish U. have led to such a bad end?

King crabbing on the *Flood Tide* way, way before the *Deadliest Catch* TV show: that amazing herd of crab in a thousand feet of water on the edge of the Aleutian Trench. The holds full and another 10,000 pounds on deck: the pile of grasping claws and spiny legs sliding back and forth in the stark light of the mast lights: as weird a scene as any science fiction movie. Finally after a discouraging season, hitting it big: putting that elusive "winter money in my ass pocket," and more—enough for me to buy a really nice salmon boat.

The magic of being one of the lucky ones on the docks of Seattle's Fisherman's Terminal: getting a really nice boat ready for a long season in the north. Meeting other young couples doing the same thing: after working on others' boats, at last making enough to go north in your own: heady stuff.

And finally, finally, finally, after years of dreaming and wishing and planning: through the locks in my own great boat, decks still cluttered with gear and supplies to be put away. Waking up that second morning in the British Columbia coastal wilderness, the rush of the tide echoing off the canyon walls. Six days of picking our way through the wonder that was the Inside Passage: coming around the turn in some winding channel revealing yet another twisting passage, steep walls lost in the low clouds overhead.

Port Protection/Point Baker days: the older fishermen welcoming and mentoring us young bloods: showing us the ins and outs of gillnetting and trolling, suggesting good places to fish.

The Cabin at Port Upton: carving our little place out of the wilderness. Another fisherman once told me, "If you can look out your living room window and see your boat on the mooring you're living your dream." We could and we were.

Exploring the hidden reaches of Southeast Alaska: the ice at the head of Tracy Arm, the raw gash in the mountain wall that was the entrance to Ford's Terror. Laying there that night in a cove so remote and lost that even radio signals couldn't go in or out: that was my bell, ringing, ringing, ringing!

Wrapping up our season in October in stormy Lynn Canal, ice on the corkline and snow stinging our faces as we picked the last salmon of the season out of the net. Our little cabin at last after three hard days of traveling and six weeks away. Lighting a fire, finding the rum bottle, looking out at our boat on the mooring in front in the last mean light of the day: the moment filling us up in a way we never felt in the south.

Joining the Whitney Fidalgo Petersburg cannery team: buying fish with Kari on the *North Wind*.

Herring days on the coast of Maine with *Amaretto*.

Emily Jane days with my wife, Mary Lou: the characters we met and how lucky we were to have those two exciting seasons together in The North before we started our family.

Fishing winters in Maine: the wolf at the door and breaking ice to drag for mussels.

And finally late one winter night: the call that brought me back to Alaska and Bristol Bay.

And all the wild twists and turns that the Bay turned out to be.

My "Day Job,"—starting a publishing company to sell books and illustrated maps to the hundreds of thousands of folks that had started coming to Alaska each year on the big cruise ships was finally taking off. After three hard years of fruitlessly knocking on the doors of all the big cruise lines, someone finally called back, the vice president of one of the biggest lines: "Hey Joe, we saw one of your illustrated Alaska maps. How much would a million of them be?"

I acted casual, didn't tell him that our biggest previous corporate map sale had been 1,500 maps. We finally came to a price. Not a big price, but when you multiplied it by a million, it adds up pretty quick. But then the kicker: I figured that now that I had a guy like that on the line, why not go for the gusto:

"But what you really should do is to let us make a book to go along with the map." Then I really went for it: "And to make the numbers work, you need to buy 20,000 books."

To my absolute amazement, he bought it, and a whole new career opened up for me, one that would allow me to spend all summer with my family at the cabin my wife and I had built on a Maine island.

On the back deck, the guys were laughing about something with our son as they picked salmon out of the net.

The boat, the place, the moment: I wasn't sure if for me, fishing would ever be any better. A fine, fine boat. A crew of great young men who'd worked together with me for years. And now the best part of all—our son aboard, with these guys as mentors, experiencing all that had brought me to Alaska in the first place. The grandeur of the place. The drama of the fishery. And best of all, the camaraderie of a great crew working together.

And just like that, our season, and my fishing career was over.

EPILOGUE

T HE SUCCESS OF THE BRISTOL BAY fishery is due to two elements: strong and independent management, where the fish's and not the processors' needs always come first, and pristine watersheds with essentially no development.

A significant threat to the latter began in 1988 with the discovery of a large body of gold, copper, and molybdenum ore in the northern part of the Bristol Bay watershed. The proposed Pebble Mine would be a massive open pit that over the course of its projected life would produce over 10 **billion** tons of toxic waste that would remain on the site forever, possibly leaching or escaping into the headwaters of the bay's biggest salmon producing river system, the Kvichak. Fishermen and natives were shocked that such a damaging project would even be considered.

And so the battle waged, with powerful mining interests fighting commercial and sports fishing organizations, native tribes and environmental groups. For more than a decade filled with court cases, surprise revelations from supposedly secret meetings, and intense lobbying, it seemed that eventually the mine would receive all its permits and begin operations.

But then a surprise turnaround in August 2020:, the all important Army Corps of Engineers which must approve of the mine determined that it could not be built without significant damage to the region.

The mine could still possibly go forward on a much smaller scale. However opponents to the original mining plan are working on some sort of protection arrangement that would protect the area forever.

As fishermen fighting to keep a huge molybdenum mine out of Southeast Alaska, and others trying to stop clearcutting old growth in the Tongass National Forest learned, these battles never cease unless you can get some sort of permanent protection of the resource.

Matt ended up going to law school to study maritime law, got a job as a "fish lawyer"—attorney for U. S. Seafoods—with nine big boats in Alaska and an office in their own shipyard in Seattle. The dad caught fish; the son sells fishing advice. Who's smarter?

And how things had changed in the fish biz! Did the first cannery that I worked for, Annette Island Packing Co, in the native village of Metlakatla in 1965 even have a lawyer on the payroll? I doubt it. Matt's company had two attorneys on staff, and a full time lobbyist back in Washington, DC.

I was going to Alaska a lot in those days promoting my book and sometimes crossed paths with Matt. Occasionally in his travels guys would come up to him, "Hey, Matt, I used to fish with your dad."

Meanwhile, in the Bay, volume and prices trended generally upwards.

What was particularly surprising was that in recent years catches in other major salmon fishing districts of Alaska were slumping, blamed on changing ocean conditions, while Bristol Bay, amazingly, continued to have record returns.

When I fished The Bay, a season of anything over 250,000 pounds was considered very big, and annual catches were in the 20–30 million fish range. After I got out and the century turned something remarkable began happening. Bristol Bay runs just kept getting bigger and bigger. In 2020 there was the rumor of the first 500,000 pound season. Then this year, 2022, the biggest run in Bristol Bay history showed up—a total run of 76 million fish, and a catch of 56 million: mind boggling numbers. One friend said the new guy in their group (with 4 years experience) had over 600,000 pounds, and a young man, whom I'd known since he was in diapers had 489,000 pounds in Ugashik after the fleet settled down to under 50 boats!!! My Maine neighbor Mike Mesko, who'd also fished The Bay, and I talked about those numbers and wondered what hands and fingers would look like after such intense and continued picking.

But sadly, the nearby runs of chum and king salmon to the Yukon Rivers, important as winter food to upriver natives were disappointing.

My earlier shipmates, Marvin and Eric, all went on to be successful

Bristol Bay skippers and boat owners. Jake Magel went on to be a respected physical therapist, and Bruce McGowan became a small town fire chief, sadly to die in an automobile accident.

My little publishing company prospered and in 2015 I began working with Dan Kowalski, an Alaska commercial fisherman and filmmaker, traveling with him and shooting short videos—essentially me telling stories—in different places around Southeast Alaska. You can see them on www.alaskacruisehandbook.com/videopage.html.

And this was all the path that old Mick, on the *Sidney*, back in 1965 started me down when he sat up with me night after night on my wheel watches in the pilothouse sharing stories with me.

Thanks, Mick, I'm still telling the stories!

Joe and Matt Upton, Katmai, Alaska, 1997.

IN 1965 JOE UPTON was one of those teenagers walking up and down the docks of Seattle's Fishermen's Terminal, eager to get on one of the Alaska bound fishing boats. In his first job, the 70-year-old mate filled Upton up with tales of a life-time working on the coast, and set him on his career path: commercial fisherman, but story teller as well. After 20 years of working up and down the Alaska coast in all kinds of boats in all kinds of weather, Upton started a publishing company to share with Alaska visitors some of the drama he had seen and experienced as a commercial fisherman. Recently he began working with fisherman/filmmaker Dan Kowalski traveling around Southeast Alaska and making short story telling videos.